THE MYTH OF THE HISTORICAL JESUS AND THE EVOLUTION OF CONSCIOUSNESS

*SOCIETY
OF BIBLICAL
LITERATURE*

DISSERTATION SERIES

Saul M. Olyan, Old Testament Editor
Mark Allan Powell, New Testament Editor

Number 179
THE MYTH OF THE HISTORICAL JESUS
AND THE EVOLUTION OF CONSCIOUSNESS

by
Hal Childs

Hal Childs

THE MYTH OF THE HISTORICAL JESUS AND THE EVOLUTION OF CONSCIOUSNESS

Society of Biblical Literature
Atlanta, Georgia

THE MYTH OF THE HISTORICAL JESUS AND THE EVOLUTION OF CONSCIOUSNESS

by
Hal Childs
Ph.D., Graduate Theological Union, 1998
Lewis R. Rambo, Dissertation Advisor

Library of Congress Cataloging-in-Publication Data

Childs, Hal, 1946–
    The myth of the historical Jesus and the evolution of consciousness /
Hal Childs.
        p. cm. — (Dissertation series ; no. 179)
        Originally presented as the author's thesis (Ph.D.)—Graduate Theological
Union, 1998.
        Includes bibliographical references.
        ISBN 0-88414-029-6
        1. Jesus Christ—Historicity. 2. Christianity—Psychology. I. Title.
    II. Dissertation series (Society of Biblical Literature); no. 179.

BT303.2.C47 2000
232.9'08—dc21   00-061929

08 07 06 05 04 03 02 01 00   5 4 3 2 1

Printed in the United States of America
on acid-free paper

To my mother, Inga

and my father, Henry

and

Kathleen, Gregory and Steven

TABLE OF CONTENTS

LIST OF TABLES

PREFACE

Over twenty years ago, my work with Walter Wink and Ann Ulanov at Union Theological Seminary led to a Master of Divinity thesis on a Jungian interpretation of the son of man, in both the Hebrew and Christian scriptures, as a principle of incarnation, with a focus on Jesus' possible use of the term. That discovery of a Jungian approach to biblical interpretation gave new life to my understanding of sacred texts, of myself and the world of the psyche. This led to over twenty years of work with the Guild for Psychological Studies in San Francisco where I have studied and led seminars on the historical Jesus of the synoptic gospels within a Jungian and experiential context.

Combined with the historical Jesus work were studies in mythology, the arts and meditative and spiritual practices. The work was profoundly rich, stimulating and life giving, but its long duration enabled a creeping dissatisfaction to gradually develop within me concerning the use of the idea of history in the study of Jesus. It slowly dawned on me that a positivist idea of "history," that is, that the "historical" Jesus is the actual and original Jesus, was unintentionally being manipulated to promote a certain Jesus-ideology. And I began to sense that the "historical Jesus" was just as much a construction of theological and christological agendas as of so-called historical facts.

The idea of "the myth of the historical Jesus" was not present at the beginning of this work. This perspective emerged as I worked more deeply with critical historiography and philosophy of history in relation to Jung's thought. But the insight that "history is myth" was also a personal crisis, because suddenly something that was solid and secure, "history," could no longer be a naive foundation. It seems that to probe deeply intellectually entails the same risks as those early explorers who feared they could sail off the edge of the world.

The present work is an attempt to develop a new conception of history and myth in order to address both the problem of the historical Jesus in relation to the methodological crisis suffered by historical crit-

ical method as well as the crisis within myself. But at the beginning of
the work I did not know I would encounter this inner crisis. The positivist, or modernist, split between history and myth (and history and
theology) is for me not just an intellectual problem, but first of all a
problem of *being*. This project is part of an ongoing work of integrating
the split aspects of being I have inherited from my intellectual and religious traditions.

The profession in which I have engaged these human and divine
splits is psychotherapy, and I have been active as a psychotherapist for
over fifteen years. I see first-hand the effects of the split between fact
and meaning, and the loss of the value of myth, on the lives of many individuals. But psychology has traditionally participated in the split between science and religion, so for me, the only meaningful psychology
is a spiritual psychology that views psyche, world and God as an integrated whole.

There have been many people along the way who have guided
and encouraged me, without whom this work would not have become
an actuality. I am deeply grateful to them all. Thanks to John Hitchcock
for some crucial early conceptual clarification, and ongoing support of
the value of these ideas. I am grateful to John Petroni for always asking
the personal question about the meaning of the work from an archetypal
perspective. Richard Naegle provided ongoing support, and perspective
when continuing sometimes seemed impossible. And appreciation to
John Gallagher for warmth and depth. I am grateful to the Guild for
Psychological Studies for nurturing the original seeds of this work.
Wilhelm Wuellner, my first advisor, whose counsel I lost to retirement,
encouraged my thought and liberally shared his bibliographic research
in New Testament and psychology.

Dreams have been crucial and supportive throughout this work.
The dissertation is, in part, an amplification of two dreams that predate
this particular project—they have always been present as part of my
own historical psychic background undergirding the work. A conversation with John Dourley early in the project affirmed an interpretation
of a key and supportive dream. To my analyst during most of this project, James Yandell, I owe a profound debt of thanks for helping to
keep ego and soul embodied.

My colleagues at the California Counseling Institute, both my
psychotherapist cohorts and the Board of Trustees, have been tremen-
dously supportive. Thanks to Lynn Bjork Mannix, with whom I co-

direct the Institute, for supporting my reduced work load while I wrote the dissertation.

And to my family I owe a special debt. To my two sons, Gregory (7) and Steven (4), who proved—by being born during this project—that having an impossible load on one's plate actually makes for more efficiency—and who, as they grew older and watched the pages pile up, helped me realize that "Daddy's book" would soon be finished. I am grateful to my wife Kathleen whose care for relationship and loving support and understanding were lifelines nurturing this work. I am deeply appreciative of my father and mother for help and support at many levels. And a special note of thanks to my mother whose generosity in caring for our children made many hours of research and writing possible.

My advisor Lewis Rambo, and committee members Joel Green and James Jarrett, were more than generous with their time, advice and helpful criticism. And while their guidance was excellent, I am responsible for any errors in the present work.

Vallejo, California
Friday, February 13, 1998

Hal Childs

Books are food for God

Author's Dream

CHAPTER ONE

INTRODUCTION

The Problem

The problem this book will address is the increasing variety of images of Jesus appearing in contemporary historical Jesus studies. This is the symptom of what some scholars perceive to be a significant methodological crisis in Jesus historiography. The cause of this problem seems to be the lack of, and the inability to agree on, a standardized and coherent method, and the inability to control, with method, the role of the scholar's subjectivity in the resulting Jesus image. My focus will be on the nature of the relationship between historical critical method and the scholar's hermeneutic preconceptions or bias (i.e., their subjectivity) in historical Jesus studies.

I will approach this problem through an investigation of the psychological, epistemological, hermeneutic and ontological assumptions embedded in the relationship between method and subjectivity. In exploring these assumptions I will compare and contrast the unconscious Cartesian and Enlightenment expectations of method and epistemology with an alternative offered by a phenomenological reading of Jung's depth-psychology that will suggest a different understanding of both method and subjectivity. This study is limited to one methodological problem in the quest for the historical Jesus, but it also has significant implications for the traditional conflict between historical criticism and theology. I also believe the hermeneutic implications of this study may reach other fields of inquiry, including the humanities, the social sciences, and the natural sciences.

My thesis is that a comparative analysis of Jung's psychological method and Crossan's historical method in relation to Jesus, and the Jesus tradition, will help set the foundation for a hermeneutic paradigm that will critique and reinterpret the epistemological assumptions that form the basis of the "scientific" historical paradigm that has guided the quest for the historical Jesus since its inception. This hermeneutic paradigm will integrate a phenomenological analytical psychology with historical critical methods, modifying each in the process. Historical critical methods currently function within the assumptions of Cartesian epistemology and ontology and the attendant tradition and authority of scientific knowledge and facts. What will happen if historical critical methods are placed within a different ontological world, one that is fundamentally hermeneutic, archetypal and psychological, without sacrificing historical reality? This is not meant to discredit historical critical methods, but to fundamentally reorder their heretofore privileged relationship to historical knowledge and truth.

My approach to this problem of the multiplicity of Jesus images and the subjectivity of the scholar involves an investigation of the relationship between subjectivity and method, and between method and interpretation, or epistemology and hermeneutics. I will propose a solution to this problem that is psychological and archetypal, through a phenomenological reading of C. G. Jung's analytical psychology. In the offense taken at the betrayal of method by subjectivity is an unwarranted expectation about the Enlightenment epistemology that informs all critical historical methods, and the Cartesian metaphysics that is its foundation. The methodological problem facing scholars in historical Jesus studies is fundamentally not epistemological, but ontological, or from Jung's point of view, archetypal. My own reply to the methodological crisis in biblical studies is not to propose a better method, but to propose an alternative ontological hermeneutic-psychological understanding of method. I want to effectively undermine the subject/object dichotomy endemic to traditional epistemology that continues to plague contemporary Jesus historiography.

Elaboration of the Problem

The problem of multiple Jesus images intensifies as more and more books and articles on the historical Jesus pour off the academic and popular presses. Since the 1980s there has been an explosion of interest in the historical Jesus in both the academic world and the public at large. In the world of academia, what has been called "a Renaissance in Jesus studies"[1] has also been named, by some, the "Third Quest."[2] The critical quests for the historical Jesus, undertaken by scholars since the mid-eighteenth century, using basically the same sources and scholarly apparatus, have produced a multiplicity of Jesus images. However, it is the contemporary Third Quest's production of such a variety of images of Jesus that is prompting serious method-ological concern on the part of scholars. Helmut Koester states that "the vast variety of interpretations of the historical Jesus that the current quest has proposed is bewildering."[3] And William Telford, referring to a reviewer's comment that "dozens, perhaps hundreds of different Jesuses can be constructed" using the same texts and scholarly apparatus, suggests that perhaps this is "the problem and challenge of Jesus Studies today!"[4] There are several overviews of this contemporary variety, including Wright,[5] Telford[6] and Borg.[7] In the next section I will look more closely at examples of four scholars who have examined this Life of Jesus multiplicity while explicitly raising questions of method.

Examples of the Problem

Irvin Batdorf, in a 1984 article,[8] examines in depth the approach-es of eleven scholars to the historical Jesus. He highlights the different interpretive results in relation to the methods used. With five of these scholars he notes significant "agreement on basic methodology," yet "what amazingly different portraits of Jesus emerge!"[9] On the other hand, Batdorf also finds that several scholars using very different methods and approaches come to very similar results with regard to the picture of Jesus they draw.[10] Batdorf wonders if there is any necessary relationship at all between method and resulting image of Jesus. He

---

[1]Borg (1994) 3-17.
[2]Neill and Wright (1988) 379.
[3]Koester (1994) 544.
[4]Telford (1994) 46-47.
[5]Neill and Wright (1988) 379-97.
[6]Telford (1994) 52-55.
[7]Borg (1994) 18-43.
[8]Batdorf (1984) 187-215.
[9]Batdorf (1984) 206.
[10]Batdorf (1984) 205.

concludes it is really the personal hermeneutical bias of the Jesus scholar that determines the final outcome.

Daniel Harrington's 1987 article[11] examines three, and notes seven, different images of Jesus that have appeared in recent years, all in the context of taking seriously the Jewishness of Jesus.[12] His terse point is "the more we know, the less we know,"[13] and as our historical knowledge grows and becomes more complex, our methodological problems deepen. Adding to this complexity is our new knowledge that Judaism, in and around first-century Palestine, was not a single monolithic norm in decline (as Christian theology has traditionally portrayed it), but a complex mix of multiple and vital Judaisms.[14] In the face of a much more richly textured picture of first century Judaisms, how do we know what kind of Jew Jesus was and within which particular Jewish context he existed? Harrington recognizes that the historical, methodological and theological issues are considerable.

Another biblical scholar, Dennis Polkow, in a 1987 article,[15] notices "a *hopeless* diversity of historical Jesus pictures in modern scholarship."[16] He locates the cause for this in the inability of recent scholarship to clarify and standardize a single method and specific set of universally recognized criteria for historical Jesus research.[17] His article is not a review of multiple Jesus images, but an attempt to standardize method and criteria for historical Jesus research. It appears that in the face of hopeless diversity, there is a hope that a standardized (singular?) method would fix the problem. However, Batdorf's findings, that method and picture of Jesus are not necessarily related, would seem to negate this hope of a unified method.

John Crossan, in a 1988 article,[18] comments that historical Jesus research is "something of a bad joke," and notes that there are a "number of competent and even eminent scholars producing pictures of Jesus at wide variance with one another."[19] Referencing Harrington's

---

[11]Harrington (1987a). See also 1987b for an expanded version of this article. These are the articles Crossan cites in relation to his own comments about the Jewish context of Jesus and multiple Jesus images.

[12]Harrington (1987a) 3-4, 7-8.

[13]Harrington (1987a) 5.

[14]Harrington (1987a) 7; Charlesworth (1988).

[15]Polkow (1987) 336-56.

[16]Polkow (1987) 356 (italics added). He is quoting P. Hollenbach.

[17]Polkow (1987) 356.

[18]Crossan (1988a).

[19]Crossan (1988a) 3.

1987 article (noted above), he says, "Even when one disciplines oneself by attempting to envision Jesus against his own most proper Jewish background it seems we can have as many pictures as there are exegetes," and refers to this situation as an "embarrassment."[20] Later, in his 1991 book, *The Historical Jesus,* he calls it an "academic embarrassment," and says, "The problem of multiple and discordant conclusions forces us back to questions of theory and method."[21] In the article he proposes that "materials and methods" must be discussed "ever more stringently" before undertaking a search for the historical Jesus. His proposed solution is two-fold. First he sketches the methodological principles which should guide one's approach to the relevant historical Jewish and Christian materials. Second, he suggests, but does not develop, that probably the "most important" principle for the historical Jesus researcher is to admit one's own "inaugural hypothesis" about Jesus. No one initiates a study of Jesus without already having ideas about Jesus. Crossan says, "There is and should be always an initial hypothesis that one tests against the data. What is one's inaugural hypothesis and can one see how it was obtained?"[22]

Crossan appears to be attempting to make a place for the personal and conscious point of view of the scholar in his method. But not everyone recognizes this as a positive direction for method. Polkow never mentions the possibility of making the issue of the scholar's subjectivity an explicit dimension of method. His entire dense and detailed discussion of method and criteria remains focused on the scholarly apparatus used to determine outer historical objects, and never considers the role of the internal judgments of the scholar as something method should address.

Crossan addresses the issues of method, objectivity and scholarly subjectivity in *The Historical Jesus,* but remains ambiguous about his own solution. He is concerned about the seemingly irresponsible nature of Jesus historiography when he says, "It is impossible to avoid the suspicion that historical Jesus research is a very safe place to do theology and call it history, and do autobiography and call it biography."[23] Worried that his book not "add to the impression of acute scholarly subjectivity in historical Jesus research," he felt it "had to

---

[20]Crossan (1988a) 3-4. See Crossan (1991) xxviii, for a slightly different version of this same point.
[21]Crossan (1991) xxviii.
[22]Crossan (1988) 10.
[23]Crossan (1991) xxviii.

raise most seriously the problem of methodology and then follow most stringently whatever theoretical method was chosen."[24] Throughout the opening paragraphs of his Prologue, Crossan explicitly and implicitly links the problem of "multiple and discordant conclusions" with the problem of "acute scholarly subjectivity," as effect and cause. Therefore, it would appear that the function of Crossan's method is to control "scholarly subjectivity" and "multiple and discordant conclusions" and thereby produce something better, but what exactly? *The* objective result or *a* more objective result? And how are we to understand "objective" in this context?

After Crossan describes his method in detail (which I will examine in chapter two), he says, "It is clear, I hope, that my methodology does not claim a spurious objectivity, because almost every step demands a scholarly judgment and an informed decision. I am concerned, not with an unattainable objectivity, but with an attainable honesty."[25] This statement would appear to be in conflict with his methodological attempt to control "scholarly subjectivity." Or, does Crossan mean that an "honest subjectivity" is attainable? What might this really mean in relation to Jesus historiography? It is not clear whether the function of Crossan's method is to structure his own subjectivity (scholarly judgment), thereby making it explicit, disciplined, and therefore honest(?), or whether the method's impressive structures simply end up authorizing his subjectivity. It appears Crossan is walking a thin line. Does his method function in a positive way to make the scholar's subjectivity honest as the guiding light of the whole enterprise, or does it function to cover up his subjectivity and hide it behind the method's own forms of rhetoric?

Adding to the sense of Crossan's ambiguity about how the scholar's subjectivity is to be handled is his failure to mention in *The Historical Jesus* the one methodological principle he claimed, in his 1988 article, was "most important": "Principle 5: Admit inaugural hypothesis." Although he makes no explicit mention of this principle in the book, he does begin the book immediately with a section titled, "Overture: The Gospel of Jesus." This turns out to be his own working hypothesis about Jesus, but it is not declared as such. Is this an oversight; or is the subjective dimension of his methodological principles being left somewhat in the background for a reason? These questions about Crossan's work cannot be answered directly, and they are not

---

[24]Crossan (1991) xxviii.
[25]Crossan (1991) xxxiv.

meant to raise suspicion concerning his conscious intentions. However, they do reveal the ambiguity that remains in spite of his attempt to be clear methodologically.

The concern about the multiplicity of Jesus-images in relation to a methodological crisis is not new. Ernst Käsemann, in his now-famous 1953 lecture, raised this specter as well. Because his talk is historic in the New Testament field for having inaugurated the New Quest of the historical Jesus it is worth considering here. He noted that historical criticism had shattered the "good faith" that the gospels contained large portions of reliable tradition about the earthly Jesus. All levels of the Jesus tradition were now suspect with regard to the historic Jesus, and the burden of proof had fallen to demonstrating genuineness. As Käsemann noted, this historical criticism that established the doubtful nature of the Jesus traditions could only propose modifications at the level of the kerygma, and could never establish the certainty of "a word or action of the earthly Jesus himself." He then says,

> The inevitable consequence is a bewildering confusion of allegedly trustworthy portraits of Jesus: now he appears as a rabbi, now as a teacher of wisdom, now as a prophet; or again, as the man who thought of himself as the Son of Man or the Suffering Servant, who stood for an apocalyptic or realized eschatology: or finally, as some sort of a mixture of all these.

This situation leads Käsemann to say that "only radical criticism can therefore do justice to the situation with which we are faced whether we like it or not." He considers the inability to establish any criteria by which to distinguish authentic Jesus material "the embarrassment of critical research."[26] The criterion he believes will provide "more or less safe ground under our feet," is what has come to be called the criterion of dissimilarity. He hopes this single criterion will at least establish the minimum of distinctive authentic Jesus material with which to begin historical research. My point is that the embarrassment of multiplicity and undecidability leads to a search for a methodological solution because the problem is assumed to be epistemological.

Crossan and Polkow, 37 years later, are again pointing to inadequacies of method as the source of the problem of multiple Jesus images in critical scholarship. Polkow argues for unified and standardized method and criteria. Crossan claims, at least, to want to make the scholar's critical judgments and their rationale explicit and visible

---

[26]Käsemann (1964) 34-36.

through following a standardized method. The claim, explicit or implicit, is that if only such a method could be agreed upon and applied then the problem of multiple Jesus images and the implicated scholar's subjectivity would be neutralized, or at least controlled, and supposedly, the definitive historical Jesus could and would emerge from critical historical scholarship (eventually).

Batdorf comes to a somewhat similar conclusion as Crossan regarding the place of the scholar's subjectivity in method, but Batdorf wants to make the hermeneutic bias of the scholar not only explicit but prominent as well. Coming to the conclusion that there is no "necessary connection between method and result" and that methods themselves do not account for the differing results in portraying Jesus, he claims it is the interpreter's preconceptions about Jesus that determine the outcome. He says, "What we are observing in the case of the quest for Jesus is an unacknowledged tension between a preconceived personal image of Jesus and consciously adopted method."[27] As a solution to this dilemma Batdorf endorses "methodological eclecticism," and proposes that any method should be pushed to its limit as skillfully as possible, for then its adequacy can be tested and judged in the public forum of scholars.[28] He wants to bring the personal bias of the interpreter into the foreground:

> We need as participants in the quest (1) to abandon the myth of objectivity, (2) to formulate for public inspection what our personal hermeneutic prejudices are, (3) to formulate for public inspection the total image of Jesus on the basis of which our investigations proceed, and (4) to make explicit how personal bias and total Jesus image are related to each other and to the canon's insistence on reading the story of Jesus in its totality.[29]

Batdorf's almost casual comment, "to abandon the myth of objectivity," is easier said than done. *Hopelessness* and *embarrassment* are strong feelings in the face of the diversity of Jesus images, and I believe these strong feelings point to frustrated, unconscious expectations on the part of Jesus scholars about what historical critical method *should* be able to do. What is the "myth of objectivity," as Batdorf calls it, and what are its origins? And, how does the very desire for objectivity influence our understanding of method and our understanding of subjectivity? The call to bring "personal hermeneutic prejudices"

---

[27]Batdorf (1984) 205.
[28]Batdorf (1984) 212.
[29]Batdorf (1984) 212.

into the foreground of Jesus historiography is a positive ideal, but how is it to be done and how much of him or herself is the scholar expected to reveal? How much self-knowledge is required, and can we ever know all of our hermeneutic prejudices? How are we to understand "subjectivity"? Is subjectivity limited to what I consciously know about myself, or is there more? Perhaps there is a "myth of subjectivity" that is just as problematic as the "myth of objectivity." Is there a method that will help us deal with hermeneutic preferences that are unknown to us, that are quite unconscious? And what is the role of imagination and emotion in our "hermeneutic prejudices"?

In my view, the problems of "objectivity" and "subjectivity" in the quest for the historical Jesus require an investigation of the philosophical and psychological dimensions of epistemology, that theory of knowledge traditionally concerned with determining facts, and hermeneutics, that theory of interpretation traditionally concerned with interpreting the facts. I will examine the unconscious Cartesian and Enlightenment ontological assumptions embedded in historical critical method that continue to privilege epistemology over hermeneutics, and rational knowing over imagination and emotion as sources of "knowing." Here I use the term "unconscious" as an epistemological concept, that, as we will see in chapter four, is in line with Jung's own understanding. The term "unconscious" refers to the limit of what we know about ourselves, and this is based on the empirical observation that people act in ways that are in conflict with their conscious aims and self-perception. The "unconscious" refers to those factors that influence the personality, both behavior and thought, that are outside the horizon of consciousness. And, as we will see, there is in Jung's view, a personal unconscious and a collective unconscious. With regard to Cartesian and Enlightenment ontological assumptions about epistemology I am referring to cultural and historical dimensions of the collective unconscious implicitly shared by all those whose cultural home is Western civilization.

The scholar's conscious and preconceived ideas about Jesus, and the scholar's more general personal subjectivity as both biography and social location are one set of problems. But to my mind, the greater and deeper problematic is the cultural and historical epistemological and ontological assumptions upon which historical critical methods are founded. These are the assumptions of Cartesian and Enlightenment rationality and positivism. Briefly, positivism can be characterized as maintaining a particular theory of knowledge (epistemology) and a particular theory of reality, i.e., being, (ontology). Its theory of knowledge asserts that a researcher, using rational principles and methods, can determine objective and value-neutral facts without bias or interpretation, and can employ the facts without influencing them. This theory of objective knowledge rests on the ontological assumption that the researcher and the object of research are discrete and separate entities (the Cartesian subject-object split). And one basic assumption of historical positivism is that the historian can accurately report what actually happened in the past. While almost no one in the Third Quest would claim a naive historical positivism, and would even claim to be beyond positivism, I believe the Third Quest remains bogged down in unquestioned assumptions about method and history that derive from Cartesian and positivist traditions. Even though Crossan is at pains to avoid an "unattainable objectivity," his insistence on certain historical methods and his dependence on traditional methodological discourse betrays a kind of tacit positivism subtly influencing his theory of knowledge (epistemology) in general.

The criticism of historical materialism and positivism from within in the fields of biblical and theological studies has come mainly from a theological perspective, and also maintains a predominantly theological program.[30] The problem with the theological criticism of historical positivism is that it preserves an interpretive dualism in the approach to biblical texts in general, and Jesus studies in particular.[31] On the one hand, a "positivist" historical criticism is supposed to establish the facts, and on the other, theology interprets the meaning of the facts. This is the traditional view of epistemology as that which determines the foundation of objective, rational knowledge upon which interpretation can then proceed; hermeneutics is the handmaiden to epistemology. This interpretive dualism is founded on an ontological dichotomy that lies unconsciously embedded in the terms of any discourse between the fields of historical method and theological method. It is the ontological split between the two that dooms the argument to endless futility. What I am tentatively referring to as a post-Cartesian Heideggerian and Jungian perspective abolishes the ontological dichotomy between method and interpretation, between object and subject,

---

[30]Braaten and Harrisville (1964); Robinson and Cobb (1964); Robinson (1959/79). More contemporary approaches like Meyer (1979) and Wright (1992 and 1993) I also view as theological projects attempting to maintain a positivist element in history.

[31]Nations (1983) 71.

and makes epistemology dependent upon hermeneutics. This means that interpretive modes of being are prior to, and influence, our ways of knowing and how knowledge is created. This perspective marks what in contemporary philosophy is called the "interpretive turn"—a shift away from philosophy's two hundred year preoccupation with epistemology to a new interest in interpretive activities.[32] This contemporary situation in philosophy was heralded by Nietzsche's declaration one hundred years ago in *The Will to Power*: "Against positivism, which halts at phenomena—'There are only *facts*'—I would say: No, facts is precisely what there is not, only interpretations."[33] I will touch on this matter again below when I discuss the importance of Heidegger's work in interpreting Jung.

As I read the Third Quest's use of historical critical methods and the resulting historiography about Jesus, I detect these unwitting (i.e., unconscious) presuppositions that assume that historical method, and social science methods in general, as a kind of "science" under the influence of the traditional mode of positivism, can and will accurately determine *the original* historical Jesus.[34] Such presuppositions lead the researcher to claim and/or assume that personal bias, as well as the bias of the social, political and historical context of the researcher, can be eliminated from historiography by the right use of method. Again, no one writing today about the historical Jesus makes such claims in the direct and naive manner of the nineteenth century historians. However, I am targeting what I believe to be a much more subtle legacy deriving from Enlightenment metaphysics that still haunts an implicit understanding of the ability to gain knowledge of the past. As we will see in chapter three on critical historiography, this unwarranted but still influential general epistemology of history does not only trouble the quest for the historical Jesus, but is a problem for the discipline of history in general.

At this point I will make some suggestions about the nature of the philosophical and psychological problems that arise from questioning the adequacy of traditional epistemology. If the traditional Car-

---

[32]Hiley (1991) 1-14.

[33]Nietzsche (1967) 267.

[34]Among the recent works consulted, see Borg (1984, 1987, 1994); Breech (1983, 1989); Charlesworth (1988); Chilton and Evans (1994); Downing (1987); Fiorenza (1983); Harvey (1982); Horsley (1987); Johnson (1996); Mack (1988); Meier (1991); Meyer (1979); Riches (1982); Sanders (1985); Scott (1981); Theissen (1987); Vermes (1973, 1993); Witherington (1994, 1995).

tesian epistemological and ontological assumptions are at bottom in-
sufficiently warranted, what becomes of the utility of historical critical
method? If Jung is correct about the unconscious, especially the collective unconscious—that what is unconscious, unknown, always
shows up via projection—is it possible to disentangle projection and
knowledge? Is this a desirable goal? If we are so unconsciously identified with cultural assumptions about knowledge and reality that they
simply function independently of our conscious judgments, are not
Cartesian epistemology and its derivative methods helpless in the face
of such phenomena? In the light of such problematic phenomena it is
my view that the ontological dimension of the assumptions that guide
the quest for the historical Jesus requires theoretical investigation. A
critical investigation of the ontological dimension, that in chapter four
I will show has significant overlap with Jung's concept of the collective unconscious, takes us below the level of personal psychology
and engages that upon which personal psychology, thought and
knowledge are founded. Jung's understanding of the collective unconscious gives an archetypal dimension to the concept of projection. I
will suggest that the archetypal understanding of projection overlaps
with Heidegger's ontological and phenomenological interpretation of
the hermeneutic circle. If Heidegger's ontological interpretation of the
hermeneutic circle is correct, and subject and object are always fused
hermeneutically at every level, what are the implications for historical
critical method and its claim to "know" the past?

It is the purpose of this book to suggest that Jung's work contains an implicit critique of the ontological assumptions underlying the
Cartesian epistemology that informs historical critical methods. Jung,
read in the light of Heidegger's similar hermeneutic critique, will help
move toward a solution of the problem of scholarly subjectivity and the
multiplicity of Jesus images.

Albert Schweitzer and the Scholar's Subjectivity

Contemporary scholars are not the first to recognize the presence
of subjectivity in historical Jesus research. Albert Schweitzer, one-
hundred years ago, noted the predominantly self-reflective quality,
both cultural and personal, that characterized the study of Jesus when
he said, "But it was not only each epoch that found its reflection in
Jesus; each individual created Him in accordance with his own charac-

ter. There is no historical task which so reveals a man's true self as the writing of a Life of Jesus."[35]

Schweitzer did not view this aspect of Jesus research as a methodological problem, but rather as inevitable and necessary. Not only did each era of theology have to find its own thoughts in Jesus, "...that was, indeed, the only way in which it could make Him live." Schweitzer presses further with this thought in regard to the individual who writes a life of Jesus: "No vital force comes into the figure unless a man breathes into it all the hate or all the love of which he is capable. The stronger the love, or the stronger the hate, the more life-like is the figure which is produced."[36] With these words Schweitzer implicitly entertains an historical method that requires intense emotion, and he tacitly gives a kind of "epistemological" privilege to hate when he goes on to say, "For hate as well as love can write a Life of Jesus, and the greatest of them are written with hate...." He is referring to Reimarus and David Friedrich Strauss, and observes that "...their hate sharpened their historical insight. They advanced the study of the subject more than all the others put together. But for the offence which they gave, the science of historical theology would not have stood where it does to-day."[37] Schweitzer's use of the word "hate" in this context is perhaps better understood if we read "critical insight" for "historical insight," and realize that the interest in an historical Jesus at the time was not a purely neutral historical interest. The Jesus of history was an "ally in the struggle against the tyranny of dogma." As Schweitzer puts it so eloquently,

> It was not so much hate of the Person of Jesus as of the supernatural nimbus with which it was so easy to surround Him, and with which He had in fact been surrounded. They were eager to picture Him as truly and purely human, to strip from Him the robes of splendour with which He had been apparelled, and clothe Him once more with the coarse garments in which He had walked in Galilee.[38]

Reimarus and Strauss would not have, and could not have, publicly declared their "hate" as part of their epistemological method. Even so, they both suffered greatly as a result of their historical investigations of Jesus, a task undertaken against the prevailing and dominant cultural and institutional adherence to the dogmatic principle of

---

[35]Schweitzer (1906/1968) 4.
[36]Schweitzer (1906/1968) 4.
[37]Schweitzer (1906/1968) 4-5.
[38]Schweitzer (1906/1968) 4.

the theological Christ. Reimarus suffered more privately. He did not publish his work during his lifetime, because his father-in-law was a clergyman. Strauss saw his teaching career ruined. But who today in the field of Jesus research, in our intellectually liberated and psychologically enlightened era, would dare begin a study of the historical Jesus with a claim for the methodological and epistemological privilege of their personal emotion, hate or love, in relation to the subject at hand? Perhaps less radically, but certainly no less determinative, who would begin their historical study declaring their passionate commitments and show how their commitments shaped their methods? This, of course, in large measure, is what Batdorf is calling for when he suggests that historical Jesus scholars "abandon the myth of objectivity" (see above p.8).

The original nineteenth century quest for the historical Jesus, presented so well by Schweitzer, was clearly part of the general Enlightenment project of rational thought freeing itself from the tyranny of dogma. It is my contention that the contemporary quest is implicitly still engaged in this Enlightenment project even though the Third Quest explicitly disavows any such anti-dogmatic ideology.

I will suggest that what sets the stage for scholarly judgments in the quest for the historical Jesus about the nature of the sources, establishing the ancient and historical context of Jesus, and the resulting image of Jesus, is first emotion and secondarily reason. By this I mean that our primary orientation is either a For or an Against[39] with regard to the Jesus traditions, and this orientation matters to us personally and deeply. And usually this emotional orientation is not a simple For or Against, but a more complex situation in which a scholar is For one image of Jesus Against another image of Jesus. I will suggest that emotion is a complex and powerful component of the hermeneutic nature of meaning and value, that it is at the heart of making anything significant, and that it is what brings us to work on Jesus in the first place. If it is accepted that emotion is making primary decisions and influencing critical methods, this does not mean critical methods do not have a positive role to play in relation to the primordial emotion guiding interpretation. In fact, this makes the need for a critical psychological method all the more important in relation to historical critical method.

---

[39]Nietzsche (1967) 267.

If interest in Jesus, whether historical or theological, has a strong, if not predominant, emotional dimension, this is usually not acknowledged, nor named as such. Emotion has a bad name in scholarship, and both methods and literary style have been designed to apparently exclude it from scholarly pursuits and results. If scholarship can be said to have repressed emotion, then, as Freud said, it returns in other forms, perhaps as ideology or dogmatism. It is always present as an invisible hand guiding interest, commitment, choice, judgement, and the framing of meaning. According to Hayden White, this is the level of being that guides any real history writing. Citing H. I. Marrou, he says, the historian "will not pass his time in splitting hairs over questions which do not keep any one from sleeping.... He will pursue, in his dialogue with the past, the elaboration of *the* question which *does* keep *him* from sleeping, the central problem of his existence, the solution of which involves his life and entire person."[40] What keep us from sleeping are not calm and bloodless ideas, but issues that matter emotionally, and emotional conflicts that may escape our awareness.

Another scholar at the turn of the century, George Tyrrell, seemingly borrowing from Schweitzer's insight, put the problem of subjectivity this way, "The Christ that Harnack sees, looking back through nineteen centuries of Catholic darkness, is only the reflection of a Liberal Protestant face, seen at the bottom of a deep well."[41]

This image of the historian's face at the bottom of a deep well is so well known in the field of historical Jesus research that it is referred to at times without citation.[42] In Tyrrell's context, the use of the word "only" signifies that this image is meant to be dismissive. The truth of the metaphor cannot be contested, but what might help this discussion is deeper reflection on the nature of the "reflection" at the bottom of the deep well. Could this "reflection" be more than what common sense implies and dismisses? This is what Jung provides—an archetypal view of subjectivity that reveals it as both constituted by, and participating in constituting, a world that becomes known through a process of mirroring, or projection.

For these reasons I will propose the theoretical integration of analytical psychology and historical critical methods as one way toward a deeper understanding of the subjectivity of the interpreter that includes the conscious, unconscious, and collective unconscious di-

---

[40]Cited by Gossman (1978) 28.
[41]Tyrrell (1909) 44.
[42]Loughlin (1984) 325. Loughlin also qualifies reflection as "only" personal.

mensions of the scholar. This perspective envisions a creative role for subjectivity in the epistemology of historiography, and brings a critical hermeneutic and psychological perspective to the totality of the person involved in interpretation. Analytical psychology takes an archetypal perspective on the phenomenon of emotion, thereby giving to emotion a reality status and value in its own right. This does not privilege emotion over other factors, but it does rescue such subjective passions from the skeptical suspicions of Cartesian and positivist methodology. Yet critical methods still have a central and crucial role within both method and interpretation in relation to emotion and its dynamism of projection. It is emotion, positive or negative, that creates our meaningful involvement with texts, and compels our interest or disinterest in them. The emotional meaning of texts is not merely personal, but archetypal and ontological first of all.

Jung's understanding of emotion differentiates it from the conventional psychological concepts of feeling and affect. Jung indicates that emotion "is not an activity of the individual but something that happens to him."[43] Emotion is a decisive presence no matter what our methods, and we need an approach that appreciates the ontological and hermeneutic value of its presence. Not just any psychology will do in this situation, because most psychological theory remains individualistic and reductive. Jung's analytical psychology offers us an approach to emotion that is both critical and hermeneutic, searching out its personal and archetypal meanings.

Why Crossan and Jung

I have chosen to compare a prominent Jesus historian, John Dominic Crossan, and a prominent psychologist, Carl Gustav Jung, because I am investigating problems in which subjectivity, method and Jesus historiography all intersect.

Crossan is important because he is representative of "Third Quest" Jesus scholars who are attempting to employ historical critical methods in order, *inter alia,* to control the impact of the scholar's personal preferences on their work. Crossan is explicit about the need for methodological integrity and what his method is, and he is a prominent figure in, and shaper of, contemporary Jesus research. Crossan

---

[43]Jung (1951) 15. All notes to the Collected Works (CW) cite the numbered paragraphs.

is not a mere historical positivist by any means. He even advocates an "hermeneutical Jesus" in contrast to an "historical Jesus."[44] Nevertheless, there is an unresolved tension in his work between the traditions of positivism and hermeneutics. I will explore the philosophical and psychological implications of his method as representative of contemporary historical critical Jesus research.

Jung is important because he is the only major psychologist who has made the figure of Jesus Christ a focus of his work. While his formal writings focus his psychological method on the Christ as mythic symbol, he also makes many comments about the historical Jesus. I am interested in both aspects of his work. His comments about the historical Jesus, like that of most other psychologists who have approached Jesus,[45] clearly express his own interpretive viewpoint. Jung does share the historical and critical view of the biblical texts of his time, but he shows little interest in the careful, critical textual and historical methods that characterize the work of most historical Jesus scholars. Nevertheless, psychological discourse about Jesus, Jung's as well as others, has an historical verisimilitude that is often quite engaging, even at times seductive, not unlike a good historical novel. Why this is the case is one interest of my study.

Jung's general psychological approach engages, explicitly and implicitly, major philosophical issues of the Western tradition, most especially, epistemology, hermeneutics and ontology. Although Jung was not a professional philosopher, he struggled with philosophical problems from a psychological perspective that is most compatible with the deep hermeneutic perspective of Heidegger's existential phenomenology. Ironically, though contemporaries, Jung had no interest in Heidegger and was dismissive of his thought. Several authors have explored Jung's philosophical significance.[46]

---

[44]Crossan (1983).

[45]Among the psychological treatments of Jesus and Christ consulted, see Berguer (1923); Cramer (1959); Dolto and Severin (1979); Dourley (1981); Edinger (1987); Garvie (1907); Hall (1917); Hitchcock (1907); Hobbs (1962); Howes (1984); Hurt (1982); Kunkel (1952); Leavy (1988); Leslie (1965); McGann (1985); Miller (1981); Rizzuto (1979); Rollins (1983); Sanford (1970); Schweitzer (1948); Stein (1985); Ulanov (1975); Wuellner and Leslie (1984); Wolff (1987).

[46]Brooke (1991); Clarke (1992); Jarrett (1981, 1990, 1992); Kelly (1993); Nagy (1991); Steele (1982).

Method

This study is a comparative analysis of those texts of Jung and Crossan, wherein they specifically focus on the figure of Jesus. I will describe and critically evaluate their respective methods, how their methods influence their view of the relationship between history and myth and their view of the psyche, or human nature.

In the light of this analysis I will compare the multiple images of Jesus that emerge from these two twentieth-century critical approaches to the traditions about Jesus. My method will be phenomenological and critical in relation to both Jung's and Crossan's methods and the resulting images of Jesus.

My approach to, and use of, Jung will be guided by several critical interpreters of his work, such as Homans, Heisig, Steele, and Brooke. Heisig and Steele both show that Jung's work is not narrowly scientific, but humanistic and hermeneutic. Brooke claims Jung must be read as a phenomenologist, within the context of Heidegger's hermeneutic phenomenology, in order to be understood, and not as a Cartesian psychologist. Homans applies the concepts of "repudiation" and "assimilation" to interpret Jung's approach to the religion of his father and his own childhood. I will apply the same concepts to interpret how Jung handled the problem of historical materialism. In my view, Jung attempted to repudiate historical materialism, but paradoxically ended up assimilating its core meaning into his overall depth-psychological hermeneutic.

I will view Crossan as carrying on a tradition of historical positivism that dates from Descartes and the Enlightenment. He shares these basic methodological assumptions with many others in the "Third Quest," such as Marcus Borg, Robert Funk, Richard Horsley, John Meier, E. P. Sanders, and others. Even those critical of Crossan, his historical methods, and resulting historiography, like James Breech, N. T. Wright, and especially Ben Witherington, I believe, still lay claim implicitly to some basic positivist presuppositions about historical method and historiography.

My approach to critical historiography will be guided by the theoretical orientations developed by Brian Stock, Peter Munz, Paul Veyne, and Hayden White, among others. They are among the critical theorists who discuss the inescapable role of the historian's personal and cultural *psyche* in the writing of history. Certeau notes that history writing is involved in creating "history" much more than it might appear to be discovering it. And Stock states, "Historical writing does not treat reality; it treats the interpreter's relation to it."[47] The "interpreter's relation" to "reality" is the place where depth-psychology enters, both practically and theoretically. The contributions of critical historiography are explored in chapter three.

The philosophical context of my approach is the hermeneutic circle, and the psychological context is an archetypal understanding of projection. Heidegger's view of the hermeneutic circle and Jung's view of projection, transform the traditional problems of Cartesian episte-mology, and fundamentally change our view of the relationship be-tween subject and object. This hermeneutic shift within epistemology has crucial implications for historical method and history writing because it shows us the inescapable hermeneutic foundation of episte-mology. Heidegger's ontological interpretation of the hermeneutic circle and Jung's archetypal view of projection also have important implications for psychology. They radically alter our view of the rela-tionship between psyche and world; it is not so much a *relationship* as it is an ontological and archetypal unity. Within this new view the nature of our relationship with the world must be explored.

This book explores these problems and issues through the following five chapters. Chapter two examines Crossan's historical critical method as described in *The Historical Jesus, In Parables* and *Raid on the Articulate.* I will make explicit the dichotomy between epistemology and hermeneutics that runs throughout his work.

Chapter three presents perspectives on history that are missing in Crossan's work from the points of view of several critical histori-ographers. Their views highlight the fundamentally hermeneutic and constructive nature of historical method and historiography. This chapter sets the stage for chapter four which is an exploration of the philosophical implications of Jung's general psychological method and an examination of his approach to the Jesus tradition at the level of the Christ symbol. This chapter reads Jung as a hermeneutic phenome-nologist in the light of Heidegger's fundamental ontology, and seeks to show Jung's relevance to the view of history held by the critical histo-riographers of chapter three. Jung's view of the psyche includes a deep historicality because his definition of the archetype incorporates a his-torical phenomenology. And it is his view of the archetypal priority of

---

[47]Stock (1990) 80.

imagination in how we apprehend reality that contributes to reordering the traditional role of epistemology.

Chapter five examines the images of the historical Jesus in Crossan's and Jung's work and suggests an evaluative criteria based on a phenomenology of history and myth. I suggest a phenomenological approach to the *image* of the historical Jesus as *image*, in contrast to the unwarranted positivist attempts to establish facts about the historical Jesus. Chapter six summarizes the themes running through this book and proposes to integrate analytical psychology and historical criticism. I will suggest that such an integration provides an alternative role for historical criticism in the quest for the historical Jesus—namely, to participate in the differentiation and evolution of consciousness. Rather than establish the facts about the original Jesus of Nazareth, which historical criticism cannot do, it can evaluate and create the meaning of history in the present

CHAPTER TWO

JOHN DOMINIC CROSSAN'S HISTORICAL METHOD

Introduction

John Dominic Crossan's historical method is my point of entry to the problem of the unwitting and subtle presence of historical positivism in the quest for the historical Jesus and within the Third Quest in particular. Crossan relies heavily on positivist presuppositions in his historical approach to Jesus. I realize this is an unusual claim to make in relation to Crossan who's work on Jesus and the Jesus traditions is marked by strong affinities with literary, structuralist, hermeneutic and postmodern sensibilities. But even in his inaugural literary works on Jesus, *In Parables* and *Raid on the Articulate*, there is a strong positivist influence in his efforts to use historical critical methods to determine the definitive *voice* of Jesus. I will undertake a close reading of his method in *The Historical Jesus* and show that the assumptions guiding his view of history, of time and of historical critical method are thoroughly positivistic. Uncovering the positivist presuppositions that guide his work will also point to the underlying hermeneutic and narrative, i.e., mythic, perspectives that in fact contextualize and create every so-called historical "fact."

Crossan inherits a legacy of historical positivism that is an important part of the context of the origins of the quest for the historical Jesus as well as a significant condition of its continuation. By way of introducing Crossan I will first present a brief overview of the quest that is generally understood to have begun in the eighteenth century. This is also the historical context of the contemporary Third Quest in which Crossan participates.

Historical Context

In this section I will review the three phases[1] of the quest for the historical Jesus commonly referred to as the "Old Quest,"[2] the "New Quest,"[3] and the "Third Quest."[4] It is a scholarly convention to use the year 1778 as the beginning of the Old Quest, the year of the posthumous publication of Herman Samuel Reimarus' (1694–1768) *The Aims of Jesus and His Disciples*. One reason Reimarus is significant is that, as Schweitzer states, "Before Reimarus, no one had attempted to form a historical conception of the life of Jesus."[5] The notion that Jesus as an historical person could have aims of his own was itself an important and new historical development in relation to thought about Jesus. By and large, any idea of Jesus was identified with the Christ of theological dogma, who functioned as an agent in a divine drama in which the course of all the action is known in advance. Prior to Reimarus, the culturally prevailing theological view of the Christ made it impossible even to raise the question of a historical Jesus with personal thoughts.

Schweitzer makes it clear that the tone of this period of historical Jesus investigation (1778–1906) was anti-dogmatic. The Jesus of history was "an ally in the struggle against the tyranny of dogma."[6] The quest for the historical Jesus was an extension of the Enlightenment and the rise of rationality as the basis of understanding in all areas of reality. Historical phenomena had to be explained in terms of material causes and effects, and not in terms of divine supernatural interventions. So, Jesus too was to be understood in the light of history explained rationally. Reason took its stand, as a liberating force, against authority of all kinds, especially political, ecclesiastical and scriptural. The idea of historical study was to understand the past independently of philosophical or theological assertions.[7] The step to base the validity of knowledge on rationality was a major epistemological development epitomized by the Enlight-

---

[1]Tatum (1982) presents a convenient overview of the history of the quest.
[2]Schweitzer (1906/1968) is the definitive study of the Old Quest.
[3]Robinson (1979) presents a detailed analysis of the shift from Old Quest to New Quest in the light of a changing conception of history and the self.
[4]There are several overviews of the contemporary situation, among which are Neill and Wright (1988), Borg (1994) and Charlesworth (1994).
[5]Schweitzer (1906/1968) 13.
[6]Schweitzer (1906/1968) 4.
[7]Krentz (1975) 16-30.

enment. I explore the significance of the Cartesian epistemological legacy in chapter four.

Schweitzer's own book, *The Quest of the Historical Jesus*, published in 1906, is considered to have brought this first phase of the quest, conventionally called the "Old Quest," to a close. Schweitzer is credited with exposing the subjective nature of all the liberal lives of Jesus produced during the nineteenth century.

A hiatus, or period of "No Quest" (1921–1953), is generally understood to have coincided with the work of Rudolf Bultmann. Bultmann held a pessimistic view of the possibility of ever getting back to Jesus because of the extensive theological, or kerygmatic, nature of the gospel traditions. This period in general was interested in unraveling the theological traditions of the gospels and operated under the assumption that retrieving the historical Jesus was both not possible and not necessary. It was not necessary because Christian faith should not be, and never had been, based on the changeable and unreliable results of historical research. Bultmann sought to reinterpret the basic message of the gospels by demythologizing the ancient kerygma. He brought a Heideggerian existential interpretation to what he saw as the mythological and antiquarian language of the gospels. Unfortunately, for New Testament historical critical studies, Bultmann's existential interpretation of Heidegger has obscured the profound hermeneutic and historicist significance of Heidegger for ontology in general, and the ontological foundations of historical studies in particular. I address this aspect of Heidegger, in relation to Jung, in chapter four.

Bultmann's influence was considerable, but in 1953, Ernst Käsemann, a former student of Bultmann, challenged the prevailing skepticism about the historical reliability of the gospels and inaugurated what became known as the "New Quest." He claimed, in a lecture, "The Problem of the Historical Jesus,"[8] delivered before a group of Bultmann's students, that the gospels did preserve authentic historical material about Jesus, and that it could be recovered.

The fundamental criterion Käsemann used for determining the authenticity of the distinctive material about Jesus was that of dissimilarity. The criterion of dissimilarity holds that statements attributed to Jesus in the gospels that can be shown not to derive from either a Jewish or an early Christian context are considered to be authentic

---

[8]Käsemann (1964) 15-47.

Jesus material. This criterion was considered to be the basis of the New Quest's attempt to use the historical critical method to establish bedrock Jesus tradition.

The adequacy of this criterion has undergone and continues to attract serious questioning in the light of the perspective of Jewish scholars interested in Jesus, a greater sensitivity to the historical complexity of multiple Judaisms at the time of Jesus and the need to see Jesus more in continuity with both Judaism and early Christianity. To view Jesus as only distinct and dissimilar from his socio-historical context invites the danger of making him so different that he would have been unintelligible to those around him. While it is true that Jesus was distinctive, contemporary historical awareness wants to also view him as embedded in, and in continuity with, the specific historical processes and constraints of his time and place.[9]

In spite of the New Quest's use of historical critical method to attempt to establish authentic Jesus material its real concern was theological. The focus of Käsemann's lecture was a general theological problem arising out of the extreme skepticism of the Bultmann period. The theological problem was, and continues to be for some, that if the identity between the earthly Jesus and the exalted Christ, which the gospels assert, is broken by radical historical skepticism, then we are left with a Christ that is docetic and mythic. Myth then replaces history, and a heavenly being replaces the man from Nazareth.[10]

Docetism, an early Christian heresy, held that Jesus Christ was really divine and his humanity only an appearance. The theological concern is that if a historical understanding of Jesus is not necessary for faith, then the Christian faith becomes merely docetic and mythic, faith loses its connection to history, and history itself loses its fundamental value. Therefore, it was theology's need that reasserted the historical reliability, in part, of the gospels with respect to Jesus, and sought to reestablish the historical continuity between the preaching of the man Jesus and the preaching of the first primitive Christian communities about Jesus.

The New Quest had a sharp awareness of the distinction between the Jesus of history and the Christ of faith, as well as the serious historical and theological breech between the two established by historical criticism of the gospels. The New Quest's agenda was to reestablish historical links between Jesus of Nazareth and Christ, in order to avoid

---

[9]Harvey (1982) 8.
[10]Käsemann (1964) 25, 34.

docetism and the reduction of Christianity to myth. The motivation for this task was theological and not historical.

Depending on the perspective one takes, the New Quest either died out in the 1970s[11] or continues in continuity with the current flurry of Life of Jesus research that began in the 1980s and remains active today.[12] N. T. Wright cites with approval his predecessor, S. Neill, who said in 1962, "the *historical* reconstruction of the life and history of Jesus has as yet hardly begun."[13] Wright himself states in 1988 that "actual historical enquiry after Jesus" only started a few years ago.[14] This contemporary resurgence of Jesus research activity is generally referred to as the "Third Quest." Wright states that these scholars work as *historians,* implying that they do not have theological axes to grind, either against dogmatic Christianity as in the Old Quest, or for theological continuity as in the New Quest. And these contemporary scholars also have "no doubt that it is possible to know quite a lot about Jesus of Nazareth and that it is worth while to do so...."[15]

The Third Quest has several general characteristics that serve to distinguish it from the first two quests: (1) its primarily historical orientation without the explicit theological motivations of the first two quests, as well as its confidence in the possibility of an historical account of Jesus' ministry (but not his life); (2) its historical orientation leads to the explicit and strong emphasis on Jesus' Jewishness and the awareness of the necessity of attempting to know the nature of the Jewish context in which Jesus lived and worked; (3) a broader view in general of the historical problem that does not just focus on whether or not individual units of gospel text are authentic Jesus tradition; (4) its critique of the New Quest's over-emphasis on traditio-critical analysis (what Crossan calls "transmissional analysis") of gospel texts, and the critique of both form criticism and the criteria of dissimilarity; (5) a general openness to interdisciplinary methods, and especially to engagement with the social sciences.[16]

While many consider the current development in Jesus research refreshing, it has done little, if anything, to minimize the historical and hermeneutic difficulties that bedevil the quest for the historical Jesus,

---

[11]Witherington (1995) 11.

[12]Telford (1994) 56.

[13]Neill and Wright (1988) 379.

[14]Neill and Wright (1988) 380.

[15]Neill and Wright (1988) 379.

[16]Telford (1994) 57-58; Neill and Wright (1988) 397-99.

among which is the problem of multiple images of Jesus discussed at the beginning of Chapter One. In fact, the complexity and confusion have only seemed to increase. However, the general aim of Jesus research is clearly stated by Telford: "The various elements of the Jesus jigsaw—his place in Judaism, the sayings tradition, the narrative tradition, the miracle tradition, his death, the emergence of Christianity and, I would add, the development of Christology—*all need historical explanation*."[17] Why this is the case, that all need *historical* explanation, is not itself addressed by Telford. Is the *need* itself for historical explanation self-evident? And if is it self-evident, why is it self-evident? And what is *historical* explanation expected to do for the Jesus jigsaw puzzle? I believe it is precisely the problem of the nature of "historical explanation" that needs to be addressed. The philosophical questions about the nature of history and historiography, while approached in a variety of ways by a few, are largely left unexplored. For example, the following scholars have touched on various problems of historical criticism in relation to the quest for the historical Jesus. Kelly (1991), J. Martin (1987) and Wink (1973) argue for a role for subjectivity in interpretation but do not address the problem of the collective unconscious, nor do they address wider problems of history and historiography as such. Meyer (1979) and Robinson (1979) both critique nineteenth-century positivist views of history, but ironically, still seek certain historical knowledge about Jesus. Oakman (1986) simply argues for the distinction between historical and theological approaches to Jesus, and for the inclusion of sociological models in historical Jesus research. Meier (1990; 1991) attempts to clarify historical concepts and limits but does not address the narrative and subjective nature of historiography. Ott (1964) and B. Martin (1990) touch on significant aspects of the ontology of history and the importance of self-understanding in historical research respectively, but do not delve into the subjective and narrative essence of history and historiography.

My aim in this work is to explore the following three interrelated areas that are missing from philosophical discussions of the quest for the historical Jesus, and to make them explicit: (1) the fundamentally constructive, hermeneutic and narrative, i.e., mythic, nature of historiography and history as discourse; (2) the relationship between the narrative structure of history and Jung's view of subjectivity, what I will call either deep-subjectivity or archetypal-subjectivity; and (3), the re-

---

[17]Telford (1994) 61; italics added.

lationship between Jung's view of archetypal-subjectivity and Heidegger's ontological analysis of Dasein. I will utilize these three interrelated themes to draw together a hermeneutic and historicist view of history with the deep structures of both narrative and subjectivity into a new understanding of the term *myth*.

Because the quest for the historical Jesus, in general, has not deepened its understanding of the necessarily narrative, i.e., mythic and subjective, structure of historiography, it continues blithely along, seemingly oblivious to the dangerously thin epistemological ice on which it skates. With this in mind, that my own focus is on the philosophical issues that condition Jesus historiography, I will now turn to the examination of Crossan's historical method.

Crossan's Method

In this section I will examine Crossan's historical method as he describes it in his major works on Jesus, *In Parables, Raid on the Articulate*, and *The Historical Jesus*. For Crossan there is a distinction between historical method and literary critical method, or diachronic analysis and synchronic analysis, and there are different but related claims each makes. There is also an unwitting dichotomy between these methods in Crossan's work that lends his overall method a split quality, that is, a method in which the left hand seems not to know what the right hand is doing. I will focus here on his historical method and the explicit and implicit claims it makes, as well as on examining the problematic nature of the dichotomy in his method. Later, in chapter five I will examine Crossan's image of Jesus.

By singling out Crossan from among a large group of Third Quest Jesus scholars, I do not mean to imply that only Crossan's historical method is in error, and others have a better, or less flawed, approach. Quite the contrary, Crossan's approach to Jesus historiography probably holds the seeds to a more creative hermeneutic method than many other contemporary Jesus scholars, once the internal conflict between epistemology (traditional historical-critical method) and hermeneutics (literary, comparative and structuralist methods) is overcome. I take the view that Crossan is representative of contemporary Jesus historiography, in general, not the least because he is sensitive to the subjective nature of historiography, and of Jesus historiography in particular. There is probably no Jesus scholar writing today who is not explicitly and keenly aware that all historical research is colored and influenced by the personality of the historian. But this awareness never seems to penetrate deeply into the overall approach and methods that then shape the historical writing of the scholar. The Jesus scholar proceeds to write about Jesus as if he or she is writing about Jesus, that is, the original Jesus "back there" in history. This problem also appears in contemporary historiography as well, as we will see in chapter three.

I will begin with an examination of the methods of Crossan's *The Historical Jesus*. The reasons for starting here are threefold: (1) it is his magnum opus on the historical Jesus; (2) it attempts to account for all the levels of the Jesus tradition and to locate them historically; and (3) its method is made explicit in response to specific methodological problems. After examining the formal method of *The Historical Jesus* I will examine the methods of Crossan's *In Parables* and *Raid on the Articulate*, which antedate *The Historical Jesus* by almost twenty years. These two books enable a closer look at the epistemological and hermeneutic conflicts I and others[18] perceive Crossan struggling with, and yet, of which he seems to be still largely unaware.[19]

---

[18]Brown and Malbon (1984); Wright (1993).

[19]In *Who Killed Jesus* (1995), Crossan draws on clear, modernist distinctions when he states, "The questions or objections put to me after public lectures or on radio call-in shows are usually theological rather than historical, usually personal and autobiographical rather than methodological and theoretical, usually more about faith than about fact"/(211), implying that his work is based on historical method that discovers facts. At the very beginning of this book he states, "It is about the historicity of the passion narratives..."/(xi). But then he also states, "It is not (in a postmodern world) that we find once and for all who the historical Jesus was way back then. It is that each generation and century must redo that historical work and establish its best reconstruction..."/(217). He asserts that all humans live out of the depths of myth and metaphor and that these are the foundations on which we build our lives/(218). And again, he asserts that faith is based not on fact, but on interpretation, and faith cannot turn interpretations into facts/(217). And yet, as we will see, it is Crossan's "faith" in Cartesian epistemology that turns his historical interpretations into "facts." The ontological nature of myth, metaphor, history, and historical facts, and their interrelationship, remain ambiguous and conflicted throughout Crossan's work.

Method in *The Historical Jesus*

Crossan's *The Historical Jesus* is a marvelous, and in many respects, convincing achievement, weaving together many complex strands of tradition and scholarship in order to reconstruct the historical Jesus in his historical setting. It is an example of painstaking scholarship that is also passionate about its subject. In undertaking this particular work Crossan is explicitly concerned with methodological integrity. In his short "Prologue," he describes both the methodological problems he believes are plaguing Jesus research, the multiplicity of Jesus images and scholarly subjectivity, and the method he will use to deal with these problems. In eight pages[20] of this Prologue Crossan describes his formal method. Eight pages do not seem like much in a book with 426 pages of text, but this Prologue functions as a Preface, and as such, seeks to instruct the reader, and therefore control the reader, in how the book is to be read. This short Prologue describes the formal structure of his method, and the rest of the book is what Crossan calls the "material investment" in the formal structure of his method. I will focus on the explicit and implicit claims made by this formal structure of Crossan's method. I will not examine here the specific content of his material investments nor their results. I am examining the epistemological claims of the method.

Crossan states that his "methodology for Jesus research has a triple triadic process," three major components with three subheadings each. On first reading such a scheme seems overly complex. For clarity, I present its components in the table below (next page).

I will discuss the triple triadic process in the light of Crossan's description of how each triad functions in the general plan of his method. He refers to the three major triads as "campaign," "strategy," and "tactics" respectively. Why does he characterize his method with military terms? What kind of epistemological position does this suggest? To attack an enemy and emerge a winner? It remains to be seen, but this imagery does not only suggest careful planning at several levels. It also suggests a certain kind of struggle in which an adversary must be conquered.

---

[20]Crossan (1991) xxvii - xxxiv.

Crossan's Triple Triadic Process

I. First Triad: Campaign—overall plan
    A. Macrocosmic level: comparative social *anthropology*
    B. Mesocosmic level: Greco-Roman *history*
    C. Microcosmic level: ancient *literature* about Jesus

II. Second Triad: Strategy—organizing the Jesus tradition
    A. Inventory: sources, texts—historical situation and literary
        relationship
    B. Stratification: chronological sequence of sources and texts;
        30–150 C.E.
    C. Attestation: multiple and *independent* for each Jesus
        tradition complex

III. Third Triad: Tactics—using the Jesus tradition
    A. Sequence of strata: must begin with the first stratum
    B. Hierarchy of attestation: must begin with highest count of
        independent attestation
    C. Bracketing of singularity: avoid single attestation

The First Triad establishes a kind of overall epistemological process in which the three areas of knowledge, anthropology, history and literature (I,A,B,C) are to interact fully and equally in order to achieve an "effective synthesis." The three levels represent knowledge from three different disciplines, and they are to interact not only cumulatively but also as check and countercheck on each other. This First Triad seems to propose an epistemological integration suggesting that the interaction of these three levels will yield knowledge about Jesus. But while Crossan demands equal sophistication at each level, he states that "any study of the historical Jesus stands or falls on how one handles the literary level of the text itself."[21] Can we determine in what sense Crossan means "stands or falls"?

The Second and Third Triads of his method, two-thirds of his triadic structure, are focused on the Microcosmic level of the Jesus tradition. Does how one handles the literary level of the text determine the validity of the study or the plausibility? Is it epistemological veracity or convincing interpretation that stands or falls? Or is it one's

---

[21]Crossan (1991) xxiv.

honesty or dishonesty that stands or falls? It will become apparent that Crossan means the *epistemological validity* of the study stands or falls on how the Jesus texts are handled. This is an important question because the way the issue is framed here, standing and falling, while not stated explicitly, actually opposes fact and interpretation. The distinction between "epistemological validity" and "interpretation" is crucial to Crossan's results. Yet, he remains ambiguous about his own stand on this distinction and which form of validity he is relying on. Further, while he focuses most of his method on handling the *problematic* nature of the Jesus tradition, he treats the Macrocosmic level, social anthropology and sociology, and the Mesocosmic level, Greco-Roman history, and history itself, as if they are *completely unproblematic.*[22]

The Nature of the Jesus Tradition

The Jesus tradition is highly problematic, and Crossan conceives of this tradition, in both the gospels and other sources, as composed of "three major layers." He refers to these layers as "original, developmental, and compositional layers, or [as] retention, development, and creation."[23] The original layer is considered to be the preservation of "at least the essential core" of the words and actions of Jesus. The developmental layer is when this recorded or remembered original material is applied by others to new situations and problems. The final layer of creation includes both the creation by others of new sayings of Jesus and stories about Jesus, as well as the creation of larger complexes, or narrative contexts, that thereby change the content. In other words, it is the working hypothesis of biblical scholars like Crossan that the gospel stories about Jesus as the Christ are based on an actual, historic Jesus of Nazareth, but that they are both heavily amplified with mythological and legendary material and written for specific and differing theological purposes. There is debate about how much the gospels are *based* on Jesus and his actual life, and how much they *refer* to him in order to authorize their own particular vision of Jesus as the Christ. At any rate, even though the gospels are not considered history or biography by any criteria, ancient or modern, according to Crossan,

---

[22]For the social sciences, see, for example, Andreski (1972) and Rabinow and Sullivan (1987). For history, see my chapter three, "Critical Historiography."
[23]Crossan (1991) xxxi.

his working hypothesis assumes that the gospels preserve something of what the actual, historic Jesus of Nazareth said and did.

The Second Triad—Strategy

Crossan's Second Triad is how he has chosen to sort through the complex, confusing and ambiguous aspects of the Jesus tradition. Crossan's guiding image is one of "sedimented layers," and he makes reference to the methods of archeology.[24] The analogy with archeology and "sedimented layers" is worth examining for a moment because of its implications for both epistemology and the nature of history.

According to Crossan, current Jesus-research methods at the end of this century are similar to the methods employed by archeology at the end of the last century. That is, the archeologist, digging into an ancient site at random, would take what objects appealed to him as precious or unique (obviously determined by personal and cultural bias), and bring them home to "some imperial museum." This amounted to little more than "cultural looting." Today, archeology employs "scientific stratigraphy" in order to establish the "proper chronological layer" for any object in the dig. Crossan states that this proper stratigraphy prevents, or checks, "almost any conclusion" from being "derived from almost any object." Therefore, the purpose of scientific stratigraphy, in Crossan's presentation, is to prevent the archeologist's subjective and random preferences from distorting his conclusions, and by implication, to also prevent cultural imperialism. At this point, one hears the critic of ideology raising the question as to whether or not the so-called objective methods of Western science are not themselves a form of cultural imperialism. But let me continue with Crossan's imagery.

Crossan sees contemporary Jesus research as little more than "textual looting" from the "mound of the Jesus tradition." Because there is no overall stratigraphy applied to the Jesus tradition that would explain why one item is given emphasis over another in one's presentation of Jesus, the impression arises that "acute scholarly subjectivity" has predetermined the result. In order to avoid textual looting and the appearance of acute scholarly subjectivity, Crossan employs his Second Triad to propose a chronological stratigraphy for the texts of the Jesus tradition, and by implication, to give the impression of

---

[24]Crossan (1991) xxviii.

scientific objectivity. Of course, Crossan never claims scientific objectivity, but his choice of language, imagery, and the oppositions he creates, such as between "scientific stratigraphy" and "scholarly subjectivity," does imply some kind of scientific objectivity.

Crossan fails to note the significant difference between the objects of archeology—dirt, rock and human-made *material* artifacts—and the objects of the Jesus tradition—words, stories, and texts. He also does not mention the radical difference between establishing chronology in relation to material stuff like soil and objects, and establishing chronology in relation to words, stories, and texts. To complicate the matter even more, there are of course no hard texts that date back to Jesus. Scholars have to presume some kind of oral tradition for the twenty– to thirty–year gap that exists between Jesus and the first presumed texts, as well as the ongoing intermingling of oral and literary traditions. The actual hard-copy texts that do exist are centuries older, and present their own technical textual difficulties when it comes to establishing the common text of the New Testament. Language is a far more ambiguous and ephemeral phenomena to deal with than the more stable objects of archeology, more like the swirling smoke from a fire than things lying in the dirt (taking this image suggestively and not literally). Although most biblical scholars accept the historically layered image of the Jesus tradition, this may be a misleading image. It could also be argued that the final product, any gospel in itself, is such a completely integrated new literary whole, that it is just as impossible to untangle its components as it would be to separate out the water, flour, salt and yeast from a loaf of bread, or the so-called "layers" of the smoke coming from a fire. (We will see in chapter five that Jung argues for the complete integrity of the gospels but for reasons quite different from concerns for literary integrity.)

Crossan's archeological guiding image does not just influence his view of the texts, but also conditions his view of history and time. It implies that the words and deeds of Jesus are objects lying back there somewhere in time waiting to be unearthed. These overlapping connections between archeology, texts and history also leave the impression of epistemological similarity, and therefore of similar epistemological validity of results from the respective methods. Crossan never mentions the subjectivity and ambiguity inherent in archeological interpretations, nor the fundamentally interpretive nature of dating and chronology in general. Chronological structure is an interpretive model humans create, that itself creates both the kinds of information it provides and the relative value of the information. What sort of ontological assumptions determine the kind of epistemological content we might expect from chronological, sequential, and developmental models that attempt to bring a certain kind of structure to time and create a particular view of what we call history? The answer is in one's view of being and of the nature of history in general. This will influence the kind of results one would expect from historical critical method. This question is discussed more fully in chapter three on critical historiography. Let us return to the Second Triad.

The Second Triad proposes three organizational strategies that will create a certain kind of order out of the chaos of the three layers of the Jesus tradition. First Crossan identifies his "inventory" (II,A) in terms of all literary sources, intracanonical and extracanonical, that refer to Jesus. Crossan does not privilege canonical texts, such as the three gospels Matthew, Mark and Luke, and in an article on materials and methods, he speaks of disciplining canonical bias.[25]

This inventory is not just a list of sources and texts however. Each source and text has a historical situation and a literary relationship, or no literary relationship, with the other texts that must be described. As Crossan admits this does not eliminate controversy because every aspect of the inventory is a problem. Determining historical and social provenance is not a simple matter and it is continuously debated. Literary relationships are also complex and difficult to determine. The source Q, for example, is not a text but a hypothetical construct that attempts to account for certain literary relationships found between Matthew and Luke that are not in Mark, their other common source. The problem is that most assertions about Q are debatable. The gospel of Thomas text is another problem. Is it dependent or independent in relation to the canonical gospels? The status of Thomas, historical and literary, is also a continuing debate. With the inventory Crossan attempts to make clear his stand on each problem area, but the inventory does not make clear the severity of the epistemological problems that surround this kind of data, nor the degree of personal opinion that informs the inventory's judgments.

Even though Crossan rejects canonical bias, he is establishing his own "canon" relying on the relative value of the texts and sources in his inventory based on stratification (II,B) and attestation (II,C). Stratification tells us which texts Crossan thinks are closest to Jesus in

---

[25]Crossan (1988a) 6.

time, and multiple independent attestation is supposed to tell us which sayings were not created by someone else and therefore might come from Jesus.

The stratification establishes four layers, 30–60, 60–80, 80–120, 120–150 C.E. (notice the layers are unequal, 30, 20, 40 and 30 years respectivel—the reasons for which are not spelled out). Such a stratification of layers implicitly establishes specific epistemological values, such as precision, clarity, objective criteria for judgment, and the objectification of time, that is, time as an object. Even if one declares that the dating of every unit of Jesus tradition is controversial, as Crossan does, the structure itself, of time as sedimented layers, leaves the specific epistemological impression of clarity and objectification, even if only unconsciously or subliminally, that may itself be ontologically deeply problematic.

Multiple independent attestation continues in this epistemological direction. It is a commonplace of critical historical method that two or more independent witnesses of an event gives us more assurance that some such event actually happened than if we had only one witness. One witness leaves us in doubt about how much, if not all, of a report has been made up. Setting aside the notorious unreliability of even eye-witnesses and the problems of interpretation and creativity in every observation and memory, the problem with multiple attestation in relation to Jesus is that there is an absolute epistemological gap between the multiple witnesses and the actual Jesus. All the witnesses and Jesus are dead, and no hard texts come to us from Jesus' own hand. Everything we know about Jesus is at least second– and third–hand. There is no way to confirm that material from multiple independent witnesses actually goes back to Jesus. The scholar can only assume or hope it does—it is a question of probability but not necessity. But how reliable is the probability? There are no epistemological procedures by which to determine this either. It remains a matter of personal preference. Crossan also allows that, theoretically, material with single attestation from the third or fourth stratum could be closer to Jesus' voice than material with multiple attestation from the first stratum. If this is true then more doubt is thrown on the epistemological weight Crossan grants to the criterion of multiple attestation in the first stratum.

Even if we accept the common understanding today that assertions about historical process and historical facts are in the realm of probability and not certainty, even if the goal of epistemological certainty has been abandoned by the historian, the aura of probability suggests that the historical reconstruction is close to some kind of historical truth about the past. Probability still assumes the past can be reconstructed. The questions remain, Is such a task as reconstruction of the past even possible? and if allowed that it is, What *kind* of truth is probable? What are the underlying ontological views that inform the conception of truth? Will it be a probable truth or a plausible truth? Probable implies the possibility of reconstruction of the past. Plausible implies reconstruction is not possible, and that only reinterpretation of our narrative traditions of the past, in the present for the needs of the present, is possible.

Another problem is that multiple attestation is not clear cut, not simply a matter of counting and collating. It is always a judgment and judgments inevitably include some subjective elements. After sorting through multiple versions of a saying or story, deciding whether or not it is actually from multiple independent sources involves judgments about the literary relationships of the sources and texts involved.

As Crossan builds the inventory he eliminates from consideration as historical any material he views as purely metaphorical. For example, the birth and resurrection stories are, to Crossan, so obviously symbolic that any consideration of their historicity is irrelevant. However, this material is not dismissed as valueless. While its metaphoric value is great, it is simply not part of Crossan's working hypothesis for the historical Jesus.

The Third Triad—Tactics

The Third Triad, Crossan's tactics for using the now chronologically organized and multiply attested rankings of the Jesus tradition, presses further on the epistemological values implied by these criteria. They are principles that follow logically from the "sequence of strata" (III,A) and the "hierarchy of attestation" (III,B). Crossan's method requires that the first strata, being chronologically closest to Jesus, must be the starting place for Jesus research. And while he allows that, theoretically, fourth-stratum material could be historically more accurate than first stratum, "scholarly discipline and investigative integrity" demand that one begin with the first stratum. Crossan's methodological priorities are clear, and he gives the epistemological privilege to the first stratum for building the working hypothesis about Jesus, which can then, supposedly, be checked against subsequent strata. But if this first stratum has so much epistemological weight, how much checking is likely going to come from the other implicitly "less important" strata?

In a way Crossan tries to claim that his method is only an exercise in method, and not a set of predetermined value judgments. He rejects the terms "authentic" and "unauthentic" in relation to the layers of the Jesus tradition, claiming that all layers have value and importance. The irony for Crossan is that the implicit values of his epistemological hierarchies belie the explicit claim of egalitarianism with regard to the value of the layers of the Jesus tradition, and "radical egalitarianism" is one of the hallmarks of his view of Jesus.

Crossan's other major principle, "hierarchy of attestation" (III,B), requires that within the first strata one must begin with those units with the highest count of independent attestation. The operating principle for this material of the first strata is that "everything is original until it is argued otherwise." But this means he does not have to argue *for* this material being original, he only has to argue against it being original. This stacks the deck in favor of what Crossan believes to be original, and he has, in principle, already established what is original with his hierarchical rankings of strata and attestation, in other words, by fiat. The argument seems to be over before it has begun. Is this a valid epistemological procedure, or is it a hermeneutic assertion?

Following "hierarchy of attestation" is "bracketing of singularity" (III,C). Crossan's method will avoid, at least for the purposes of establishing the working hypothesis about Jesus, all units of material found only in single attestation. As Crossan states, this is a safeguard because, "something found in at least two independent sources from the primary stratum cannot have been created by either of them. Something found there but only in single attestation could have been created by that source itself. Plural attestation in the first stratum pushes the trajectory back as far as it can go with at least formal objectivity."[26] But Crossan is not exactly clear about how far back back is. "Formal objectivity" seems to mean that "as far back as it can go" is original to Jesus, and his operative principle also postulates this. But a quick look at his inventory in Appendix 1[27] shows that 43 units out of the 131 that constitute this first stratum are rejected (given a minus sign) by Crossan as not original (almost thirty percent). (This count

---

[26]Crossan (1991) xxxii-iii.
[27]Crossan (1991) 434-41.

does not include the material given a plus and minus sign to indicate it is considered by Crossan to be so thoroughly metaphorical so as to make the consideration of its historicity irrelevant.) This numerical finding suggests there are more complex and subjective issues (i.e., personal judgments) involved in accepting material as original or not original. And Crossan seems to admit as much.

After he has described his methodological structure and process, he states, "It is clear, I hope, that my methodology does not claim a spurious objectivity, because almost every step demands a scholarly judgment and an informed decision. I am concerned, not with an un-attainable objectivity, but with an attainable honesty."[28] When Crossan refers to the decisions he must make personally about his method and his material he uses the word "judgment" or "scholarly judgment," and when he refers to the personal decisions other scholars must make he uses the phrase "acute scholarly subjectivity."[29] Why is Crossan mak-ing "judgments" but other scholars are caught up in "subjectivity"? What Crossan does not say, and should say, is that every step of his methodology is infused with personal and cultural, conscious and unconscious, interpretive preferences, or bias.

He claims that his methodology is only a series of "*formal* moves, which then demand a *material* investment." But this traditional epistemological division between form and content is not tenable, as Crossan himself observed in 1973 when he quoted Werner Heisenberg in the Preface of his book *In Parables*: "The scientific method of analyzing, explaining and classifying has become conscious of its limitations, which arise out of the fact that by its intervention science alters and refashions the object of its investigation. In other words *method and object can no longer be separated.* The scientific world view has ceased to be a scientific view in the true sense of the word."[30] Crossan also cited Roland Barthes, approvingly, in the same Preface, arguing against the possibility of historical chronologies giving access to the facts, and in favor of historians who deal in structures and intelligibility rather than the misguided attempt to duplicate so-called past reality. Why, after years of literary and structuralist interpretations of the Jesus tradition, has Crossan mounted such a massive traditional historical critical analysis with *The Historical Jesus*?

---

[28]Crossan (1991) xxxiv.
[29]Crossan (1991) xxviii.
[30]Crossan (1973) xv (italics added).

The ontological conflict between traditional historical-critical epistemology and literary and structuralist hermeneutics exists in Crossan's work from the start, beginning with *In Parables*. And even though his early work emphasized literary and structuralist interpretation, seemingly against traditional historical criticism, his own interpretations were always dependent upon a confidence in the secure results of a historical critical analysis of the Jesus tradition. Crossan always holds back from saying that literary, structural analysis should replace historical analysis, that structuralism should replace history. He never does take the position that the epistemologically assured results of traditional historical criticism are illegitimate and impossible in the face of the inevitable ontological implications of the structuralist, linguistic, and literary hermeneutic perspectives Crossan marshals for his interpretations of the Jesus tradition. He still seems to want something "solid" (*the* historical Jesus) to rest his interpretations on. Crossan seems to want to join together a historical critical epistemology that derives from the legacy of positivism and the quite different epistemology of literary and structuralist hermeneutics. This would not be a problem if it were not for the fact that the ontological presuppositions of each epistemology are mutually exclusive. They are mutually exclusive because they each take incompatible views of the ontological nature of the subject-object relationship. This problem will be examined in chapter four in terms of the Cartesian legacy that informs epistemology. Naturally, historical and literary, or hermeneutic, approaches to the Jesus tradition need not be mutually exclusive. But in order for them to be coherent and not contradictory, the ontological context within which they operate must be consistent.

Crossan might contend that I have misconstrued the formal method of *The Historical Jesus*, and it might seem that I have if it is taken that I am only examining and criticizing his conscious intent, that is, his attempt to achieve a methodological honesty. But I believe the military terms and the epistemological weighting of the Jesus tradition uncovered by my analysis of his triple triadic process suggest that there is more going on here than methodological honesty. I am interested in both the conscious and unconscious epistemology at work and the concomitant ontological assumptions embedded, not only in Crossan's historical critical method, but historical critical method in general. His formal structure makes no sense except in so far as it accepts the epistemological assumption and the ontological position that historical reconstruction is possible, and that time and the past are objects that can be retrieved. The triple triadic process is an attempt to achieve an integrated *epistemological* result—the reconstruction of the probable historical past and the probable historical Jesus. Crossan does not say that he is undertaking a hermeneutic creation of a plausible historical portrait of Jesus in the present in response to personal, social, and theological needs of the present. In spite of his caveat that "there is *only* reconstruction," it seems as though Crossan believes epistemological methods can and do enable reconstruction to make a reliable contact with the actual historic Jesus of Nazareth.

Method in *In Parables*

Let us now turn to *In Parables* for a closer look at Crossan's seemingly unwitting split view of reality, that is, his split ontology. *In Parables* is paradigmatic of the ontological dichotomy that exists in Crossan's work, between, on the one hand, the historical critical epistemology used to retrieve and reconstruct the original language and parables of Jesus, and on the other hand, the literary and structuralist hermeneutic used to interpret this "original" language of Jesus. Crossan's literary and structuralist hermeneutic is brought to the fore in *In Parables, The Dark Interval, Raid on the Articulate,* and *Cliffs of Fall,* but it is nowhere to be found in *The Historical Jesus.*

With the Preface[31] of *In Parables: The Challenge of the Historical Jesus,* Crossan explores the meaning of the book's title. The term "historical Jesus" is limited to the language of the parables of Jesus. Crossan reminds us "that we have literally no language and no parables of Jesus except and insofar as such can be retrieved and reconstructed from within the language of their earliest interpreters [i.e., the gospels and other sources]." In fact, Crossan suggests that we might consider the word "Jesus" as the name for "the reconstructed parabolic complex itself." The parabolic complex is the systemic unity of the parables that can be understood on its own terms without needing to know all the parables Jesus ever told. But Crossan does not say he is attaching the name "Jesus" to "*Crossan's* reconstructed parabolic complex." He asserts that the reconstructed parabolic complex is from *the* historic Jesus himself. Crossan arrives at both the reconstructed parable and the reconstructed parabolic complex using

---

[31]Crossan (1973) xiii-xvi.

the "methodological principles" of the "new quest for the historical Jesus," which he later comes to call "transmissional analysis."[32] I will undertake a close look at Crossan's transmissional analysis shortly. First I will look at what he means by "in parables."

For Crossan, the phrase *in parables* is ontological in that it represents the nature of reality itself. And not just any reality, but true reality. Parables can only be understood within their own world. They reveal a world only to those who are formed in them, that is, have the direct experience the parable itself is meant to be; these are the ones who have learned to live in parables. Those who have the *experience* of the parable's world are the "in-group," not a predetermined group, but a group created by the experience.

Crossan extends this sense of *in parables* to reality in general by saying that perhaps the only way to live and the only way to know reality is *in parables,* that "in parables" equals "in reality," that reality is parabolic. Crossan then cites three poets to amplify this parabolic ontology: "Only the imagination is real!" (William Carlos Williams). "So, say that final belief/Must be in a fiction" (Wallace Stevens). "Truth is knowing that we know we lie" (W. H. Auden). Crossan then cites Roland Barthes, who declares that historical positivism's claim on the facts is dead, historical narrative is dying, and history has more to do with intelligibility than with chronology. Following Barthes is the citation from Werner Heisenberg, noted above: "...method and object can no longer be separated." Crossan himself goes on to say that when we realize reality itself is parabolic, then we know reality "as images projected on the white screen of chaos...."[33]

This is an interesting litany of reality: imagination, fiction, lying, the end of chronological historical narrative as the image of reality, the fusion of method (and therefore of subject) and object in science (and so obviously in the social sciences and humanities), and finally, the identification of reality as only images projected on an ultimate ground of chaos. If this is reality, then what happens to the clearly positivist aims of the historical critical method and transmissional analysis? This view of reality, this ontological perspective, raises serious problems for the epistemological view of truth Crossan relies on to retrieve and re-construct the so-called original voice of the historic Jesus.

Such a view of reality, in which imagination, fiction, intelligibility and the fusion of method and object define the ground of

---

[32]Crossan (1983a) 246-48 and (1985) 7-10.
[33]Crossan (1973) xiv-xv.

being, is clearly an ontology in which subjectivity will have a prominent and central place. In this world view, the traditional positivist
ideal of rational, objective and neutral methods, leading to the attain-
ment of certain and indubitable knowledge, that is, true knowledge,
that unequivocally represents its object, is thoroughly undermined. In
this case, it is the historical critical method, of which transmissional
analysis is a part, that is informed by the positivist ideal of rational
epistemology, and its object is the historic Jesus. If the ground of being
is imagination, and method does not simply discover its object, but
shapes it, on what basis can Crossan be certain that he can retrieve the
original voice of Jesus? With these concerns in the background I will
examine Crossan's use of the historical critical method in this particular book.

He describes the method in five steps:[34] (1) A careful,
comparative and critical reading of Mark, Matthew and Luke reveals
the degree to which creative reinterpretation has been applied to the
Jesus tradition. All material attributed to Jesus has been revised,
rephrased and reframed by the gospel authors, as well as by anyone
else before or after the gospel authors who has handled the Jesus tradition. This first step establishes the problem that must be dealt with, the
so-called layers of reinterpretation and restatement that make up the
sources. (2) At this level any judgments about historicity or authenticity must be bracketed, because "...one does not even have a definite
saying on which to pass such judgments." All one has at this point are
multiple forms of sayings and stories. (3) This step is crucial: "...one
must attempt to write a history of the transmission of the piece of
tradition under discussion. This will trace its successive steps of
development and will isolate its earliest form." (4) Apply the criterion
of dissimilarity to this "earliest form" of the tradition in order to be
"methodologically sure that it stems from the historical Jesus and not
from the creativity of the church." The criterion of dissimilarity
depends on a sharp contrast between the form of the saying attributed
to Jesus and the Jewish and earliest Christian contexts. As Crossan
puts it, "...a rigorous negativity must be invoked to separate what
Jesus said or did from what the tradition records of his words and
deeds." (5) Extend the criterion of dissimilarity, especially in relation
to the parables, to determine not just content, but even more
importantly, style and form. Crossan knows he cannot legitimately

---

[34]Crossan (1973) 4-5.

claim to recover the actual words of Jesus, especially Jesus as an oral teacher, but he is confident that the structure of Jesus' parables, as metaphor and paradox, can be recovered.[35]

One problem with the criterion of dissimilarity is that the contrasting elements it depends on, both the reconstructed saying and then the forms of Judaism and early Christianity at the time, are all historical reconstructions. The type of Judaism and the type of Christianity with which Jesus is supposed to stand in contrast have to be built up by the historian. How confident can Crossan be that he has defined without remainder the contrasting contexts used to authenticate a saying of Jesus? Scholars can unwittingly reconstruct the historical context of Jesus in order to enable their idea of Jesus to stand out in particular ways. This circularity of historical reconstruction in relation to Jesus is inescapable.

To demonstrate the criterion of dissimilarity Crossan looks at Jesus' reply to the request for a sign found in all three synoptic gospels (Mark 8:11–12; Luke 11:29–32 and Matt 12:38–41). In Mark Jesus says, "...no sign shall be given to this generation." In Luke and Matthew this statement is softened to "...no sign shall be given to it [this generation] except the sign of Jonah." Crossan claims that Mark's version, "no sign," is an "absolute," "unconditional," and "radical denial" of a sign, while Luke and Matthew shift the saying "toward Judaism and its interest in signs."[36] The question then raised by the criterion of dissimilarity is, Did Mark's version of Jesus' statement come from Jesus or from the church and placed by it on the lips of Jesus? Crossan's reply is, "In this case the answer is a strong affirmation of authenticity." But the contrast that leads to Crossan's complete confidence in authenticity depends on Judaism's being interested in signs and Jesus' being absolute and radical. This analysis does not discuss the problem that these images of Judaism and of Jesus are constructs, nor does it entertain the possibility that Mark's version of the saying, "no sign," could have been created by Mark's author just as the Lukan and Matthean versions are assumed to have been created.

This strongly intimates that the criterion of dissimilarity, far from being an epistemological method that yields secure knowledge, is a creative and hermeneutic process involving assumptions and imagination. But even before this step there is step two, the transmissional analysis of the saying in question, that is, the reconstruction of the

---

[35]Crossan (1973) 5.
[36]Crossan (1973) 7.

history of the Jesus tradition. What kind of historical and epistemological assumptions does this procedure rest on?

Transmissional Analysis and Freud's Dream Interpretation

Crossan uses the term "transmissional analysis" to refer to a widely used, standard scholarly method "variously termed tradition-critical or traditio-historical or history-of-traditions analysis."[37] Transmissional analysis is at the heart of Crossan's reconstruction of the Jesus tradition—everything depends on its results. This method is the foundation of most of Crossan's work, also including *In Fragments* (1983), *Four Other Gospels* (1985), and in a more complicated way, *The Cross That Spoke* (1988). And of course, it stands behind the results of *The Historical Jesus,* determining the core of any Jesus tradition complex Crossan believes to be historical. This analysis assumes that the Jesus tradition has undergone a historical development, reflected in the "layers" of interpretation and reinterpretation that constitute the gospels and other sources. It proposes to reconstruct this development, working backwards from the given texts we now possess to a reconstructed earlier version of the story or saying. This process of reconstructing backwards raises problems of epistemology. How does the scholar know he or she is reconstructing an earlier version of the saying, as opposed to creating a new version and calling it "early"? I believe there are unwarranted epistemological assumptions embedded in this process. In order to highlight the fundamentally hermeneutic nature of this particular method I will compare Crossan's characterization of transmissional analysis with Robert Steele's analysis of Freud's method of dream interpretation.[38]

The structure of Crossan's transmissional analysis and the structure of Freud's method of dream interpretation are similar enough so that Steele's analysis of Freud's misleading claims about finding the "cause" of the dream reveal the epistemological ambiguities inherent in Crossan's claim to recover the earliest form of a saying. This comparison will reveal similarities between what Freud claimed he was doing with dreams and what Crossan claims he is doing with the Jesus tradition. First I will present Steele's analysis of Freud's method of dream

---

[37]Crossan (1985) 7.
[38]Steele (1982) 135-41.

interpretation, and then I will compare it with Crossan's method of transmissional analysis.

In interpreting a dream Freud distinguished between a "manifest dream" and a "latent dream." The "manifest dream" is the dream we remember upon waking, and for the purposes of this comparison the "manifest dream" is equivalent to the textual version of a Jesus saying. And the "latent dream," alleged to be the source of the "manifest dream," is, for this comparison, equivalent to the "original voice of Jesus." In *The Interpretation of Dreams* Freud wanted to show "how dreams, when interpreted, express wishes which, before the process of interpretation, had been unconscious."[39] Therefore, the "manifest dream," as the text of the remembered dream, was considered to be a changed and distorted version of a more original, "latent dream." The task of dream interpretation, according to Freud, is "investigating the relations between the manifest content of dreams and the latent dream-thoughts, and of tracing out the processes by which the latter have been changed into the former."[40] For Freud it was the "dream-work" (a sub-conscious censor) that modified and distorted the latent dream thoughts into the manifest dream. The four mechanisms used by the dream-work to disguise the original infantile wish of the latent dream were thought to be condensation, displacement, considerations of representability (distortions that arise through translating visual image into verbal narrative), and secondary revision (telling the dream changes it by trying to make it consistent and coherent, that is, by turning it into a narrative). The first two were considered most important by Freud as they are the work of the dream censor. Condensation assumes that an image is so compact as to be unclear, the result of several lines of dream-thought. Unpacking the image through free association and in-terpretation expand it and make it intelligible. Displacement refers to both the elimination of disturbing elements and the change of, or relocation of, emphasis.[41]

The manifest dream is considered by Freud to be incomplete, discontinuous and incomprehensible. Free association by the dreamer to the manifest dream provides access to the latent dream thoughts that do not appear in the manifest dream. Next, interpretation by Freud created narrative coherence and meaning that not only connected the dream meaningfully to the history of the dreamer's life, but also turned

---

[39]Steele (1982) 135.
[40]Steele (1982) 136.
[41]Steele (1982) 140-141.

the latent dream into the "cause" of the manifest dream. What is really a hermeneutic process throughout was turned, by Freud, into a mechanistic process of cause and effect.

The manifest dream is the real origin of this whole process, and the so-called "latent dream" is actually a creation of interpretation. The latent dream has no independent existence that can be checked against the interpretation. It is a creation of the interpretive narrative, and, according to Steele, has more to do with "historical explanation" than "scientific analysis." It is the manifest dream that gives rise to the story of the latent dream through the collaboration of the dreamer and the psychoanalyst in the present. Because Freud asserts that the wish of the latent dream is always infantile, it is connected with the dreamer's past, and thereby the idea of the latent dream is given the impression of being a historical cause. As Steele says, "Dominated by the principles of nineteenth century natural science, he [Freud] recast his interpretative methodology into a theoretical system that was causal and mechanistic by transforming origins [manifest dream] into results and results [latent dream] into origins."[42]

Although transmissional analysis is not identical to Freud's method of dream interpretation, not least because Jesus really existed and the latent dream did not, there are surprising structural similarities. Crossan begins with suspicion of the manifest form(s) of the saying, and then works backwards to an original, or latent form. The saying (like the manifest content of the dream) cannot be trusted as it presents itself in the gospels to the reader (the dreamer), because "creative reinterpretation by the primitive church is the presupposition of the whole problem."[43] An intervening process of reinterpretation (dreamwork and censorship) has modified and distorted the original latent (i.e., Jesus') form of the saying. Therefore, Crossan says, "one must attempt to write a history of the transmission of the piece of tradition under discussion. This will trace its successive steps of development [*backwards*] and will isolate its earliest form."[44] This needs to be done because it is assumed that the modified and distorted manifest saying hides an uncomfortable and disturbing original (latent), form of the saying. Freud also claimed that the infantile wishes of the latent dream were so disturbing to the conscious adult mind that dream censorship was required in order for them to be accepted in the form of the mani-

---

[42]Steele (1982) 141.
[43]Crossan (1973) 5.
[44]Crossan (1973) 5.

fest dream. Does transmissional analysis really discover the original form of Jesus' sayings, or does it create new forms of Jesus' sayings in the present, in the same way that Freud's so-called latent dream is not really discovered, but a creation of interpretation?

In the gospels, according to Crossan, the mechanisms that modify the Jesus tradition, similar to the dream-work mechanisms, operate at every level in the same way: "...such processes as expansion and contraction, relocation and elimination, work in exactly similar ways on parable and miracle, on passion and resurrection."[45] Freud's mechanisms of condensation, displacement, considerations of representability, and secondary revision sound similar to the "mechanisms" Crossan assumes operate on the original Jesus tradition. Steele makes it clear that Freud's "mechanisms," alleged to operate in the unconscious of the dreamer, are really his own hermeneutic tools used to make sense of the dream and give it a historical reading. This in itself does not invalidate the resulting interpretation, but it does let us see that what is claimed to be an epistemology of the dream *cause*, is really a hermeneutic of dream *meaning*. Could this be the case with Crossan's transmissional analysis? The following diagram illustrates the structural similarities between Freud's dream interpretation and Crossan's transmissional analysis.

Cause vs. Interpretation

Freud's Dream Interpretation	Crossan's Transmissional Analysis
Manifest Dream (visible)	**Gospel Text** (visible)
↑ ↓	↑ ↓
(!cause) (?interpretation)	(!cause) (?interpretation)
↑ ↓	↑ ↓
Dream Work (invisible)	**Creative Reinterpretation** (invisible)
Condensation	Contraction
Displacement	Relocation
Representability	Expansion
Secondary Revision	Elimination
↑ ↓	↑ ↓
(!cause) (?interpretation)	(!cause) (?interpretation)
↑ ↓	↑ ↓
Latent Dream (invisible)	**Jesus' Voice** (invisible)

[45]Crossan (1985) 186.

The exclamation point in front of "!cause" is to indicate that cause is alleged to be definitive and "known." The question mark in front of "?interpretation" is to indicate the fundamentally ambiguous and finally unknown nature of the alleged development and the alleged origin. And although Jesus' voice and its creative reinterpretation really did happen and the latent dream and the dream work do not exist, Jesus' voice and its creative reinterpretation, from an epistemological perspective are just as invisible as the alleged unconscious dream processes. To talk about such things as Jesus' voice and its creative reinterpretation is hermeneutic speculation, not epistemological discovery, and not even epistemological probability.

One objection to this comparison could be that there are multiple variants of the Jesus tradition that seemingly cluster around a common core, while there is only one version of a dream. But, in fact, the free associations of the dreamer create alternate versions of the dream that have to be taken into account in the narrative interpretation and explanation of the dream. Freud believes the imagery of the dream and the imagery of the free associations cluster around a common core of meaning that is brought out by the interpretation. Freud knew that symbols are overdetermined, that is have multiple meanings, and so even if a "common core" is "discovered" it is the result of interpretation, and remains fluid and open. In the same way, what gets isolated by Crossan as the common core of a Jesus tradition complex is the result of interpretation and not value-free discovery.

Another objection could be that while dream censorship never takes place, the "creative reinterpretation" of Jesus really did take place. I am not arguing against the real "expansion and contraction" of the Jesus traditions. I am arguing against any positivist claim to know how this took place and to be able to reconstruct the original voice of Jesus. The reality of history is far too irrational and contingent to be able to claim to *know* how any particular tradition or textual variant developed. What I am emphasizing is the hermeneutic nature of transmissional analysis.

Perhaps all variants of the Jesus tradition, including contemporary reconstructions, should be thought of more in terms of "free association" on an original "dream" rather than in terms of modification and distortion. From such a perspective we might look at the Christian story about Jesus as a cultural "manifest dream" that has become fragmentary, discontinuous and incomprehensible to modern consciousness. Then Crossan's transmissional analysis and historical reconstruction would be his own "free associations" and interpretations that seek to explain and understand what has broken apart. Within this view, one might say that once the *mythical* declaration, "In the beginning was the Word," was sufficient for meaning and understanding. However, today the *historical* declaration might be, "In the beginning was expansion and contraction, relocation and elimination." Thus, through a methodological coherence that is itself a kind of narrative, Crossan attempts to create meaning and understanding of our origins in terms of a new myth, but a myth none the less, the myth of historical reconstruction, perhaps the myth of history itself.

The Shift from *Ipsissima Verba* to *Ipsissima Vox*

In the same way as there is no way to check the so-called latent dream with an original hard copy, there is no way to check the reconstructed parable or saying with some original hard copy of Jesus' own words. Of course, the latent dream never existed. It is an interpretive creation of Freud's. Yet, while the original Jesus did speak actual words once, from an epistemological point of view there is an absolute chasm between us and those words—they do not exist now and cannot be checked. And just as everyone recognizes that it is impossible to recapture those actual words, it is equally impossible (in any positivist sense) to recapture the *voice* of Jesus. Crossan's attempt (and he is not at all alone in this move) to shift from the *ipsissima verba* to the *ipsissima vox* of Jesus is an epistemological sleight of hand that attempts to avoid facing the absolute historical gap between any saying or action attributed to Jesus and the actual words and actions of the actual Jesus. The shift to the *ipsissima vox* seems to be driven by the positivist need to have a historical object that one can claim to *know* with some certainty. Like the water in a river, that original Jesus is gone forever, and forever irretrievable. I emphasize the absolute nature of this gap for two reasons. One, it highlights, in relation to epistemology (what can be known), the incommensurability between the goals of historical positivism (to retrieve the historical object with some measure of certitude) and the historical object itself, in this case, the language, or voice, of Jesus. And two, it points to the fundamental and inescapable hermeneutic nature of historiography.

That Crossan is fascinated by, and brilliant with, language is evident throughout his work. However, it leads him to place far too great a historical burden on linguistic objects, that is, the voice of Jesus. The shift from *ipsissima verba* to *ipsissima vox* has not lessened the epistemological emphasis. For example, in a 1988 article, Crossan seems intent on finding and locating a kind of "cause," or at least the source, for the multiform manifest versions of Jesus' sayings in the original *voice* of Jesus. He proposes the "criterion of adequacy" to replace the criterion of dissimilarity as the first principle in historical Jesus research. He defines it thus: "that is original which best explains the multiplicity engendered in the tradition. What original datum from the historical Jesus must we envisage to explain adequately the full spectrum of primitive Christian response."[46]

The problem that arises with this criterion is that it is not an epistemological criterion at all. It is really a hermeneutic principle that Crossan tries to have function epistemologically when he claims it will tell us what is "original." In fact, it is no more epistemologically valid than the criterion of dissimilarity, which also has more to do with hermeneutic principle than epistemological criteria. When Crossan says, "What original datum from the historical Jesus must *we envisage* to explain adequately the full spectrum of primitive Christian response [emphasis added]," he is really providing an *interpretation* of the multiplicity of the earliest Christian response, and is not establishing its cause, and is certainly not establishing knowledge about the original voice and deeds of the historic Jesus.

Crossan also seems to verge on what is a kind of concretistic historical fallacy in assuming that "the full spectrum of primitive Christian response" can only have its origin in, and therefore must be traced back to, the original words and deeds of Jesus. This becomes an inadvertent historical materialism if the only conceivable historical agent for the great variety of cultural creativity that did have the figure of Jesus Christ at its center are the words and deeds of the original person of Jesus of Nazareth. The symbol of Jesus Christ has inspired the individual and cultural imagination in a tremendous variety of creations and directions for two thousand years quite independently of the historic Jesus.

---

[46]Crossan (1988b) 125.

Method in *Raid on the Articulate*

Crossan's book, *Raid on the Articulate: Comic Eschatology in Jesus and Borges* (1976), is also imbued with the dichotomy between traditional Cartesian epistemology and a hermeneutic ontology. It is all the more ironic in this book because, as we will see, Crossan points out a similar dichotomy in the work of Johan Huizinga, on whom he relies heavily for his ontology of play.

Crossan begins *Raid* with a critique of the ascendancy of historical criticism as the *only* valid methodology for biblical studies. He tells us, "For the last hundred years biblical criticism has meant historical criticism,"[47] and refers to the "successes" that have derived from both understanding the Bible as a historical document and reading it critically as a product of historical and human factors. Although he does not identify the "successes" explicitly, he is affirming historical consciousness and historical criticism as positive developments in understanding the Bible. Although Crossan does not mention it, the *historical* understanding of the Bible is a major shift away from the theological perspective that views the Bible as a product of ahistorical, infallible, divine inspiration.

Crossan is arguing in favor of making literary criticism an equal partner in biblical research. He allows that literary criticism itself is a little too aggressive in asserting "the primacy of language over history," and he himself does not appear to want to subordinate historical research to literary criticism. However, he goes on to say, "Literature reminds history that it is language and text that binds the historical student with the historical subject and that it may be terribly naive to ignore that medium in which we all live, move and have our being."[48] If, as Crossan is affirming, language is the common medium that "binds the historical student with the historical subject," serious questions about the epistemology of historical research arise. What happens to the epistemological assumptions that guide traditional historical analysis? What happens to the ontological status of historical objects in relation to the researcher? Without addressing such questions Crossan is left with the problematic dichotomy in his work between the ontological assumptions inherent in the epistemology of historical research and the ontological assumptions inherent in the epistemology of structuralist literary criticism. This dichotomy is

---

[47]Crossan (1976) xiii.
[48]Crossan (1976) xiii.

serious because the ontological assumptions that guide these two different epistemologies are mutually exclusive. They are mutually exclusive because they each take incompatible views of the ontological nature of the subject-object relationship.

One would not at first expect such a dichotomy in Crossan's work because his emphasis is turned toward the "ontological priority of language," and this in turn aligns him with what he calls "a shift in the master paradigms" of biblical research.[49] In fact, Crossan claims to be a part of this paradigm shift by making this whole book a structuralist and comparative literary analysis of "systemic and generic relationships within the possibilities of language,"[50] specifically the language of Jesus of Nazareth and Jorge Luis Borges. He is trying to add another paradigm, structuralist literary criticism, to an already existing paradigm, historical criticism. This is not a true paradigm shift, and simply echoes the traditional dichotomy between historical criticism and theological interpretation in biblical studies, already noted by scholars.[51]

The dichotomy is established in *Raid* with the following statement, "[The book] also presumes, acknowledges, and appreciates the results of historical investigation into the teachings of Jesus. It will never use texts except those supported as authentic by the vast majority of the most critical historical scholarship."[52] In other words, Crossan establishes the credibility of the historical Jesus material he will rely on by saying it is authenticated by traditional historical critical epistemology, which ironically, the entire thrust of his book implicitly undermines. What I want to touch on here is that Crossan is subject to the same ontological inconsistency that he himself sees in Johan Huizinga's *Homo Ludens,* the classic study on culture as play.

My demonstration of this point does not require an extensive presentation of Huizinga's argument. Crossan's own presentation is adequate. Huizinga's aim in *Homo Ludens* is to show that play is not simply one among many aspects of culture, but that culture, in its own being, *is* play. Crossan accepts this brilliant thesis, but he also notes that Huizinga's "argumentation suffers from a vacillation between the historical and the ontological, between proofs showing how culture came *from* play and is therefore somehow successive to it, and how culture arose *as* play and is therefore absolutely simultaneous with

---

[49]Crossan (1976) xiv.
[50]Crossan (1976) xv.
[51]Nations (1983) 70-71.
[52]Crossan (1976) xv.

it."[53] Huizinga also has a tendency to set play, as "not serious," over and against "ordinary reality," that is "serious." But this dichotomy between "ordinary reality" and "playful reality" is just what Huizinga is trying to argue against. He wants to say that all reality and culture are constituted as play. Crossan says, "Huizinga is still trapped in a dichotomized rationalistic world and cannot fully accept the radical implications of his brilliant intuition: reality is play, reality is make-believe, you make it to believe in and believe in what you have made."[54] Crossan is also "trapped in a dichotomized rationalistic world and cannot fully accept the radical implications of his own brilliant intuition" about the language relationships between Jesus and Borges. If Crossan wants to be consistent with the ontological priority of language then he needs to allow the epistemological claims for the historical Jesus to dissolve completely, and allow his creative picture of Jesus to be just what it is, *hermeneutic play!* But Crossan never goes this far. Crossan always claims he is reconstructing *the historic* Jesus, and never allows that what he is really doing is painting a "historical" portrait of *Crossan's* Jesus. Now there are valid ontological claims that can be made for Crossan's "historical" portrait of Jesus, but it is very important to distinguish these claims from claims about the original historic Jesus.

Crossan also gets himself in philosophical trouble by limiting Huizinga's intuition to the idea that reality is the play of only human language. He says, "reality is make-believe, you make it to believe in and believe in what you have made." If all of reality, without remainder, is play, then why does reality and play have to be limited to human play? Crossan presses on and says, "To be human is to play. Our supreme play is the creation of world and the totality of played world is termed reality. This reality is the interlaced and interwoven fabric of our play. It is layer upon layer of solid and substantial play and in this and on this play we live, move, and have our being."[55] Recall Crossan's earlier statement, that language is that "medium in which we all live, move, and have our being."[56] With these statements Crossan has established an identity between language, play, reality and world, and if he has not slipped into solipsism, he has come danger-

[53]Crossan (1976) 25.
[54]Crossan (1976) 26.
[55]Crossan (1976) 27.
[56]Crossan (1976) xiii.

ously close with a linguistic fallacy that reduces reality, i.e., being, to language. But this is exactly what Crossan means to do.

For Crossan, play and structure are connected. Within any game that we play self-consciously there is structure, so play in general has structure, and structures therefore, are the forms of play. Crossan views the structure of play as a system of transformations that is itself a whole, maintained by internal relationships and regulations. Crossan then says, "it is the playful human mind which establishes and imposes structure. I do not think of structures as already existent in 'reality-out-there' and discovered or acknowledged by our obedient minds. What is there before or without our structured play strikes me as being both unknowable and unspeakable."[57] The problem with this view is that it preserves a traditional ontological split between "reality-out-there" and the human mind. Crossan's view seems to assume that the human mind has an ontological existence independent of the so-called outer world, or outer reality. Crossan implies that the existential world of language and play exists independently of so-called physical reality, or the rest of the universe.

He presents the view of French theologian, Georges Crespy, in order to make his own point. Crespy states that, "In the beginning was the structure. It was everywhere in the world and the world had been organized by it." According to Crespy, this structure is in everything, minerals, crystals, plant and animal life, and then in human rhetoric. Then Crossan says, "It is a beautiful thought but unfortunately the opposite may be just as true. I would prefer to reverse his paragraph and say: In the beginning was human rhetoric and it proceeded forthwith to structure all things."[58]

Now perhaps Crossan simply wants to be epistemologically modest regarding any claims about ultimate reality and that is fair. But in pressing this modesty as far as Crossan does he ends up with an ontologically split universe. Crossan seems to be arguing with a secret adversary, but he does not tell us directly who or what it is. He gives us a clue when he says, "I do not think of structures as *already existent* in "reality-out-there" and discovered or acknowledged by our *obedient* minds [italics added]." It sounds like he is arguing against some kind of traditional theological metaphysical system in which human beings are passive recipients of ontologically other divine determinism. The

---

[57]Crossan (1976) 34.
[58]Crossan (1976) 35.

theological metaphysical system would be medieval Catholicism, a view of reality Crossan tells us he was steeped in as a young man.[59]

This is simply to say that Crossan's extreme linguistic position with regard to structuralism and reality has a legitimate reason, but that it is hidden in his own life experience. This is by no means to reduce his argument to subjective psychology. In fact it is my position that the subjective dimension has ontological value and needs to become a legitimate factor in our arguments. But there is no need to posit preexistent structures of play in terms of a fixed and determinant, ontologically "out-there" reality that are then only discovered by merely "obedient minds." As we will see in chapter four, Jung, working with the same problem, takes a significantly different view. For Jung, the archetypes (Crossan's structures of play) are not created by the human mind, but as inherited *possibilities* they are not merely immutable determinants that must be obeyed. In fact, the archetypes and human consciousness exist as a complex ontological whole, and mutually effect each other in a dialectic inter*play*. There are interesting points of overlap between Crossan's and Jung's points of view, but one of the problems with criticizing Crossan here is that what he means by "human mind" is not clear. Crossan does not give us an explicit psychological theory, and his philosophical point of view is sketchy.

Summary

This examination of Crossan's historical method in relation to the historical Jesus has revealed a subtle and unwitting positivism pervading his so-called formal method in *The Historical Jesus*. His criteria used to isolate allegedly historically reliable bits of the Jesus tradition in terms of chronological closeness to Jesus is a desire to establish definite *knowledge* about the historic Jesus. What Crossan does not say is that one, the formal method is not formal, but an interpretive matrix imposed on the Jesus traditions, and two, whatever is isolated in this way is a pure abstraction and by itself tells us nothing about the once living human situation in which the original Jesus of Nazareth lived and spoke. The formal method itself is embedded in an unspoken narrative of meaning that gives it its intelligibility in the first place. This "narrative of meaning" is positivism. Crossan's view of

---

[59]Crossan (1996) 214.

time and the texts as sedimented layers suggests he is after definite historic facts and not just interpretations. But even this view of the texts and time is a positivist interpretation and not, as assumed, a given objective fact.

Whether Crossan is dating texts and Jesus tradition complexes (stratigraphy), or whether he is isolating an alleged saying or action at the core of a Jesus tradition complex (multiple attestation), Crossan is interpreting ambiguous textual situations and not digging objects out of the soil or discovering what actually happened.

In comparing Crossan's main historical critical tool, transmissional analysis, with Freud's method of dream interpretation, we are able to see the fundamentally hermeneutic and ambiguous nature of the attempt to analyze the history of the Jesus textual traditions. Its hermeneutic nature stands in strong contrast to the positivist epistemological claims it makes to recover the original *voice* of Jesus.

The examination of *In Parables* and *Raid* highlighted the ontological dichotomy between fact and interpretation that runs through the heart of these works. Crossan attempts to ground his own creative literary interpretations of Jesus-tradition texts in the original *voice* of Jesus. It is ironic that Crossan, for whom "in parables" means life has no foundations and "comic eschatology" means the Holy is known in the shattering of foundations, has to ground his own interpretations in the "foundation" of the historic Jesus of Nazareth. The goal of a historical foundation in the original Jesus is a clear legacy of historical positivism, but it is also something else.

One of the themes I will develop in the next chapters, particularly four, five and six, is that the figure of Jesus is an object of personal and collective projections. This means that Crossan does not merely create Jesus in his own image, but that he also projects the Holy, or to use Jung's term for ultimate value, the self, into the historic figure of Jesus. This is a very important development historically and psychologically as the myth of the heavenly Christ (the legacy of Christianity for almost two-thousand years) becomes the myth of the historical Jesus (the legacy of historical consciousness for approximately the last three-hundred years). I view this shift from heavenly Christ to historical Jesus in terms of a historical and psychological transformation of archetypal cultural *images* that has great significance for the psyche. But Crossan, of course, does not view it this way. He believes he is talking about the historic Jesus of Nazareth, and this belief is crucial for him.

Throughout his work Crossan fails to address the unwarranted assumptions that guide the historical critical quest for the historical Jesus and yet, he does acknowledge in part the inescapable hermeneutic relationship between the historian and history. This however leads to his ontologically split approach to Jesus. On the one hand, his literary approaches to the Jesus traditions are creative, playful and inventive, while on the other hand, his playful and hermeneutic sensibilities have not had any impact on his Jesus-historiography—he continues to write about Jesus as if he were writing about the actual Jesus. As we will see in the light of critical historiography, this is an untenable way to continue to do Jesus-historiography. For some reason, the fundamentals of historical critical method and historiography remain unproblematic, and this is surprising in the light of Crossan's sophistication about the metaphoric, playful and hermeneutic nature of language, and his familiarity with thinkers like Barthes and Heidegger. There are no references in Crossan's work to philosophy of history in contrast to his sophisticated explorations of language and story.[60]

In the next chapter I will explore the fundamental limitations and ambiguity of history as discourse, or story, in contrast to history as the real past. We will see that historical methods do not lead to knowledge of the past as much as they create the past. The problematic of positivism's influence in the historiography of Crossan and the Third Quest is not limited to historical Jesus studies, but has been a theme of discussion for several decades in the field of historical studies. This will pave the way for chapter four in which I will explore Jung's method as another alternative to positivism in continuity with the perspectives raised by critical historiographers.

---

[60]Crossan's most extensive theoretical reflections occur in *The Dark Interval: Towards a Theology of Story*. However, his reflections on story and myth in this book never include history or historiography. Similar to his work in *In Parables* and *Raid* this work is oriented toward interpreting the parables of the historic Jesus and the same ontological split between fact and interpretation is implied. The implication from Crossan's overall work is that "story" and "history" are somehow significantly different.

CHAPTER THREE

CRITICAL HISTORIOGRAPHY

The Problem of History

As seen in the previous chapter, the structure of Crossan's formal method in *The Historical Jesus* focuses all of its attention on the epistemological problems of the Jesus tradition, while appearing to treat both social anthropology and history as completely unproblematic. This chapter will explore the nature of history and historiography from the perspective of contemporary critical historiographers, specifically in relation to what I think Crossan overlooks in the presentation of his own Jesus-historiography. My purpose here is to discuss the historiographical alternatives to the "myth of objectivity" that Batdorf suggested be abandoned by those participating in the quest for the historical Jesus. The "myth of objectivity" has its roots in Cartesian metaphysics and the legacy of historical positivism. This chapter focuses on the problem of historical positivism, and chapter four will discuss Cartesian metaphysics in connection with Jung's analytical psychology and Heidegger's hermeneutic phenomenology.

The aim of this chapter is to show that the historical positivism uncritically assumed throughout Crossan's own approach to the historic Jesus has long been problematic in historiographical theory and is rejected outright among many philosophers of history.[1] As Peter Munz observes,

> Sir George Clark once described history as a hard core of fact surrounded by a pulp of disputable interpretations. E. H. Carr, wittily and with greater perspicacity stood the statement on its head.

---

[1] For this discussion in the U.S., cf. Novick (1988). More generally, see the survey in Breisach (1994).

'History', he wrote in *What is History?*, 'is a hard core of interpretation surrounded by a pulp of disputable facts.'[2]

Conventionally, "history" has been viewed as "an activity that transcribes facts from reality to a piece of paper, an activity that is solely guided by the concern for truth."[3] It is this perspective that has been foundational in the quest for the historical Jesus in the twentieth century and persists today even among those practicing in the Third Quest. However, developments over the past few decades in the philosophy of history point in a quite different direction.

In Hellenistic antiquity, history writing became concerned with making a distinction between fact and fable, or myth. This concern for "objectivity" was primarily interested in resisting the temptation to flatter, but did not diminish the importance of "interpretation" or even "instruction" in historical narratives. The historical positivism that developed in the eighteenth and nineteenth centuries grounded in Cartesian metaphysics, went further and attempted to insert an ontological wedge between "fact" and "meaning." The nature of historical truth became identified with an overvaluation of supposedly rational facts, and the attempted elimination of interpretation. It is this view that persists generally today, and that enjoys a taken-for-granted status among many historians of Jesus. It is inevitable, then, that my engagement with Crossan's project take up the question of the nature of history and, in particular, of the relationship between "history" and "myth."

In what follows, I will redefine both "history" and "myth." Here at the outset, though, I want at least provisionally to make clear what I do not mean by the term "myth." I do not mean only a fable about gods, goddesses and other imaginary beings and creatures, although such stories are included in my larger conception of myth. And by myth I do not mean a falsehood, illusion or superstition, which is the general and colloquial pejorative connotation of the word. My meaning of myth will come closer to a *way of thinking* about dimensions of reality that have their own psychological and ontological truth. As will become apparent in chapter four on Jung, myth, imagination and emotion all share the same archetypal and ontological status as foundational modes of being. History too will come to be redefined more in terms of a *way of thinking* about the human experience of time. History will be seen to have more in common with myth than not. In relation to critical histori-

---

[2]Munz (1977) 248.
[3]Munz (1977) 246.

ography, I will engage and redefine the conventional polarization of the terms history and myth.

The conventional positivist view of history creates a strong contrast between history and myth, with history representing the facts, the real and the true, and myth, along with other forms of fictive literature, representing the imaginary, and therefore, the unreal, and the false. This view also establishes a strong and hard ontological dichotomy between history as the real and objective, and myth and fiction as the imaginary and subjective. The ontological dichotomy also entails value judgements. Historical knowledge, based on objective facts, is considered superior, and mythology, as a subjective expression, is viewed with contempt by the epistemological perspective of positivism. We tend to accept that myth and fiction are created by the human mind and thus are appropriately imbued with the subjective. And we tend to think of the discipline of history as aligned with science and traditional ideas of objectivity, with the result that the subjective should play no role in historical reportage.

Crossan participates in this strong dichotomy when he sets up the opposition between history and theology, and biography and autobiography.[4] This is the same dichotomy we saw him establish, and then rely on, between the epistemology of historical criticism and the hermeneutics of literary criticism. Even when the meaning of myth as referring to something false is rejected, and is viewed, as Crossan does, in terms of metaphor, as holding a valid and profound quality of truth, history is still supposed to be superior epistemologically, and precisely because of the rational and empirical methods it supposedly employs.

The conventional view of historical method, that relies on the broad assumptions of positivism, assumes that historical objects as facts and events can be retrieved as discrete entities by historians who are also conceived of as discrete entities, and that the past can be reconstructed or reconstituted. Positivist historical method and historiography assume that "what actually happened" in the past can be objectively reported. Crossan implicitly relies on such a view of historical critical method when he confidently says it can and does retrieve the original voice of the historic Jesus.

In the following pages I will present an alternative view of history by showing (1) that historical objects do not exist as such, and that so-called facts and events of history are actually interpretations and

---

[4]Crossan (1991) xxviii.

constructions; (2) that "document," interpretation, historian, cultural context, and history form an ontological unity that cannot be discretely separated; (3) that the past can be neither reconstituted nor reconstructed as such; and (4) that "historicity is simply one of the many possible ways of being aware of the past,"[5] and as such, historical awareness is itself a kind of myth of time created and held by the present. If these points can be shown to be true, then it will follow that we must learn to think of "history" in a completely different way, and come to see that "history" is itself a form of "myth." Of course, such an understanding of history is more complex than this simple assertion allows. But I will show that a closer look at history and historical writing establishes a much closer relationship between history and myth than conventional thinking allows. In this chapter and the next I will show that history and myth share the same ontological structures and concerns, and that their hard separation is unwarranted, as well as damaging to deep self-understanding.

The Ambiguity of the Word *History*

The word *history* itself is problematic. As Hayden White has noted, the term is ambiguous because of a "failure to distinguish adequately between an object of study (the human past) and discourse about this object."[6] The word history refers to both the reality of the past and those texts that are written about that past. Our basic access to the past is through documents and texts, which gives history a decidedly literary dimension.[7] In an important way history *is* historiography. But the word historiography is also problematic. Michel de Certeau sees the same ambiguity in the word historiography that White sees in the word history when he says that it "bears within its own name the paradox—almost an oxymoron—of a relation established between two antinomic terms, between the real and discourse. Its task is one of connecting them and, at the point where this link cannot be imagined, of working *as if* the two were being joined."[8]

---

[5]Munz (1977) 121.

[6]White (1987) 57.

[7]For the purposes of my discussion I omit considerations of oral recording, cinema and video, which are characteristic of only the most recent past. However, these media as remnants of memory, suffer the same hermeneutic problematic as texts in being fragmentary, selective and interpretive.

[8]Certeau (1988) xxvii.

The ambiguity between "history" as the real past and "history" as literary text leads to their uncritical identification. It is the *words* of historical discourse that conjure up the sense of the real, and it is this *reality* of the past that is created by words that is peculiarly hard to shake. It takes a real effort of critical consciousness to bring the literary nature of "history" into the foreground. Certeau is concerned in his own writing to avoid the illusion that our words are adequate to the real, but concedes that this "philosophical illusion lies hidden in the requirements of historiographical work." And he cites Schelling's acknowledgment of the tenacious nature of the dogmatism of the real: "For us the tale of actual facts is doctrine."[9] The fascination with the equation of "facts" and the "real" is a more general epistemological preoccupation in the West that has metaphysical roots in the Cartesian legacy. Chapter four will explore the view of being in Cartesian epistemology that gave rise to positivism.

The problem of the relationship between historiography and literature has been of interest to critical thinkers since the Greeks. Lionel Gossman, in a 1978 essay titled "History and Literature: Reproduction or Signification," traces the relationship between history and literature from the Greeks and Romans to the present, with a focus on the modern era. Only recently has the relationship between history and literature become problematic. For many centuries, "history was a branch of literature." Not until the eighteenth century, when the idea of literature itself began to change, did history become something distinct.[10] The dichotomy established between history as the representation of the real and literature, or fiction, as the expression of the imaginary, heightened the epistemological emphasis placed on history as a discipline. History was believed, and expected, to be the simple and direct copying and representation of "what actually happened." As White noted, "Getting the 'story' out of 'history' was therefore a first step in the transformation of historical studies into a science."[11] And this historical "science" was required to follow the ideals of positivism.

---

[9]Certeau (1988) xxvii.
[10]Gossman (1978) 3.
[11]White (1987) 169.

The Ambiguity of "Facts" and Historical Knowledge

Gossman points out that in the mid-eighteenth century "the epistemological basis of [history's] ideal of impartially copying or representing the real was put in question." The idea of point of view was seen as fundamental to all historical narrative. However, it was also thought that combining points of view would yield an objective view of the historical object. Further reflection on historiography, "particularly in Germany, was overwhelmingly preoccupied with discovering a more comprehensive theory of historical objectivity than naive realism, one that would include and subsume subjectivity." This thinking

> led to a conception of historical knowledge that emphasized its peculiarity with respect to the knowledge provided by the natural sciences. Positivist theories of history, on the other hand, aimed to bring history as close as possible, epistemologically and methodologically, to the natural sciences. Reflection on historiography was thus becoming more concerned with the problems of historical knowledge, and very rarely, or only incidentally, with the problems of historical writing.[12]

Even though this distinction of the qualitative difference between knowledge in the historical sciences and knowledge in the natural sciences was emerging, the continuing emphasis on epistemology reveals the prevailing and predominant influence of positivism. Maintaining a focus on problems of historical *knowledge* results in not seeing the literary nature of history as discourse. This in turn fails to see that historical writing is what constructs the historical past. Crossan's own heavy emphasis on epistemological method in *The Historical Jesus* obscures (not necessarily intentionally) the essentially literary and creative nature of his historical narrative. Keeping the literary nature of historical discourse in the background invites our unconscious positivist assumptions to continue unchallenged to imagine history as a kind of *thing*, full of other objective, distinct *things* called facts and events. We continue in this vein to imagine unwittingly that "scientific" historical critical method can extract these fact-things from the past as if it were mining metals, or engaged in an archeological dig. We further assume that such facts can be definitively established independently of the subjectivity, containing both cultural and personal perspectives, of the researcher and history writer. This idea of the past as something "objectively fixed" that can be objectively "discovered and reconstituted"

---

[12]Gossman (1978) 6-7.

is now under serious question not only in historical studies, but in depth-psychology and memory studies as well.[13] But if the goal of objective knowledge of the past is rejected as unattainable in principle, is the *ideal* of a definitive objective knowledge of the past still worthy of being a guiding principle of historical research? As we will see, the answer to this question is negative because the very ground of such an ideal is still a traditional positivist epistemology. The ground of historical being should be conceived in fundamentally hermeneutic terms, and historiography needs to be seen as a hermeneutic process whose concerns have more to do with consciousness, ethics and practice, rather than some kind of "scientific" method that establishes absolute and objective facts.

The general idea that the "forthright empiricism" of historical method is somehow objective is actually faulty. I include the following long quotation, in which Gossman cites Murray Murphey, because, among other things, it highlights the fundamentally interpretive nature of Crossan's "formal" method at every level of its triple triadic structure:

> ...It has often been argued by philosophers that the historian's objects are not unproblematically situated on the other side of the evidence, as it were, but constructs, whose function is to account for the present evidence. "George Washington," one such argument runs, "enjoys at present the epistemological status of an electron: each is an entity postulated for the purpose of giving coherence to our present experience, and each is unobservable by us." According to the same argument, "the forthright empiricism which has generally prevailed in the historical trade" has laudable objectives, "but its view of the process by which historical knowledge is attained is naive. In holding that external and internal criticism yield statements from which facts are determined, and that the function of interpretation is to account for all, or a preselected few, of these facts, it badly distorts the actual practice of historians. In fact, interpretation enters at every step along the way. External criticism is really a process of testing classificatory hypotheses about objects and so depends upon such interpretative hypotheses being made. Similarly, the attribution of meaning and reference to an inscription is an interpretative or hypothetical process. Historical facts are not established from pure data—they are postulated to explain characteristics of the data. Thus the sharp division between fact and interpretation upon which the

---

[13]Gossman (1978) 7. For depth-psychology see Spence (1982), and for memory see Schacter (1995) and (1996).

classical view insisted and which the revisionists have accepted, does not exist."[14]

What we commonly refer to as "facts" and "events" of the past can only appear to us after a process of selection involving both history itself and the historian, that removes them from the vast, dense and seamless reality that constituted the "life" of the so-called fact. But even to say that "facts" and "events" of the past exist, and can be selected out of the past, still relies on a positivist view of reality, time and memory. A positivist view suggests that, first, things exist in the past and are discontinuous with the present such that recollecting them or reconstructing them does not change them, and that they in turn have no real influence on the present. And second, that it is possible for facts and events that had their own existence within a dense web of significance that constituted their historic being, most of it unconscious even in its own time and place, to be somehow (magically? dogmatically?) more than a mere abstraction. Here I am borrowing from theologian Heinrich Ott who in a 1964 essay stated, "Facts in the sense of *bruta facta* do not exist at all. They are mere abstractions arising from a disregard of the significance which first and foremost constitutes historical being."[15] And "significance" has a complex subjective dimension that is obscured by the rhetoric of positivist epistemology.

These arguments suggest that it is our current contexts, with their own needs and purposes, including epistemological needs and purposes, that actually create the "facts" of the past. This hermeneutic perspective encourages us to see that so-called "facts" and "events" of the past are in fact abstractions (not reality itself) that then find their meaning in the present through new contexts created by the language and texts of historiography. As Gossman notes, "One of the most effective and radical criticisms of historical realism has been made by highlighting the linguistic existence of historical narratives, by emphasizing that history constructs its objects, and that its objects are objects of language, rather than entities of which words are in some way copies."[16] And of course, history is written by a historian who has, not a neutral relation, but a meaningful and significant relation to both language and the past she or he is trying to write about.

---

[14]Gossman (1978) 27.
[15]Ott (1964) 157.
[16]Gossman (1978) 29.

Brian Stock notes that in the positivistic tradition, the historian views events as related to fact, and not to relation. The positivist view cannot see that the writing of history is itself an event. Furthermore, an event can only be a "historical" event if it has a relation to a subject—it had to have been perceived, remembered and recorded, and last but not least, it had to have value and significance, in order to be so treated. In this way events are "subjectivized." Stock goes on to say,

> They are not as subjective as a text of pure fiction created for an occasion, but have more in common with such a narrative than with the event-structure of the external world. Let us not be deceived by the skepticism of much historical writing, that arid criticism of documents that pretends to take the reader behind their rhetorical facades and into a world of sober facts. Historical writing does not treat reality; it treats the interpreter's relation to it. For an event does not stand alone as an isolated object of thought, except by abstraction. It can only be understood as one element in a narrative that is stated or implied.17

Not only is the word *history* itself ambiguous, but the words *event* and *fact* that point to the content of history are also ambiguous and problematic. The word history functions with no clear referent and, in fact, history is its own subject and object. Its object, the human past, no longer exists as such. As discourse, it is a kind of subject, or at least produced by a subject, and while this subject writes about the past, he or she is also a product of the very past about which he or she thinks and writes. History writing, in the sense that its object does not exist in the present, creates its object as discourse. History in this sense does not really reconstruct the past. History, as discourse, creates ideas about the past in terms of *writing* that is about the historical. As Peter Munz states, "History is not what happened but what people think happened"; and, "Our historical knowledge...is of historical knowledge—not of what actually happened."18 There is no getting away from the textual and subjective nature of history, and its fundamental circularity. As we will see in chapter four, Jung and Heidegger accept such circularity, not as a methodological problem to be overcome, but as the basic and only way of being within which "knowledge" is possible.

17Stock (1990) 80-81.
18Munz (1977) 208, 205.

The Tacit Superiority of *History*

The word history is also equivocal in that it inescapably posits a nonhistory that is different from that period of time considered to be prehistory, and different from the history of nature. White observes that the object of history, that which is historical, can only be conceived of on the basis of the "equivocation contained in the notion of a general human past that is split into two parts one of which is supposed to be 'historical,' the other 'unhistorical.'" This split is based on the common observation that cultures that used and preserved written records are historical cultures. But White suggests it is unwarranted "to further divide [the human past] into an order of events that is 'historical' and another that is 'nonhistorical.' For this is to suggest that there are two orders of humanity, one of which is more human—because it is more historical—than the other."[19] This valuation inherent in the word history is subtle but nevertheless influences the historian. It operates at an ontological level by bestowing more reality (more being) on the *historical* and less reality on the *nonhistorical*.

In this sense the word *history* itself points to a grand story that takes up everything considered historical into its world of meaning, and implicitly devalues what is left out. But even so-called historical cultures do not preserve in writing the totality of their historic reality, everything that has ever happened. And, even elements of what has been preserved can be easily forgotten and relegated to the "nonhistorical." For example, Crossan's own efforts throughout his work to include extracanonical sources in the building of his basic Jesus tradition are an attempt to make historical again material so long ignored as to be practically nonhistorical, almost non-existent. But in his efforts Crossan may be bending over backwards in his attempt to right what he considers a historical wrong. One scholar notes a consistent tendency in the source database Crossan develops, to date extracanonical sources earlier than canonical sources, and so by his own criteria, increase the authority of the extracanonical, and decrease the authority of the canonical sources.[20] In attempting to avoid canonical bias, one of Crossan's own historical critical principles, he may unwittingly tend toward an extracanonical bias.

Crossan may be struggling with the theological division between secular history and salvation history that parallels the separation be-

---

[19]White (1987) 55.
[20]van Beek (1994) 84.

tween history and nonhistory. As canonical texts belong to salvation history and extracanonical texts to secular history, within the Christian tradition these two sets of texts cannot possibly have the same value or authority. It is not inconceivable that a scholar desiring to balance this theological imbalance in valuing the texts would seek to give the extracanonical texts more historical weight by dating them closer to the historic Jesus. Whoever takes up the problem of thinking historically about Jesus has to contend with these ambiguous and equivocal meanings of the word history. The problem is that the ambiguity and relative values that constitute what the word history refers to tend to remain unconscious in the historian, and as such, can exert their subtle influences against the historian's best conscious intentions.

History is a True Novel

Paul Veyne asserts, "History is not a science, and has little to expect from sciences; it does not explain, and has no method. Better still, history, about which much has been said for two centuries, does not exist." For Veyne, "historians tell of true events in which man is the actor; history is a true novel."[21] And like the novel, "history sorts, simplifies, organizes, fits a century into a page."[22]

By "true" Veyne means that history is an account of events that have happened, but by no means does the historian grasp events "directly and fully." History is "always grasped incompletely and laterally, through documents" that are themselves not events—history is written from "traces, impressions"—and Veyne cites the useful distinction of Genette: "history is *diegesis* and not *mimesis.*"[23] In this light Veyne states that "history is mutilated knowledge,"[24] which stands in strong contrast to the illusion that history should be "the integral reconstitution of the past." Veyne believes this illusion derives "from the fact that the documents, which provide us with the answers, also dictate the questions to us; in that way they not only leave us ignorant of many things, but they also leave us ignorant that we are ignorant."[25]

---

[21]Veyne (1984) x.
[22]Veyne (1984) 4.
[23]Veyne (1988) 4-5.
[24]Veyne (1984) 13.
[25]Veyne (1984) 13.

Because we are largely unconscious of this limit to history it takes an effort to realize that "historical knowledge is cut on the pattern of mutilated documents."[26] The effort to realize this is difficult, and seems to go against nature, so natural is our sense that historical discourse is the real as the objective report of "what actually happened." This problem is not simply one of methodology, but involves our fundamental sense of being and our deepest sense of self. The idea that the documents that provide the answers also dictate the questions reveals the unconscious ontological situation in which the historian is embedded. The history we wish to write has, in an important way, already constituted us as the writer. In this way, a certain level of historiography simply "happens" independently of the conscious intentions of the writer. However, the unconscious influence of the documents on historiography does not point to a need for a psychology of the historian, but to the need for a critical ontology of historiography that will include the psyche.

The Production of History

Michel de Certeau recognizes that writing history is itself "historical practice." He examines, among other things, in the modern period of Western history, "the current system of the historiographical 'industry,' which articulates a socioeconomical site of production, the scientific laws of a form of mastery, and the construction of a tale or a text." This leads to, in Certeau's words, "a *writing that conquers*."[27] This recalls the military terms—"campaign, strategy and tactics"— Crossan used to characterize the triple triadic process that determined the epistemology of his Jesus-historiography. We might wonder what Crossan, with his method and his writing, wants to conquer?

Certeau illuminates how the establishment of sources is itself a production process that does not just receive or discover information. Transforming certain objects into "documents" by "photocopying, transcribing and photographing" changes their location and status. This "collection" of documents "exiles them from practice in order to confer upon them the status of 'abstract' objects of knowledge. Far from accepting 'data,' this gesture forms them."[28] Here we can recall Crossan's

---

[26]Veyne (1984) 13.
[27]Certeau (1988) xxv-xxvi.
[28]Certeau (1988) 72-73.

database of the Jesus tradition and its own specialized structure and form. Sayings attributed to Jesus in ancient documents are treated as isolated, discrete entities and given numbered rankings within an over-all stratigraphy. Contrast this construction and its attendant, implicit interpretation of this material that now becomes a "database" (and the technological manipulation of "data" associated with the world of computers), with the actual social and personal contexts in which these sayings were originally spoken or written. Obviously databases and hierarchical stratigraphic rankings have nothing to do with the historic Jesus. But even if Crossan's method, in isolating common themes and structures from out of the mass of the sayings tradition attributed to Jesus is allowed to be in some measure phenomenological, that is, descriptive and comparative, as in fact it is, the so-called *voice* of Jesus is still a creation of this procedure. Everything attributed to the *voice* of Jesus by Crossan is an interpretation made out of the elements of Crossan's contemporary world, not Jesus' world, which is long gone. However, as I maintain throughout this work, it is not just Crossan's personal voice that we hear in the *voice* of his Jesus.

The Invisible Role of Theory and Worldview

Larger theoretical structures also play their role, usually unbeknownst to the historian:

> *History furnishes "facts"* destined to fill formal frameworks determined by an economic, sociological, demographic, or psychoanalytical [or other] theory. This conception tends to direct history toward "examples" which must illustrate a doctrine which has been defined elsewhere.[29]

In this way, "facts" serve to illustrate norms and doctrines that remain invisible, not only to the historian but to the reader. It is the invisible norms, shared by historiographer and reader, that lead to the impression that an objective reality is being represented by the historical text. This sense of "reality" is further enhanced by the global and unconscious ideal of epistemologically rational and objective facts that gives modern history texts their ontological status as the "real." To the extent that we all share the sense that historical explanation and description convey the real, we will experience little conflict with Crossan's narrative

---

[29]Certeau (1988) 119.

whether we agree with any of its specifics or not. And further, to the extent that one unconsciously or consciously shares the norms of the specific sociological models that Crossan utilizes in portraying first century Mediterranean and peasant worlds, so much the stronger will be the sense of the reality of his narrative. This should let us see that historical events are ambiguous because they are constituted by, and joined together by, meanings, that is, thoughts and ideas, which, by definition, are changeable. This fundamental ambiguity of historical events leads Cook to assert that, "What counts as an event is in itself initially unstable and cannot be fully stabilized."[30]

In spite of the growing awareness of the subjective, hermeneutic and creative aspects of historiography, Gossman has a remarkable thing to say about an opposite tendency:

> ...despite decades of demonstrations by philosophers and by historians themselves that history is a construct, the belief that it is an immediate representation of reality, and the historian's own complicity with this belief, have remained remarkably vigorous. Indeed, the tenacity of the belief itself is something that requires explanation.[31]

Gossman attempts to explain this fascination with history as "an immediate representation of reality" in terms of Barthes' analysis of the modern tendency to make an idol of the real. Among other things, Barthes states that the enormous development of photography has contributed to the modern popularity of realism, and the fetishism of the "real" has become an escape from the human responsibility to be a creator of meaning. The problem of what counts as the "real" however, has metaphysical roots that Gossman does not touch on.

A tenacious belief has its roots in an ontological perspective, that is, a worldview, or what we will later see can also be an unconscious projection, that is, by definition, not immediately available to intellectual criticism. It is experienced as if it were a given; it is the real. As a tacit assumption about the nature of our core self-understanding such a belief constitutes our very being. Such unconscious beliefs are connected to deep self-images that are created by particular metaphysical systems. In this case it is the legacy of positivism that leaves the lingering belief that history is the immediate representation of reality. But what makes positivism possible is a Cartesian metaphysics that ontologically splits subject and object, individual and world, and, as Stev-

---

[30]Cook (1988) 4.
[31]Gossman (1978) 32.

enson notes, establishes the *clear and distinct idea* "to be *the* criterion of all knowledge, including the knowledge gained through history." The "objective fact," Stevenson observes, became the historical equivalent of the "clear and distinct idea."[32] Our contemporary conscious intellectual criticism of such a positivist epistemological and ontological perspective as outmoded and inadequate does not easily alter its unconscious and emotional hold on us. It is the *unconscious* ontological perspective that predetermines our epistemology—*being* determines *knowing*. As Ott notes, "Usually the historian is unaware of being determined by the positivistic axiom. It is not a conscious presupposition of his historical study."[33] Our unconscious Cartesian legacy and Jung's response to it are the subject of chapter four.

This dichotomy between what we know consciously and how we continue to behave unconsciously is further drawn out in Gossman's description of the difference between the developments in fiction writing and history writing during the modern period:

> Many modern historians…have repudiated the goals and premises of historical realism, and certain aspects of the rhetoric of the old historical realism have in fact disappeared from modern historical texts. But there seems to have been no radical reform of the *historian's mode of writing* comparable with the changes that have affected literary writing and fiction in the last half-century. *Historical texts continue to recount calmly events and situations located in the past as though the 'age of suspicion' had never dawned.*[34]

This problematic dichotomy is a common theme of the critical historiographers presented here, and it pervades Crossan's Jesus-historiography as well. Indeed, Crossan's creative use of literary criticism, comparative literature and comparative folklore in interpreting the Jesus tradition stands in marked contrast to his confidence in his historiography to reconstruct the past of the historic Jesus. His own mode of historical writing conveys the assurance that he has secure facts in hand that he uses to tell his story about Jesus. And not just his facts of the sayings tradition that go back to Jesus, but the facts of the history of Greco-Roman society, and the facts of the sociology of Roman and Palestinian society, the people of whom of course, never thought of themselves in "sociological" terms. Crossan never allows in *The Historical Jesus* that his overall story and sub-stories are what have

---

[32]Stevenson (1969) 5.
[33]Ott (1964) 152.
[34]Gossman (1978) 36; italics added.

created his "facts." The assumption that is allowed to remain is that his "facts" have led him to the story.

So-called facts have no meaningful existence without a story that constitutes their *historical* being, which must be differentiated from their original *historic* being. The distinction between *historical* being and *historic* being is important. *Historic* being refers to the reality or actuality of everything that has happened in the past (and that, by definition, cannot be recaptured). *Historical* being encompasses the meaningful stories about the historic past that are told within the particular perspective of historical consciousness. This distinction between historic and historical is suggestive of the distinction and relationship I am developing between history and myth. This distinction takes the ambiguity embedded in the term history, as both the real past and discourse about the past, and distributes it between the terms history and myth, with history standing for the reality of the past and myth as the varied discourses about that past. This is not meant to be a hard and fast definition, but suggestive of the complex overlapping meanings I am trying to clarify and relate. Later we will see Hayden White do something similar with the terms history and fiction when I discuss the role of narrative in history.

The Historical, Finality and Narrative

It is generally understood that what distinguishes historical discourse from the natural sciences is its concern for understanding and meaning. Veyne introduces the idea of "finality" as that which specifically characterizes historical understanding, but he also says that the idea of finality "entails no consequences for the epistemology of history"[35] because it is not introduced by the historian, and belongs to actual experience. The "final" viewpoint, that we always have aims and purposes in everything we do and say, is also what characterizes the nature of narrative. But to say that the final viewpoint "entails no consequences for the epistemology of history" can be misleading unless it is made clear that how the final viewpoint is handled by the historian can have dramatic consequences for the historical narrative.

Narrative is always structured with an end and a beginning, and the beginning is always oriented toward the end. But, in real life the

---

[35]Veyne (1984) 4.

"end," or outcome, is not always known nor predictable, and in historical writing the "end" is both known and selected. Munz cites Namier's maxim that "the historian is a man who knows the future and imagines the past."[36] The historian's final viewpoint is always based on hindsight, that as Munz notes, "is a superior quality of which the historian has a monopoly."[37] The historian selects where in time the historical story will end, and to this extent the historian knows the outcome of the historical actions in a way the original participants could not. Those original participants, and we ourselves now as historical actors, acting with the same human desire for a future possibility, must be content with the inferior and limited quality of foresight.

It is the quality of finality that introduces predictability and causality into historical narrative, and they are unavoidable features of any historical narrative that is going to be intelligible. But predictability and causality do not have to be deterministic. It is for this reason that Munz speaks in terms of an "air of predictability" that will characterize any historical narrative. A historical account that merely reported events as purely contingent, like a strict chronology (even though such a list is also selective and interpretive) would be meaningless. But predictability does not need to be rigidly enchained or imposed, nor does the whole historical story need to be predictable, but the general air of predictability is necessary in order to make the "story" intelligible.

Too much predictability in a narrative leads to determinism, that in literary terms, is a kind of foreshadowing that reduces the present moment to a mere preparation for the end. Michael Bernstein, in *Foregone Conclusions: Against Apocalyptic History*, argues against foreshadowing, especially in the narration of the Shoa.[38] The important concept he introduces against foreshadowing is "sideshadowing." This idea refers to "a present dense with multiple, and mutually exclusive, possibilities for what is to come."[39] The impulse to predictability and foreshadowing is natural, but it can become so dominant that it creates "a closed universe in which all choices have already been made, in which human free will can exist only in the paradoxical sense of choosing to accept or willfully—and vainly—rebelling against what is inevitable."[40] On the other hand, "sideshadowing stresses the significance of

---

[36]Munz (1977) 244.
[37]Munz (1977) 245.
[38]Bernstein (1994) 10. This is Bernstein's preferred term for the Nazi genocide.
[39]Bernstein (1994) 1.
[40]Bernstein (1994) 2.

random, haphazard, and unassimilable contingencies, and instead of the power of a system to uncover an otherwise unfathomable truth, it expresses the ever-changing nature of that truth and the absence of any predictive certainties in human affairs."[41]

The concept of sideshadowing contains an ethical implication in preserving the value of the prosaic and the individual by refusing to subsume their worth under some foreclosed future. What Bernstein calls "prosaic ethics," or a "prosaics of the quotidian," refers to two important dimensions of sideshadowing: (1) that we not see "the future as pre-ordained," and (2) that we not "use our knowledge of the future as a means of judging the decisions of those living before that (still only possible) future became actual event."[42] We need to learn to tell our histories in terms of an "unmastered future," struggling to construct the meanings of our lives without resorting to the "absolute and inevitable."[43] The implications of sideshadowing also argue against the unconscious epistemological tyranny of the legacy of positivism that locks history into objective, and therefore fixed and discrete, facts. When facts are objectively fixed they are endowed with an absolute inevitability, a deterministic hardened realism, in sharp contrast to the probabilistic, unruly and fluid realism implied by sideshadowing.

To employ sideshadowing in one's reading of history results in a more realistic understanding of the process of life, the historic. It is also an ethical stance. Bernstein identifies himself as part of "a newly emerging critical counter-tradition that unites ethics and exegesis from an anti-utopian and anti-systematic perspective."[44] In this light, Crossan's *Who Killed Jesus?* can be read as participating in this critical mode of "ethics and exegesis." But Crossan also tries to base his ethical argument on traditional "positivist" epistemological grounds. Crossan appears to base his ethical aim, to combat the anti-Semitism of the Passion narratives, on an outmoded epistemology of historical facts that is philosophically untenable.

I believe the concept of sideshadowing also introduces a problematic element into Crossan's transmissional analysis of sayings attributed to Jesus. Crossan's transmissional analysis depends on a predictability of the historical process of textual development that can be determined through the comparison of similar texts. The concept of

---

[41]Bernstein (1994) 4.
[42]Bernstein (1994) 16.
[43]Bernstein (1994) 125.
[44]Bernstein (1994) 129.

sideshadowing applied to this particular "narrative" of text and saying development introduces unpredictable and unknowable historical, social and psychological factors into the appearance of texts that renders null and void any attempt to date with certainty textual variants. For example, an isolated second- or even third-century textual community could produce, on its own, without any literary dependence, quite "early sounding" sayings material. In the light of sideshadowing, it is quite impossible to know the historic vagaries that contribute to textual formation and transmission. Sideshadowing should emphasize for us the dense, vast and unpredictable nature of reality at all times, present and past. As such, it should alert us to how much the historian's selections, hypotheses and interpretations of historic materials subjectivize the historical narrative.

History and Memory

The problems of selection and construction lead us to the relationship between history and memory. Memory and historical narrative select from experience and construct stories in similar ways. Munz continually emphasizes that "The narrative that results from the historian's work is not a portrait of what happened, but it *is* the story of what happened."[45] As Munz reminds us, the

> totality of what happened is so large and broad that it cannot be surveyed, and the mere subdivision of that totality into definable and specific events distinct from one another is part of the historian's activity. ... The historian's narrative is history.[46]

This unavoidable process of selection in historiography parallels the function of memory, and contemporary memory research points to a psychophysical dimension to historiography. Memory must be able to select, forget and generalize from the overwhelming totality of daily detailed experience. This process is the basis for the development of a coherent self as well as the basis for successful adaptation to the real world. It has been discovered that memory, at the neurological level, while usually more often accurate than not, is also fundamentally constructive, creative and vulnerable to distortion. Schacter, referring to psychophysical studies of the brain and the subjective experience of memory states that,

---

[45]Munz (1977) 233.
[46]Munz (1977) 233.

the idea that storage and retrieval of explicit memories involves
binding together different kinds of information from diverse cortical
sites provides a biological basis for the notion that retrieval of a
memory is a complex construction involving many different sources
of information—not a simple playback of a stored image....[47]

Memories are always being superimposed on one another, influencing our experience and being influenced by our experience. Remembering is a process of constructive interpretation, influenced by the present context of remembering, the present condition of the rememberer and the motivation for remembering. It is not a passive recall of a stored replication of some past event. The obvious, but often unrealized, point is that a memory is by definition revision. Memory cannot be "the way it really happened" because memory is first of all "the way it happened *to me.*" And secondly, memory, like a document, is not the event itself, but the memory-of-the-event. Schacter tells us, "memories are records of how we have experienced events, not replicas of the events themselves." And, "it is now clear that we do not store judgment-free snapshots of our past experiences but rather hold on to the meaning, sense and emotions these experiences provided us."[48] Memory is our significant history, and as we will see in the next chapter when exploring Jung and Heidegger, significance, emotion and meaning are bound together ontologically, thereby creating our basic sense of self, which predetermines and conditions our ways of knowing.

Clear and vivid memories are also no guarantee of accuracy. The clarity and vividness of a memory has more to do with a function of the psyche that can also produce dramatically clear and vivid dreams. Some memory may have more in common with dreams, as metaphors for the significance of emotional experiences that have strongly impacted us. Munz's statement, "The historian's narrative is history," also means that "the historian's narrative is the memory that is history." And as Veyne says, "History is the daughter of memory."[49]

---

[47]Schacter (1995) 19.
[48]Schacter (1996) 5-6.
[49]Veyne (1988) 5.

Event, *Sinngebild* and Myth

Munz points out that when the historian makes a selection of events out of the totality of what has happened, the selected events are linked in a meaningful way by thought, or ideas, and not in terms of time or nature. It should be clear that time does not connect events. Establishing dates for events simply creates a chronology. And nature by itself does not connect events. Events are connected in a meaningful way through ideas having to do with cause and intention. As noted above, one of these meaningful thoughts is the idea of finality. Even the eyewitness connects the observed events with thought. Events cannot have a meaningful existence without the connecting thoughts of eyewitness or historian. And every event is always a composite of sub-events that are linked by thought, and each sub-event can be subdivided again, and so on, *ad infinitum*. This leads Munz to conclude that historical research is not about discovering or establishing "facts" in any traditional or positivist sense. He says,

> The most factual discovery is not the discovery that a certain event occurred but that a certain *Sinngebild* occurred—that is, that there was a certain intelligible constellation of events, where intelligible refers to the people involved in the events. This kind of discovery is the most 'factual' discovery there is. 'Factual' here, includes 'thought'; but then thoughts are facts.[50]

The "thoughts" Munz is referring to here are what he calls universals, general laws, or covering laws. We all use commonly accepted general understanding to create sense to ourselves and to others. And events cannot make sense to us or to others unless they are connected by thoughts of common understanding. Munz distinguishes between abstract universals and concrete universals. By abstract universal he means those forms of ideas derived from philosophical and scientific modes of thought, and by concrete universal he means those modes of thought derived from myth. However, they each function in exactly the same way in being those general forms of thought that link the events of history and life into meaningful stories or narratives. For example, when we observe an apple fall from a tree and hit the ground we make sense of these events with reference to the law of gravity, and if we are inclined, with reference to the chemical changes in the plant cells at the point where the apple stem and tree branch connect. These abstract

---

[50]Munz (1977) 231.

universals involve us in causation and predictability, and give us a sense that we understand the event. An alternative concrete and mythic covering law might say that the tree let go of the apple, or the apple let go of the tree, because Mother Earth, in her sorrow (late summer and fall), called her child (the fruit) back to her bosom. In the Gospel stories about Jesus it is clear that mythic universals, such as God, Holy Spirit, Satan and Jesus' own supernatural powers and knowledge, along with themes of transformation involving death and rebirth and sin and redemption, are at work connecting and interpreting the action. Crossan on the other hand employs abstract universals derived from sociology, cultural anthropology and political science to connect and interpret the action of the same story.

Whether any covering law, abstract or concrete, is true or adequate by whatever standards is not the point here. The point here is to see the fundamental structure of any event in terms of the *Sinngebild*, a cluster of meaning that is held together by covering laws, or generalizations, or, the word I prefer, interpretations. That is, all covering laws, abstract or concrete, are basically hermeneutic, and therefore, fundamentally mythic. I believe the term myth is adequate to refer to all hermeneutic frameworks, and that it can function as a meta-covering law, expressing the meaning-structure of all covering laws or universals. And lest such an overarching use of a term that is so problematic and ambiguous seem confusing or overly ambitious, it is my view that giving such a role to myth, redefined as a mode of thinking, gives a more adequate sense of the real role of the hermeneutic mode of thinking, and therefore myth, in both psyche and historiography.

I prefer the term myth for such general usage for several reasons. First, I believe myth was probably the first kind of covering law used, and that abstract universals emerge with developing civilizations and rational thought. Second, there is a tendency to give greater epistemological and ontological status to abstract covering laws over and against myth in our modern Western culture. In order to subvert this unconscious tendency to privilege abstract universals I believe the use of the term myth reminds us that all covering laws, or universals, are fundamentally hermeneutic. And third, the origin of the Greek word *hermeneia* is connected with the god Hermes and therefore has its roots in myth.[51] Hermes is the messenger of the gods, psychopomp (leader of souls to Hades), god of crossroads and boundaries, as well as associated

---

[51]Palmer (1969) 13.

with the origins of language, writing and commerce. This phenomenology makes Hermes a symbol of that existential and archetypal function that connects, links, and so interprets, the unfamiliar to the familiar. Hermes makes it possible for what is beyond human understanding to come into understanding via interpretation. This is the hermeneutic function of every covering law or universal. It could be said that Hermes constitutes the *Sinngebild*.

In this sense, history and memory are "myths" or "fictions" of reality, or of actual happenings. Events are not "things," but lived experiences, and what we say about experiences are *interpretations* of those experiences, and not the experiences themselves. This states again that there is no such thing as a so-called naked and neutral, objective fact. Any so-called fact is really a cluster of meanings, connected to other clusters, and all are "unstable," that is, by definition, open to reinterpretation, revision, variation, no matter how trivial or generally obvious.

Veyne calls the "thought" that constitutes a fact the "plot": "a very human and not very 'scientific' mixture of material causes, aims, and chances."[52] The plot is infinitely variable in itself and in relation to other plots. A plot is neither a determinism nor a mere given because of its variability, and yet it is not a fiction in the sense that it is purely imagined, but it is "fictional" in that it is a story of experience made with words. It is, to a degree, imagined and created. Plot and *Sinngebild* are interpretations and points of view, and in this sense they are mythic.

The lowest common denominator of what is considered to be a historical fact is a hermeneutic construct or creation, a flexible interpretive cluster of understanding that is only thereby intelligible. The "historical fact" is not a hard and fixed absolute, but a changeable understanding. How Christopher Columbus' relation to America is understood is a good example. The bare fact that Columbus came to America is meaningless in itself, and amounts to nothing more than a truism in that many people have come to America. What makes Columbus' coming to America historically significant is the interpretation that contextualizes the event in a host of meanings associated with the origins of the United States of America. This will usually include a positive sense of the United States as the greatest nation in the world, and as a democracy, the moral beacon of the world, etc. In this context Columbus "discovered" America, and is a kind of national saint. However, another view, with a completely different plot is available and making itself

---

[52]Veyne (1984) 32.

heard. This alternative interpretation takes into account the indigenous peoples who were in the Americas before Columbus arrived. This plot views Columbus as a brutal invader and conqueror, a thief and a slave trader. He did not "discover" anything from this perspective, but invaded and stole what already belonged to someone else. This is hardly the view of the benevolent explorer taught to the nation's children. If this interpretation of Columbus is allowed to become part of the larger plot of the origins of a nation, the larger plot of the history of the nation will have to change if this new sub-plot is not to be suppressed and relegated to the status of official "non-history." This example should emphasize that plot is everything in the presentation of the *historical* in contrast to what is simply the historic. Another example is that of Jesus of Nazareth. Depending on the plot, the history of Rome, of the Jewish people, or of Christianity, Jesus is either practically nonexistent, a minor figure, or dominates center stage.

History as Myth is not Idealism

My emphasis on the interpretive nature of history should not be taken as a debate between historic actuality and some kind of interpretive idealism. As Veyne has noted, "Since everything is historic, history is what we will choose."[53] This distinction is important because the reality, or actuality, of everything that has ever happened, the historic, is not in doubt here. But what is important is to see that when we talk about history and the historical we are immediately and inescapably involved in plot, interpretation and selection.

Veyne affirms the reality of the past by saying that the subjective essence of history does not mean "arbitrariness," nor "idealism," but "nominalism." This simply means that "a fact is not created when it is discovered."[54] The fact Veyne is referring to is the discovery of preromantic themes in classical literature. He is arguing against Bergson who implies that the so-called preromantic themes are actually the creation of the romantic sensibility that later cut them out of the earlier classical context. But Veyne asserts that the preromantic themes are not put back in to the classical context by the literary historian. It is simply the fact of romanticism that enables the preromantic themes to be seen later. In this case, however, the "fact" is related to a text that exists in

[53]Veyne (1984) 42.
[54]Veyne (1984) 42-43.

the present and can be examined by many. I would consider such a "fact" a hard fact, that is, a thing that persists into the present and can be observed in the present. In this case, the words of the text. But as such, hard facts are nothing in themselves. Everything that gave the hard fact its historic being, its historic context of meaning and purpose is gone. History is not made up of hard facts. History is composed of soft facts, the plots, *Sinngebilden*, and interpretations that make up the stories of history. The soft fact or event is constituted by the description that calls it into being, and "every description implies the choice, most often unconscious, of features that will be deemed pertinent."[55] So, when Veyne affirms the *fact* and a "nominalist conception of history," it is not in terms of the old argument about whether the particular or the universal is the really real thing, but that the *fact* is a convention that "comes to us from the documents of the day, from collective memory and from school tradition,"[56] and it is this unavoidable combination of particular and universal, the plot, that is at the heart of all historiographical arrangements. As Munz has noted, history cannot be written from scratch in each generation. We are all dependent on the historical-facts, the stories, that have been handed down from generation to generation, and we can only write and rewrite our histories from these more or less common traditions.

Veyne chooses to think of history in terms of a nominalism that we might say is writ small, so as to emphasize the "objectivity" of the "facts" that subjectivity chooses in order to write history. He is very aware that subjectivity is the essence of historical epistemology, but he also affirms the reality (though ever changeable) of the historical-facts history must use to tell its story. Munz occupies the same ground but approaches history from the opposite direction and sees it in terms of an idealism writ small. Munz bases his view that it is the combination of thought and experience that creates the *Sinngebild* as the most basic and only "fact" that history deals with on the conviction that the human mind shares a universal structure. He emphasizes the simplicity of his view of this basic structure, and it is this:

> the basic structure of the human mind consists in the fact that we can only think by referring particulars to universals, by subsuming particulars under universals, or by recognizing particulars as instances of universals. We can distinguish two kinds of universals, concrete universals and abstract universals. Each kind of universal has its

---

[55]Veyne (1984) 44.
[56]Veyne (1984) 44.

own mode of subsumption. But that is all. The content of the universals must differ, but the modes of operation do not.[57]

This is what Munz means by an idealism writ small. He is not
interested in the argument between nominalism and realism and the debate about the ontological status of particular or universal. He is simply
affirming that particulars and universals are always related, that universals must be employed to relate particulars, and that the combination of
particular and universal, the *Sinngebild*, constitutes the historical fact.
In no way is Munz, nor am I, interested in the proposition that the real
world is only an idea (the extreme form of idealism). In the next chapter I will relate Munz's view of the universal with both Jung's concept
of the archetype and Heidegger's ontological view of understanding.
By making these connections I will deepen our understanding of the
essentially hermeneutic nature of being and history, and my contention
that history as story is best understood in terms of myth.

Historical-criticism and Self-criticism

Critical historiography raises the question of just what is an adequate understanding of the nature of the relationship between history as
discourse and the real past. It is crucial to see its complex, problematic,
ambiguous, limited and fundamentally human nature. Criticism must be
exercised at every level, not just in relation to sources and "documents," but with the resulting histories as well. From source to narrative, every historical "document," has the same status as a human creation in need of critical reflection and interpretation.[58] In this light, historical criticism does not recover or establish definitive or absolute
facts, but raises questions about the *thought* that shapes events and facts
and bequeaths them to us in various forms. As Veyne states, "historical
criticism has only one function: to answer the question asked of it by
the historian: 'I believe that this document teaches me this; may I trust
it to do that?'"[59] But in questioning the trustworthiness of the document
to teach me something, I am really questioning *my idea*, or the *general
idea*, of what the document teaches. A document, as such, does not
teach anything. It is what *I think* the document says, or my interpreta-

---

[57]Munz (1977) 13.
[58]White's *Metahistory* (1973) is an example of a critical look at the literary forms
and ideologies that determined the writing of nineteenth century historians.
[59]Veyne (1988) 12.

tion of the document, that teaches me something. Therefore, the question of historical criticism is, "May I trust the interpretation that arises in the interaction between myself and the document?" The document is itself a product of thought, memory, imagination and cultural context, and the critical evaluation of its trustworthiness is also a complex function of thought, memory, imagination and cultural context.

Although I have not yet used the word psyche in this discussion of the subjective dimensions of historiography, it should be clear that psyche and history are intimately intertwined, if not in some measure practically identical. The psyche itself is profoundly historical (as we know from both Freud and Jung) and history, as discourse, is an expression of psyche. This relationship between psyche and history is also evident in the overlapping connection between historical criticism and self-criticism.

When we apply historical criticism to a document, a gospel text for instance, it is less the text itself that is being evaluated and more our idea about the meaning of the text, or a prevailing idea about the meaning of the text, that is being evaluated. When we critically evaluate a historic document or artifact we are critically evaluating interpretations that have been handed down and are held in the present. In this sense all history is contemporary. Krentz, in *The Historical-Critical Method,* quotes Walter Kasper as saying, "Historical criticism is a form of criticism of the present, a setting into question of the prevailing *sensus communis.*"[60] The common beliefs we all more or less share about ourselves, make up, in part, the collective psyche. The collective psyche is both culture and a deeply felt sense of self that is largely unconscious. Historical criticism as method may be, in fact, not a way to recover the past, but rather, more of a phenomenological attitude toward being that reimagines our self-understanding in the present in terms of a relationship to an imagined past. Perhaps new "knowledge" about the past needs to be conceived in terms of a newly revisioned story about our present. The critical function of historical criticism, and our separation in time from the past, give us the distance necessary for reflection on who we imagine ourselves to be. For this reason I think it is appropriate to begin to re-conceive of the "method" of historical criticism more in terms of a phenomenology of being rather than an epistemology of facts. In this sense historical criticism is a questioning of meanings and not a technology for establishing data.

---

[60]Krentz (1975) 45.

Gossman refers to Alain Besançon as arguing "that all historical research is in some measure 'recherche de soi-même…introspection.' According to Besançon, 'the fundamental operation of the sciences of human behavior is not the observation of the subject by the observer. It is the analysis of their interaction in a situation in which both are at one and the same time subjects and observers.'"[61] In a similar vein White introduces the role of imagination in historical narrative,

> How else can any past, which by definition comprises events, proc-esses, structures, and so forth, considered to be no longer perceiv-able, be represented in either consciousness or discourse except in an "imaginary" way? Is it not possible that the question of narrative in any discussion of historical theory is always finally about the function of imagination in the production of a specifically human truth?[62]

The role of the self and imagination in historical narrative and understanding, as well as self-understanding, has a deeper dimension than the merely personal, and has a function that is not merely "hu-man." To introduce introspection, the self, and imagination into the domain of historical understanding is not to seek a reduction to psy-chology. I refrain from saying the "human" imagination because, as we will see, in Jung's view, the imagination is something *sui generis*, a function of the unconscious that is independent of the ego's own aims and goals. It is more accurate to think of the human and the imagination in terms of a relationship in which each, at different times, as subject or object, influence each other. More on this in chapter four.

History, self and imagination are constitutive and interdependent aspects of each other. Gadamer, concerned with the ontology of history and self-understanding, states,

> In the last analysis, *all* understanding is self-understanding, but not in the sense of a preliminary self-possession or of one finally and definitively achieved. For the self-understanding only realizes itself in the understanding of a subject matter and does not have the char-acter of a free self-realization. The self that we are does not possess itself; one could say that it "happens."
>
> It is not really we ourselves who understand: it is always a past that allows us to say, 'I have understood.'[63]

---

[61]Gossman (1978) 28.
[62]White (1987) 57.
[63]Gadamer (1977) 55, 58.

For Gadamer, the self is never an isolate, nor a discrete subjectivity. It is first and foremost a historical tradition and it is this historical tradition that constitutes our being. Our self-understanding is always, first of all, unconsciously self-evident as a member of a family, a community, and a nation long before personal self-examination, or conscious reflection, occurs.

Our historical being is constituted far more by the "prejudices" of the historical tradition we belong to than the individual judgments we might make. For Gadamer, "prejudices" are those traditional ways of knowing and being we simply inherit because we are, first of all, in our being, an undifferentiated part of a human group before any individuality can emerge.[64] The significance that constitutes historical being as plot, as *Sinngebild*, is first of all an inherited "prejudice" or perspective (i.e., a myth) that is also selective. This historical reality is what first constitutes the individual, and it is probably not possible for the individual to divest themself of their tradition. There are options available to the individual in relation to tradition and they are to mimic the tradition, rebel against, or reject, the tradition, or become an individual expression of the tradition—but, in all cases, one is still connected to the tradition. And as the individual is a product of its history, so too is the present constituted by its history. The present cannot simply manufacture a "past" although it might try to do so in denial of the totality of its historic reality. As individuals we attempt to do this when we forget, or repress, painful episodes from our personal life history, and only remember what we believe is conducive to a "happier" self-image. The attempt to manufacture, or make-up, a history, is always done in reaction to another history that is, in some way, real. To reiterate, the subjectivity of the individual is never merely personal—there is always something historical and traditional that is fundamental to it. The realization of the introspective and imaginative aspects of historiography introduce both critical and creative factors in relation to the inherited history that we are, and should deepen our appreciation of the fundamentally hermeneutic nature of history.

---

[64]Gadamer (1986) 245.

History, Narrative and Myth

Now we have seen that written history is constituted by meaning, imagination and unconsciously inherited tradition, and, as such, has more to do with story than a scientific object of knowledge. Is there, then, any significant difference between history and myth given our new complex and hermeneutic understanding of both history and myth? Veyne states that "history is a true novel." Is it not also true then that "history is a true myth"? The issue seems to hinge on the meaning of the word "true." In Veyne's usage, "true" simply means that history refers to true human events, things that people have reportedly really done, while myth and fiction do not refer to events that have really happened, and myth, as fable, usually includes actors other than humans. But the modern novel with only human actors, reads, or sounds, just as true, in this sense, as the historical narrative. And what is the difference between the historical novel and the historical narrative? Within such an ambiguous realm of overlapping meanings what does it mean to say that "history is a true myth"? Is it meaningful to do so, or only more confusing? I believe any confusion is a valuable part of the meaningfulness of the phrase because this forces us to think consciously about their deep-seated conventional meanings.

I find part of the answer to this problem in making a shift from the *content* of myth to the *function* of myth. The function of myth, as a hermeneutic framework, involves the nature and function of narrative as it appears in both historiography, mythography and other literary forms we associate with fiction. In Greek, the word *mythos* means story, tale, legend, fable and myth, and Aristotle uses it to mean the "plot" of a play.[65] Understanding *mythos* as plot, as a literary structure, eliminates the adversarial conflict between the content of history as true and real and the content of myth as fiction and false. But the terms history and myth have served for a long time, and continue to serve, as a conventional shorthand for the polarization of the nature of reality, with history "as a kind of archetype of the realistic pole of representation," and myth (as story, novel, etc.) as the fictive, the imagined.[66] This polarization has also involved the overvaluation of history by involving it with the search for final, rational and objective foundations and the undervaluation of myth as merely subjective, arbitrary superstition. By eliminating the argument between myth and history at the level of true

---

[65]Gossman (1978) 9-10.
[66]White (1978) 42.

or false content, we can approach the problem of myth and history in terms of structure and function, particularly narrative structure, and see the value and truth about human being they share equally.

The most general structure of narrative is a story with a beginning, middle and end. It is this simple structure, a beginning and end, that distinguishes historical narrative from the mere passage of time in which one thing happens after another—the simple chronology—with no connecting links and no purpose, that is, no end, no telos. Without beginnings, that is, origins, and without endings, that is, purpose, time has no meaning to us.

As we have seen, facts and events have no meaning in themselves. They must be embedded in contexts of meaning, a *Sinngebild*, a plot. Narrative is the overall plot-structure that gives meaning, comprehension and coherence to a description of events that would otherwise remain chaotic, strange and meaningless. Narrative gives intelligible shape to time. And it is narrative that lends to historiography the experience of "reality" because narrative structure has an ontological dimension—as a structure of being, it is intimately connected with our personal experience of being real and meaningful. I conclude that the terms narrative structure and mythic structure are synonymous because both are expressions of the primordial impulse to interpret meaning that constitutes human being. It is necessary to be able to say that "history is a true myth" in order to emphasize the fundamental being of history, which is that the ultimate referent of history is not facts but meanings.

White shows that the narrative structures available to historiographers are the same as those available to writers of fiction, and they are a limited number, such as, romance, comedy, tragedy and satire.[67] It is such literary, or mythic, forms that endow historical events with the form and meaning that involve our thought and emotions in understanding the events that make up our collective experience as history. In effect, White says that the historian, in order to write a meaningful history, has to translate "fact" into "fiction."[68]

The historian and the poet or novelist are engaged in the same basic process—how, through writing, can one make sense of life and experience, especially in relation to time? White does not believe that the realization that the historian and novelist are engaged in the same fundamental process diminishes the epistemological status of historiography if we also believe that literature and imagination illuminate the

---

[67]White (1978) 54.
[68]White (1978) 53.

same human world. History (historiography) and myth, in this sense, share the same ultimate desire to understand and grasp in some measure the meaning of being. As White states,

> In my view, we experience the "fictionalization" of history as an "explanation" for the same reason that we experience great fiction as an illumination of a world that we inhabit along with the author. In both we re-cognize the forms by which consciousness both constitutes and colonizes the world it seeks to inhabit comfortably.[69]

If this view does not diminish the epistemological status of historiography it must be seen to radically relativize and fundamentally reorient the epistemology of historiography. Rather than an epistemology driven by the absolutist ideals of positivism, this is an epistemology of meaning and soul, or psyche. And as we will see in the next chapter, soul or psyche is not a private affair of the individual, but is the public and private shared world within which we all dwell and have our being. Neither does this reorientation of epistemology diminish the role of rational and critical thought, but it does reorient its function. Rather than working to establish definitive facts, it can work to evaluate the thought and assumptions that combine to build the "facts" of history.

Historicality and the Ontology of Time

History, in its concern with the past from the position of the present is concerned with time, and time is not an object we can grasp. Instruments are devised to measure time but this has nothing to do with the experience and meaning of time. As historical beings we are all confronted with "being-in-time," and time is the fundamental basis of history and historical understanding. Time is a fundamental dimension of being and world we all share. Ricoeur (as presented by White) speaks of the problem of "being-in-time" as a mystery that cannot be solved, but is, up to a point, comprehensible.[70] We comprehend time through narrative, because it is narrative that tells us what time is, what it means, with the modes of beginnings, middles and ends. The problem of time cannot be grasped directly, and because both history and literature share this same ultimate referent, they both speak symbolically, figuratively, about "the aporias of temporality."[71] Ricoeur believes that

---

[69]White (1978) 61.
[70]White (1987) 171.
[71]White (1987) 175.

"historicality" *is* the structure of narrativity because narrative reflects the structure of temporality. Time is narrativistic.[72]

White cites Ricoeur as holding "temporality to be that structure of existence that reaches language as narrativity and narrativity to be the language structure that has temporality as its ultimate referent."[73] Along with White, I believe that Ricoeur is showing us the "metaphysics of narrativity." As ontological, narrative is not merely something created and imposed by the human mind. If we view narrativity as a fundamental structure of being and therefore of reality, then we can say that it uses us to tell the meanings of our lives in time, personal and collective. In Jung's language this would mean that narrative structure is archetypal, that is, prior to human consciousness. In fact, the phenomenology of narrative overlaps with some of the characteristics of the archetype of the self in that narrative gives coherence, totality and wholeness, meaning and purpose, to a story.

Munz also suggests an ontological basis for historiography, but he approaches it in terms of an asymmetry in our experience of time and space. He states that through the experience of time we experience deprivation, lose. Things disappear in time. But in space we can experience gain and expansion. In time there can be only one thing at a time. In space there are many things at once. Therefore the impulse to convert "time into history" is based on the need to work against "the depressing experience of deprivation through time by trying to assimilate the passage of time to the extension of space."[74] This leads Munz to say,

> When we see the past as a story, we give shape to time. And since there is no absolute shape that we could give to time, it might be more appropriate to think of the transformation of time as a process of putting sets of masks over the face of time.[75]

Thinking in terms of "masks on the face of time" relativizes our positivist sense of history as the true report of what actually happened. Rather we see that as a mask on time, history has more in common with myth than not. History and myth have an intimate relationship. As traditional modes of discourse they are differentiated, but in a deeper sense, they are much closer in structure and intent than traditionally allowed. There is an interpenetration of history and myth that is both

---

[72]White (1987) 171.
[73]White (1987) 52.
[74]Munz (1977) 37-38.
[75]Munz (1977) 38.

unavoidable and problematic. I will use the term myth to mean a *structure of meaning* in order to broaden the limiting idea of myth as only a particular type of discourse or literary genre. It is myth that brings a specific ideology and worldview into a particular historical story. In principle this cannot be avoided because myth, as a kind of ideology, is almost always unconscious. I have tried to show how a particular epistemological myth has been unconsciously operative in Crossan's Jesus-historiography. In chapter six I hope to show how Jung's concept of projection can function as a hermeneutic aid in just this area of unconscious myth. In a similar vein, White hopes that acknowledging the "fictive" element in historiography will also make historians more conscious of their ideological preconceptions that function unconsciously as the dogmatic truth in their history. Seeing that the fictive element and the ideological are the same will raise historiography, and the teaching of historiography, to a new level of self-consciousness than, in White's view, it now occupies.[76] White believes that

> history as a discipline is in bad shape today because it has lost sight
> of its origins in the literary imagination. In the interest of appearing
> scientific and objective, it has repressed and denied to itself its own
> greatest source of strength and renewal.[77]

When I say that history is a myth I do mean that the traditional positivist idea of history as the definitive record of absolutely objective facts about "what actually happened" is an unwarranted illusion deriving from a Cartesian metaphysics. But I do not mean that history itself is an illusion. When I say that history is a myth I affirm Nietzsche's assertion that there are no facts, only interpretations. This does not diminish or devalue history in anyway. But it should loosen the metaphysical underpinnings of historiography that leads the quest for the historical Jesus astray. In saying that history is a myth I hope for the same increase of historiographical self-consciousness that White does when he says history is a fiction.

Crossan's own interests in relating the literary imagination with historical discourse in relation to Jesus approaches White's concerns but it does not go far enough. For White the literary imagination, and myth, are at the heart of the historiographical creation of history and cannot be separated. For Crossan, history, as the result of historical re-

---

[76]White (1978) 61.
[77]White (1978) 62.

search, and the literary imagination and literary critical method, exist side by side. For White they are necessarily integrated, for Crossan they are supposedly separate but equal partners. At the beginnings of *In Parables* and *Raid on the Articulate*, Crossan claims an objective and reliable epistemology for historical criticism to establish the authentic historic Jesus tradition, and criticizes only the self-appointed role of historical criticism to be the sole legitimate approach to Jesus. He then brings the traditions of literature and his own creative literary imagination to interpret the historically established Jesus tradition. Crossan fails to take a critical view of historiography in general and does not notice the problematic of the ontological and hermeneutic nature of history itself. Part of Crossan still seems to want to view history as the historic, that is, in this case, the "historical" as "what actually happened," and fails to see that history can not be the historic in this sense, but can only be a hermeneutic exploration of being. What is written as history is more properly understood in terms of stories that are imaginative explorations of the inherited interpretations we call history. Once we realize that history is a complex mixture of experience, meaning and subjectivity the insights of hermeneutic phenomenology and depth-psychology can contribute to our understanding of its true nature. In other words, history is not, and cannot be, "what actually happened." Rather, histories can be, and are, many, changeable interpretations of the human experience of time and being.

Summary and Conclusion

The idea of history, under the influence of positivism became associated with objective reportage about the past. Within the ideals of positivism history was to be a true account of "what actually happened" in the past, free from the bias of the historian's point of view. These ideals of scientific objectivity meant that history as discipline and discourse became disassociated from the idea of 'story,' the literary imagination and the values of subjectivity associated with meaning, significance and purpose.

Although the extreme and obvious forms of historical positivism have been critiqued and to a large extent discredited, the legacy and ideals of positivism still haunt historiography in general, and Crossan's Jesus-historiography in particular.

The critical historiographers surveyed in this chapter, White, Veyne, Munz, Certeau and others, have pointed to the fundamentally hermeneutic, imaginative and constructive nature of historiography and historical narrative. At every level, from the smallest "fact" to the grandest plot, it is variable and unstable meanings that constitute the events and narratives of history as discourse. There is no privileged epistemological vantage point outside of history by which the one true historical report could be determined. We are our history and we create our history. However, history is not an arbitrary creation by an isolated present. We inherit a heritage of historical interpretations (our history) that shape the present and are continually reinterpreted by the present.

Realizing that history has more in common with fiction and myth than not does not mean we do not have any knowledge about the past. What this perspective emphasizes is that our knowledge of the past is extremely limited, interpretive and subjective, and that it is not a replication of the past. It also emphasizes that knowledge of the past always serves subjective purposes in that it serves particular narrative purposes. But narrative purpose does not derive from only personal or private subjectivity. As White and Ricoeur suggest there is a "metaphysics of narrative" that is related to an ontology of time we all share. Looking ahead, in the light of Heidegger and Jung, I will propose the concept of *deep-subjectivity* as the ontological and archetypal source of narrative. It is in this sense that I suggest that the deep-subjectivity of historiography is fundamentally mythic.

This exploration of critical historiography makes it apparent that *history* and *myth* are overlapping and ambiguous terms. Their ambiguity resides in the fact that both must have two simultaneous and related but different referents: (1) an aspect of the *real*, and (2) *discourse* about the real. I propose the following working definitions for the terms *history* and *myth*: *history* refers to (1) the reality of the events of the past, and (2) historical discourse (stories) about the events of the past; *myth* refers to (1) structures of meaning and narrative that, though not observable in the same way that events are, are nevertheless ontologically real, and (2) varied discourses and stories that include fable, legend, fiction and historical narrative. History and myth most obviously overlap in the term narrative, and this is where they both coincide with the idea of deep-subjectivity.

By making the place of subjectivity in historiography prominent I want to broaden the role of historical criticism to include a kind of phenomenological-psychological criticism. As Veyne stated, historical criticism asks the question, "May I trust this document to teach me what I believe it teaches me?" Knowing that the historian's relationship to the document is an integral part of what the document will "teach," I suggest that historical criticism also ask, in the light of a phenomenological understanding of deep-subjectivity (to be developed in chapter four), "On what basis can I trust the interpretation that arises in the interaction between myself and this document?" A phenomenological-psychological criticism, informed by historical criticism, tries to be aware of the myth or narrative within which it raises questions of trust about documents that were created in the context of very different historic myths or narratives (other historical epochs). A phenomenological-psychological perspective understands that the narrative (mythic) purposes any so-called "facts" serve are mostly unconscious, and influence our consciously created methods. The methods themselves are crafted by unconscious narratives, that is, mythic purposes. In this sense "narrative" is not viewed as only a literary structure—it points to tacit ontological worldviews (myths) with purposes and aims that we cannot avoid bringing to our historical inquiries.

In the next chapter on Jung and Heidegger I will explore the ontological and archetypal dimensions of deep-subjectivity and its implicit narrative (mythic) structure. This leads to the implications for understanding the ontological nature of the relationship between psychological projection and the hermeneutic circle in Jesus-historiography. In this context I also address the problem of the unconscious nature of deep-subjectivity and the methodological problem of how the collective unconscious, that wide, culturally shared unconsciousness we live in together, can be accounted for in Jesus-historiography.

CHAPTER FOUR

JUNG'S PHENOMENOLOGICAL PSYCHOLOGY AND THE CHRIST

Introduction

This chapter on Jung has two main and interrelating parts. The first part will undertake a philosophical reading of Jung's general psychological method, and in so doing, revise our understanding of "subjectivity." The second part will examine Jung's interpretation of the Christ in the light of the philosophical reading of Jung in part one.

Undertaking a philosophical reading of Jung enables us to understand his work as, among other things, a response to the legacy of Cartesian epistemology and its underlying ontology, which is the primary presupposition of the unwitting historical positivism that conditions contemporary Jesus historiography. The philosophical reading of Jung, that I undertake in the light of Heidegger's fundamental ontology, is important because of my contention that the legacy of Cartesian metaphysics is the stumbling block at the heart of the methodological crisis in contemporary Jesus-historiography. Crossan, among other New Testament scholars, identifies this crisis in terms of a problematic relationship between multiple Jesus images and scholarly subjectivity. Heidegger is the contemporary thinker who most explicitly and dramatically takes the hermeneutic turn that undermines Cartesian metaphysics.

It is necessary to make clear the unconscious, ontological assumptions that have driven epistemology in general since Descartes in order that Jung's revisioning of subjectivity and the resulting challenge to both critical historiography and Jesus historiography will also be clear. By illuminating Jung in comparison with Heidegger's thought I will also make clear that Jung's work represents a different perspective on the Cartesian and Freudian epistemological traditions that posit any psychological approaches to understanding as merely reductive and personal. A central point of Jung's and Heidegger's is that subjectivity is not merely personal. The deepening of our under-standing of subjectivity will provide a fresh perspective on the so-called problem in Jesus-research that what is found in the historical Jesus is only the reflection of one's own face at the bottom of a deep well. I contend that concealed in the reflection are unconscious aspects of the self, that as archetypal potentials of consciousness, desire to manifest consciously in the individual. As we will see later in the light of Jung's interpretation of traditional Christian images, we can also say that the reflection at the bottom of the well reveals previously un-known aspects of the "face of God" that desire incarnation.

The second part of this chapter will look at what I take to be the phenomenological similarity between Jung's psychological-archetypal interpretation of the Christ in Western Christianity and the quest for the historical Jesus. I will view Jung's interpretation of the Christ as a kind of historiography of a process of progressive incarnation, or as Jung would put it, the process of individuation that develops con-sciousness by deepening its dialogue with the collective unconscious. In the light of the previous chapter on historiography and myth I hold that the quest for the *historic* Jesus cannot succeed in its traditional aim of recovering the original Jesus of Nazareth, and, more importantly, that it is the misplaced, externalization of the process of individ-uation—the quest for the historical self as the conscious realization of one's own God-given archetypal individuality. In other words, within Jung's frame of reference, I suggest that the quest for the historic Jesus is an unconscious projection of the individuation process, and as such, that there is a moral imperative from the self (i.e., God) for the project to be *consciously* so conceived.

In the light of this perspective, relying on Jung's informal phenomenology of Catholicism and Protestantism, I will suggest that Crossan's image of Jesus shows a development from a Catholic image of Christ to a Protestant image of Jesus. And that the historic development from Catholicism to Protestantism is a transformational step in the individuation process. I will discuss this idea in more detail in chapter six.

I will show that Jung's understanding of subjectivity in terms of the collective unconscious can be conceived of as a deep-subjectivity and that this term overlaps with my understanding of myth. I will view Jung's archetypal interpretation of the Christ and historiography in terms of Jung's own attempt to integrate history and deep-subjectivity, or, what I take to be another term for deep-subjectivity, myth. My position will be that the quest for the historical Jesus is most fruitfully understood, and undertaken, within the view of reality that understands history as myth, and particularly, Jung's myth of individuation and the development of consciousness.

As seen in chapters one and two, historical Jesus scholars tend to frame the problem of multiple Jesus-images in terms of epistemology, that is, that there are rational methods that can overcome this so-called problem. My guiding premise is that theories of knowledge (epistemology) are framed and controlled by *a priori*, that is, unconscious, conceptions of being (ontology). And, if our theory of being remains unconscious then our theory of knowledge, the criteria for what counts as valid and legitimate knowledge, also remains unconscious. If being is prior to knowledge, then we *are*, in our being, first of all, a hermeneutic perspective that is constituted by culture, history, imagination and emotion, all of which condition how we know, what we know, and the methods we use to gain and define knowledge.

Contemporary philosophy has undergone a shift, in its fundamental preoccupation, from epistemology to hermeneutics, or, from foundationalism to postfoundationalism. Foundationalism is the term for philosophy's epistemological preoccupation with establishing absolute and transcendent rational foundations for objective and certain knowledge. This has been the preoccupation of philosophy for the last two hundred years. Postfoundationalism is the contemporary understanding that such absolute foundations are not achievable, and that a historical and hermeneutic view of reality and knowledge, though almost completely ignored by professional philosophers, is, for the time being, more realistic.[1]

---

[1]Hiley (1981) 1-13.

I view Jung's psychology of the unconscious as participating in this fundamental shift of metaphysical paradigms, or worldviews. What I call Jung's *psychological-archetypal* method is congruent with the challenge to historical positivism undertaken by critical historiography, as seen in chapter three. I refer to Jung's method as *psychological-archetypal* in order to differentiate his general approach from Cartesian and Freudian psychology, and to keep this difference before us. Jung's method is not just psychological, that is, only personalistic and reductive, and neither is it just archetypal, that is, romantic and idealistic—it is both simultaneously. I believe Jung manages to integrate psychological and archetypal themes into a new unity that is best understood in terms of an existential, or hermeneutic, phenomenology—a philosophy of life. There is a significant difference between traditional Cartesian epistemology, its ontological splitting of subject and object and the consequent ontological status of subject and object, and a Heideggerian and Jungian orientation that hermeneutically connects subject and object at every level, conceives of world as prior to subject, and subordinates epistemology to hermeneutics, while at the same time preserving the valuable and necessary function of critical, rational thought, which is a major achievement of our Cartesian heritage.

Martin Heidegger is the contemporary philosopher who most dramatically challenges western philosophy's traditional understanding of epistemology. In *Being and Time* Heidegger critically analyzes the ontological assumptions guiding traditional Cartesian epistemology, and proposes an alternative ontology. My approach to Heidegger is guided by Charles Guignon's *Heidegger and the Problem of Knowledge*. With this work Guignon shifts the emphasis away from reading Heidegger as a mainstream existentialist "by raising to prominence the historicist and hermeneutic dimensions of *Being and Time*."[2] Guignon's work highlights Heidegger's profound ontological and hermeneutic critique of Cartesian metaphysics and epistemology.

I place Jung in this Heideggerian tradition that both criticizes Cartesian epistemology and offers a radically new ontology, and I will also draw on Roger Brooke's work *Jung and Phenomenology* for this new reading of Jung. Jung's view of the unconscious and his concept of projection function as a new interpretation of being that is consistent with Heidegger's hermeneutic phenomenology. My final purpose is to rework the ontological understanding of historical critical method and

---

[2]Guignon (1983) 4.

Jesus historiography from the point of view of Jung's psychological-archetypal method.

Historical criticism and Jung's psychology have the same historical roots in the Enlightenment, but each continues the Enlightenment project in very different directions. The Enlightenment project, which continues to this day, is to establish truth on foundations of rationality, over against non-rational foundations, such as uncritical metaphysical beliefs, dogma, tradition, commonsense, imagination, custom, emotion, subjective bias, etc. Rationality is to be the supreme, independent arbiter of truth and knowledge, and as such, rejects as invalid all forms of "knowledge" not based on clear rational and empirical thought,[3] a world-view also known as positivism. Critical historical Jesus scholarship continues to struggle with the unconscious and subtle presence of the legacy of positivism in its methods, hoping to establish something definitive about the historic Jesus. Jung's perspective explicitly and implicitly questions the assumptions that drive the need for absolute rational foundations in epistemology.

Jung takes the rational achievement of the Enlightenment in another direction. His psychological-archetypal method reinterprets both the role of rationality and traditional metaphysical concepts (here used interchangeably with theological concepts and mythological imagery) by, among other things, redistributing ontological value between them. That is, Jung gives both the rational and critical functions of the conscious mind and the mythological and imaginative functions of the unconscious equal value and weight. Jung embraces a "scientific" view of the world without embracing scientific reductionism, and he does not promote a return to traditional mythological, metaphysical or theological worldviews. Jung struggles to balance psychologically the ontological values of both a critical "scientific" attitude and the so-called merely subjective truth of religious and mythological reality.[4] Jung does this by adopting a phenomenological method that stays tied, like science, to empiricism. Jung's empiricism, however, is focused on the observation of human experience and all the cultural products of human experience, and in contrast to virtually all orthodox philosophical empiricism that limits itself to sensory experience, includes in significant measure unconscious experience,

---

[3]Hiley (1991) 2-3.
[4]Homans (1979) and Brooke (1991).

notably in dreams and reflective imagination. Of critical importance is that the phenomenological attitude in Jung's psychological-archetypal method is turned, of necessity, toward the subject, including both personal subjectivity and the deep ontological, archetypal structures of subjectivity, that have a special objectivity of their own.

The phenomenological interpretation of Jung rescues his concept of individuation from being simply a new form of individualistic piety, or a continuation of the isolated subject that derives from the Cartesian subject-object split. Jung's view of the structural unity of the ego and the unconscious amounts to an understanding of the individual and the world as a structural unity. This view means that the individual should not be conceived of as an apolitical, ahistorical, asocial, individualistic and discrete spiritual subjectivity. Jung's view of individuation is thoroughly historical and reveals a new view of history by way of revisioning the historical subject, the human person. This alters the traditional foundations of historical method because not only is the ontology, that is, our view of the reality, of the historical subject transformed, but the ontology (the reality) of the so-called historical object is also transformed.

Jung's Philosophical Psychology

Understanding the philosophical orientation of Jung's psychology is the key to grasping the significance of Jung for historical critical method, hermeneutics and historiography. Two important books that situate Jung philosophically, *Philosophical Issues in the Psychology of C. G. Jung* (Nagy, 1991) and *Jung and Phenomenology* (Brooke, 1991) take two different approaches. Nagy examines the historical antecedents of Jung's ideas in the traditions of Western philosophy since Plato and Aristotle. Brooke on the other hand places Jung in the new philosophy of existential phenomenology and Heidegger's fundamental critique of Western philosophy's traditional understanding of ontology and epistemology.

Nagy's book is valuable in looking to the tradition of the history of ideas with which Jung wrestled so intently, but her book fails to locate Jung in the present as a transitional thinker pointing to the future. Nagy positions Jung as a Kantian, or neo-Kantian, in the tradition of "metaphysical idealism."[5] As Clarke notes, Jung was deeply influenced by Kant, and was a self-identified Kantian: Jung claimed that "epistemologically I take my stand on Kant."[6] Nevertheless it does not do justice to Jung's thought to leave it at that. Such a reading fails to realize Jung's contribution to the reworking of the Western philosophical traditions which have been preoccupied with epistemology since Descartes.

Jung appreciated Kant's epistemological distinction between the *noumenon* (the fundamentally unknowable thing in itself) and the *phenomenon* (what is known in terms of what shows itself to the subject) in terms of his own understanding of the unconscious. Kant's idea of the *noumenon* overlaps with the epistemological limit that Jung called the unconscious. For Jung, the unconscious is not a place or mechanism inside us, as for Freud, but that limit, or horizon, beyond which our knowing cannot go. Jung was not explicitly concerned philosophically with the subject-object split that dominated Cartesian metaphysics and Kant's epistemology, although he wrestled with this problem implicitly and psychologically. Kant did represent an important advance over the rigid subject-object division of Cartesian epistemology by pointing out the interdependence of the mental and the physical, but he still left a fundamental split at the core of philosophy.[7] It was Heidegger who saw that "Kant took over Descartes' position quite dogmatically."[8] Kant accepted without question the epistemological problem of the subject-object relationship as the starting place for philosophy. According to Heidegger, "[Kant] failed to provide an ontology with Dasein as its theme or (to put this in Kantian language) to give a preliminary ontological analytic of the subjectivity of the subject."[9]

Heidegger explicitly challenges the unconscious ontological assumptions embedded within the Cartesian epistemological model, and develops an alternative view. Jung's psychology undertakes a similar critique and reinterpretation but most of the philosophical implications of his work remained implicit and unsystematic. By taking a

---

[5]Nagy (1991) 265.
[6]Jung (1973) 294. (cited in Clarke 28).
[7]Clarke (1992) 60.
[8]Heidegger (1962) 45.
[9]Heidegger (1962) 45.

look at the structure of the Cartesian epistemological model and Heidegger's critique of it, we will see that the Cartesian epistemological dilemma is not solved as such, but simply dissolved[10] because its starting premise, that subject and object are ontologically split, is replaced with another point of view. This view is that subject and object are an ontological unity, and that the subject can observe an object only because the subject is first of all constituted by the object. In the light of Heidegger's own phenomenological ontology it is possible to see that Jung is more properly a phenomenologist (and not a scientific psychologist). Jung did come to understand that he was a phenomenologist, but certainly not in terms of Heidegger, of whom, ironically, he was dismissive. This approach frees Jung from being read within conventional Cartesian and Freudian frameworks.

I now present the broad outline of those philosophical presuppositions of the Cartesian legacy we in the West all tend to share unconsciously. This should make explicit the philosophical underpinnings of the scientific worldview within which Jung worked and struggled to revise.

The Cartesian Model

The following presentation of the Cartesian model, upon which traditional epistemology is based, will illuminate the unconscious metaphysical assumptions of Cartesian epistemology that predetermine the nature of knowledge and being itself. The thrust of epistemology in general is to establish rational foundations as the final ground for understanding ourselves and reality. Rational foundations are constructed by the conscious mind. Therefore, the hoped-for final rational understanding of ourselves and reality is going to be a conscious and intellectual understanding. These rational foundations of understanding are supposed to be permanent and unchanging, transcending all times and places, establishing a lasting truth independent of all forms of subjectivity or bias, cultural, historical and personal.

The Cartesian Model[11] is intended to capture the general legacy of Descartes, and not the exact details of his thought. I believe it is this model that is behind Crossan's attempt to use method to overcome

---

[10]Guignon (1983) 84.
[11]Guignon (1983) 11-38.

scholarly subjectivity, so it is important to understand its assumptions about being, and the nature of reality.

The Cartesian view is characterized by a radical skepticism of our commonsense *knowledge* (as subjects) of the outer world of objects, and a radical ontological split between person and world. Descartes himself was not a radical idealist who doubted the existence of the world, and the Cartesian legacy itself is not directly concerned with this problem. Guignon describes the Cartesian legacy as "a conception of the world as consisting of minds and matter, a picture of truth as correct representation, and a belief that intelligibility is to be rooted in rationality."[12] The problem is not whether matter exists, but how can mind *know* matter because the two, mind and matter, are conceived as totally different substances. This leads to the ontological gulf between subject and object (as mind and matter). From this develops the belief that mind and rationality, as transcendent to world and matter, can observe the world and its objects rationally, that is, neutrally, and eventually achieve complete and final true knowledge of the world. These tenets make up our Cartesian common sense, and are so taken for granted that to question them seems absurd. We naturally tend to think that, of course, we are a separate subject with our own internal ideas, desires and aims, and that because we are separate from the world we can observe it from a value-free position and should be able to come to a final, objective and rational definition of the world. Given this premise, truth must be the correct correspondence between concept and object, and the ground of understanding, the intelligible, can only be rationality.

These world-view beliefs became firmly entrenched in the West and dictated the only "natural and obvious" problems for thought during the three hundred years since Descartes. This world-view not only predetermined the direction of philosophy, but permeated the culture at large and predetermined the ordinary experience of ourselves and the world. I believe these metaphysical presuppositions are what unconsciously predetermine the methodological concerns of historical Jesus research in the direction of trying to base the solutions to its problems on rational epistemology. I believe it is also the unconscious Cartesian and Enlightenment assumptions about the metaphysical superiority of rationality to determine the "facts" of history that lends

---

[12]Guignon (1983) 14.

Crossan's method in *The Historical Jesus* its tacit, but unwarranted, authority to convince the reader that he has the true "facts" about the historic Jesus (in spite of his anti-positivist caveats).

Descartes own writings appeared in an atmosphere conditioned by Martin Luther's ninety-five theses challenging the absolute authority of the church, and Montaigne's *Essays* that challenged the traditional and absolute standards of religion and morality. A shattering relativism shook the sixteenth century and Descartes' writings were an attempt to overcome the ravages of relativism. From Descartes' perspective, what was needed was a "method that will lead us to certain and indubitable truths. Descartes resolved 'to rid myself of the opinions which I had formerly accepted, and commence to build anew from the foundation.'"[13] There is a genuine fear in the face of pervasive relativism, uncertainty and the absence of absolute foundations. Certainty is one antidote for the fear of relativism. Descartes sought a foundation for knowledge that would transcend the relativism of prejudice, superstition, commonsense and tradition.

The Cartesian inquiry seeks rock-solid certainty, but it does so through rational doubt of our knowledge of the world in order to establish the thinking subject as the absolute ground of intelligibility. Descartes' methodical doubt serves to sever us from the commonsense and "vulgar" assumptions with which we understand and relate to the world. He sought to establish a new certain and unshakable foundation for knowledge and understanding based on "pure intellection."[14]

Guignon identifies three stages of the Cartesian inquiry[15] which are at the heart of all traditional epistemological arguments. Stage I is a simple description of our everyday beliefs, our ordinary knowledge of the world, and how we come to hold these beliefs. Descartes prepares himself for this stage of his analysis by becoming a disengaged "spectator" of life, and assures himself that "I have delivered my mind from every care and am happily agitated by no passions."[16] This "objective" and "unprejudiced" stance, deliberately adopted by Descartes, becomes the unquestioned and natural model of our "epistemic situation." This perspective views the subject acquiring knowledge about the world through the senses, and the senses, sight, hearing, etc., upon inspection, are notoriously untrustworthy.

---

[13] Guignon (1983) 22-23.
[14] Guignon (1983) 24.
[15] Guignon (1983) 23-29.
[16] Guignon (1983) 24.

This sets up Stage II which is to press a systematic doubt of the senses so far as to throw our commonsense knowledge of the outer world tentatively into question. The thinking subject thereby achieves a kind of citadel of internal rational ideas. But these are the sought for ground of knowledge of the world because they are certain and indubitable. However, now any connection to the world, formerly achieved through our assumptions and beliefs (i.e., our "myths," our collective belief systems of society, culture and religion) has been irreparably broken by rational doubt. How are we to reconnect with world?[17] This is the work of Stage III.

The Cartesian solution proposes to "rationally rebuild our former beliefs on a more secure foundation."[18] This foundation is to be the certainty available to the thinking subject through its rational ideas. Descartes made "the decisive move of identifying self-certainty as the self-grounding ground of all knowledge and understanding."[19] This move ensures that truth and understanding will be established through the rational construction of correct one-to-one correspondence between concept and object. Ambiguity is not to be tolerated and is a mere product of subjectivity. With logic as the model, truth is to be clear and univocal. But this "truth" is to be a product of the isolated rational mind, irretrievably cut off from matter by the Cartesian definition of being. The deep problem is that "it is not at all clear how the thinking subject can get out of the circle of its own ideas to gain knowledge of objects in the external world."[20] This Cartesian isolation of the subject dooms us finally to frustration and failure.

Traditional epistemological arguments approach these problems of knowledge through Stage II or Stage III, but *always accept Stage I as unproblematic.* Stage I is assumed to be simply the obvious and natural way things are, a separate subject observing separate objects. However, Stage I represents the very metaphysical assumptions that skew our entire picture of reality. This ontological split between subject and object is the central unquestioned assumption of Cartesian metaphysics: that we are encapsulated, rational subjects, who, detached

---

[17]Descartes himself solved this problem by coming to the conclusion that God was not a deceiver and that therefore he could trust his method for achieving knowledge of the world.

[18]Guignon (1983) 27.

[19]Guignon (1983) 24.

[20]Guignon (1983) 27.

and passive, look out on a world of objects, and assign concepts and meanings to the objects by private and internal cognitive acts. And by this process of rational thought achieve true knowledge of the world that transcends passions, subjectivity, traditions and myths. It cannot be stressed enough how deeply ingrained this view of reality is in all of us who inherit the Cartesian legacy. I believe it is this general state of affairs, here called the Cartesian legacy, that unconsciously imbues the terms "history" and "historical" with subtle, and sometimes not so subtle, forms of positivism. It is our unconscious Cartesian over-valuation of the rational establishment of material facts that lends to the term "history" its ontological status as the really real, and denigrates that other experience of reality we can refer to as myth, that imaginative, creative, interpretive and deeply felt world of meaning. In the following three sections I will show how Jung and Heidegger reverse the worldview of the Cartesian legacy and establish "myth" as that primordial way of knowing that must precede any rational epistemology. Although these sections are theoretical explorations of the structure of psyche, Dasein, projection and hermeneutics, the direction of this thought is to undermine the epistemology of historical positivism and to keep the question of the nature of history and historical knowledge before us.

The Structure of the Psyche

The reason for relating Jung to Heidegger is to explicitly empha-size the phenomenological, hermeneutic and ontological dimensions of Jung's psychological method and overall approach. In this section I will demonstrate the analogous structures shared by Heidegger's fundamental ontology and Jung's archetypal depth-psychology. This will show that Jung's psychology should not be read within the Cartesian or Freudian framework that traditionally views the psyche as an encapsulated personal subjectivity split off from an outer world. Rather, Jung's psychology should be read as a phenomenology of life that is existential, historical and hermeneutic. This will also show that terms traditionally associated with personal psychology, such as, psyche, unconscious, consciousness, emotion, imagination and projec-tion, have, in Jung's psychology, an ontological and archetypal world-related foundation, and are not to be construed as merely reductive and personalistic. This understanding paves the way for my interpretation, in the following two sections, of the ontological foundation of projection and its shared analogous structure with Heidegger's ontology of the hermeneutic circle. This will prepare us for the view of projection as a hermeneutic understanding that is revelatory of deep and "objective" aspects of world and meaning. "Objective" here simply means not created by only the personal subject, yet is not something absolute and value-neutral. Jung's understanding of the psyche suggests that the following three ideas—(1) projection as a form of deep-subjectivity, (2) the reflection at the bottom of the well, and (3) multiple images of Jesus—share an archetypal structure that cannot be avoided, and should be welcomed as containing positive value for deep historical and ontological self-understanding.

Heidegger and Jung each use a central concept with which to revision the subject-object relationship. For Heidegger it is *Dasein* and for Jung it is *psyche*. Both terms, *Dasein* directly and *psyche* indirectly, are related to Dilthey's concept of *life*.[21] While *Dasein* and *psyche* are terms deriving their definitions from the context of Heidegger's and Jung's overall work respectively, they are each at bottom reinterpretations of how we should think about and understand *life*. If psyche and Dasein are new synonyms for *life*, then these terms will also have a direct bearing on the term *history*, and especially on our understanding of historiography. As new interpretations of existence, psyche and Dasein also provide a new understanding of historiography by viewing history as a story existence tells about itself. Our understanding of psyche and Dasein, as the subject and object of history and history writing, radically changes our understanding of traditional Cartesian epistemology and delineates the limits and the ontological ground of historical knowledge. As an introduction to Heidegger's and Jung's concepts of Dasein and psyche, I will take a brief look at Dilthey's understanding of *life*.

Dilthey[22] rediscovered Hegel's concept of *life* as that totality of relations that make up the unified whole of the universe, in contrast to views that looked at life as a composite of discrete parts. For Dilthey the *meaning* of life can only be understood in terms of its totality, inclusive of past and future, memories and goals. Here we can recall that "past and future, memories and goals" are what constitute the

---

[21]Guignon (1983) 59-60.
[22]For the following I draw on Guignon (1983) 45-57.

structure of narrative in general, and historical narrative in particular. Although Dilthey does not make the connection explicitly, we can see that narrative and *life* share the same meaning-structure. *Meaning* and *life* are the total context of experience that we all share, and this shared context enables us to understand each other and the world. Dilthey also borrowed Hegel's phrase "objective mind" to refer to that collective medium within which we all live and understand each other; a shared matrix of meaning. He employed the imagery of the child within the matrix of the family to describe that preconscious historical-cultural reality we all share:

> The child grows up within the order and customs of the family which it shares with other members and its mother's orders are accepted in this context. Before it learns to talk it is already wholly immersed in that common medium. It learns to understand the gestures and facial expressions, movements and exclamations, words and sentences.... Thus the individual orientates himself in the world of objective mind.[23]

Life for Dilthey is a kind of "unconscious" foundation and context of experience. *Life* happens immediately and directly, un-mediated by thought or reflection. Dilthey states, "Behind life itself our thinking cannot go."[24] *Life* is the non-rational foundation upon which rationality is founded. Expressing a sentiment that echoes Jung's own concerns, Dilthey writes, "No real blood flows in the veins of the knowing subject constructed by Locke, Hume and Kant [and we might add Descartes], but rather only the diluted juice of reason, a mere process of thought."[25] *Life* represents the totality of the whole em-bodied, active and creative person, embedded in culture and history.

Heidegger describes the ontological structure of *life* with the term Dasein, which means literally, "there-being," or the "there-of-being." It is a common word in German meaning "existence." He deep-ens our sense of its ontological structure with the neologism *being-in-the-world* in order to emphasize the pre-subjective ontological unity of existence and world, over and against the Cartesian separation of subject and world. Jung also shifted from implying that *the psyche is in us* to saying explicitly that *we are in the psyche*. This perspective, from the Cartesian standpoint, is a dramatic dislocation of our traditional self-understanding. The traditional Cartesian dichotomy between sub-

---

[23]Dilthey (1988) 155.
[24]Palmer (1969) 99.
[25]Guignon (1983) 45.

ject and object, or world, ends up making the object dependent on the subject for its being. It is the subject, through its methods of knowing, that grants the object its ontological status, its degrees of reality. For example, what is known through rationality and logic is trustworthy and reliable, and therefore "real." What is known more subjectively via the passions, imagination or tradition is less trustworthy and therefore less "real." Heidegger reverses this situation by showing us that the subject is not first a separate observer of the world, but is in fact first constituted by a world before it can have cognitive knowledge of the world. Jung also suggests as much when he states that the conscious ego (the subject) is constituted by, and develops out of, the *a priori* collective unconscious (which, as we will see, phenomenologically overlaps with world).

Dasein and psyche show analogous structures when read phenomenologically. Dasein is both ontic and ontological and psyche is both conscious and unconscious. Dasein is both existentiell and existential and psyche is both personal and collective, or impersonal. The words "ontic" and "existentiell" are roughly equivalent in Heidegger, and refer to the specific and concrete facts and details of one's existence.[26] And in Jung, the ego, as the conscious and personal aspect of the personality, denotes the everyday empirical human being. For example, ontic and existentiell aspects of my existence include my age, gender, marital status, job, my children, as well as the specific concerns, dreams, goals, feelings, etc., with which I live my life. All the phenomenal particulars of life are ontic and existentiell. The ontological and existential refer to being itself and include those *a priori* conditions and structures that constitute and make possible ontic existence. They are the phenomenological structures of being that are considered universal and shared by all humans, and in this way overlap structurally with Jung's understanding of the collective unconscious as also universally shared but not available to direct observation.

Dasein and psyche are each simultaneously "farthest" from and "closest" to itself, unknown and known to itself, strange and familiar to itself. Both terms, psyche and Dasein, understand self and world as a unified and interconnecting web of relationships, purposes and meanings. Psyche and Dasein are the lived world of experience prior to the separation of subject and object and the appearance of the in-

---

[26]Heidegger (1962) 31-33.

dividual subject. Here we should recall Peter Munz's characterization of the universal structure of the human mind seen in chapter three. His view of the combination of particulars and universals as the basis of all thought shares structural similarities with Dasein and psyche.

Dasein is paradoxical: "Ontically, of course, Dasein is not only close to us—even that which is closest: we *are* it, each of us, we ourselves. In spite of this, or rather for just this reason, it is ontologically that which is farthest."[27] As a human being I am closest and most familiar with how to be a human being. At the same time I am farthest from and most unconscious of the archetypal (ontological) structures which make it possible for me to be a human being—to exist in that way that only a human can exist.

Dasein and psyche are not dualistic structures, but unified, dialectic structures. Existence and life are both ontological and ontic, unconscious and conscious. Dasein and psyche are not double structures of two "things" joined, nor of two "essences" mixed. Heidegger's analysis makes explicit the dynamic invisible background that makes what is visible and obvious possible. Ontically, what I do is what I am, but what I am ontologically precedes, not spatially or temporally, but preconsciously, what I do ontically. Yet, my ontical doing is the only avenue I have to discover and make explicit my ontology. This is the circular nature of Dasein, and points toward Heidegger's ontological understanding of the hermeneutic circle. In living, however, the ontic and ontological are not separate, they are one and the same existence.

For Heidegger "the roots of the existential [i.e., ontological] analytic...are ultimately *existentiell,* that is, *ontical.*"[28] The ontic *is* the showing-up of the ontological. It is the observable phenomena of Dasein that lead to the interpretation of the ontological structures of being Heidegger called *existentialia.*[29] Jung's self-identification as an empirical scientist can best be understood within the context of Heidegger's phenomenology. Jung's empiricism is "scientific" in the broad sense of phenomenology. He observes and describes phenomena from a critical perspective, and builds his hermeneutic and archetypal theory from observation. Jung rejects the ontological materialism of the traditional scientific world-view. The thrust of Jung's method is not traditional reductive explanation, but constructive and interpretive understanding. For this reason I do not think it is at all adequate or

---

[27]Heidegger (1962) 36.
[28]Heidegger (1962) 34.
[29]Heidegger (1962) 70.

accurate to classify either Jung or Heidegger as simply philosophical idealists. Each represents a new development in western thought that is attempting to integrate the traditionally polarized views of realism, or empiricism, and idealism, into a view of reality that is hermeneutic, historicist and phenomenological.

For Heidegger, Dasein as the *there*-of-being is a clearing whereby being is disclosed as existence. This means that Dasein is the clearing in which the world is noticed and apprehended with concern and intention. Dasein is a kind of illumination in which the world can appear. As Heidegger puts it, "To say that [Dasein] is 'illuminated' means that *as* Being-in-the-world it is cleared in itself, not through any other entity, but in such a way that it *is* itself the clearing." And, "*Dasein is its disclosedness.*"[30] It is best to think of this disclosedness as a kind of shared and cultural background intelligibility that makes the world noticeable and accessible.[31] Because Dasein is not an individual but a common structure of being human, the clearing or disclosure is not an individual subjective awareness. What is disclosed as Dasein is the ontical world, the specifics of our everyday living. What is not disclosed are the existential phenomena, those ontological structures that make disclosure possible. This is the project of Heidegger's fundamental ontology. He wants to lay out those fundamental existential structures that are invisible and yet, so intimate as our very ways of being.

Heidegger's word for clearing is *Lichtung*, which usually refers to a 'clearing' in the woods. *Lichtung* is a cognate of the German word for light, *Licht*, and with this we can make a connection with Jung's concept of consciousness which he always associated with light and illumination. In a way not unlike Dasein, psyche is for Jung the place where the unconscious shows up as consciousness. Consciousness is the structural aspect of psyche that illuminates the collective unconscious, that is, what is commonly lived unconsciously. Consciousness, as disclosedness, constitutes the *there*-of-psyche, just as Da-sein is the there-of-being. Consciousness too is not at first a self-aware individuality but a shared pre-reflective way of being in the world with others and things in an intelligible and concernful way.

---

[30]Heidegger (1962) 171.
[31]Guignon (1983) 70, 104.

Although Jung generally equates the *field* of consciousness with the ego, consciousness as a field contains much that is more often than not relatively unconscious in that all of it cannot be in the sharp focus of immediate personal awareness all the time. Also, because of routine, identification with collective expectations and roles, and lack of self-reflection the ego cannot always be self-conscious. Jung also thought of the ego as the *center* of consciousness and here it is the "I" as agent, the one who decides, chooses and acts. Consciousness that is both self-consciousness and consciousness of the unconscious, what I will later call deep-consciousness, is a special case that stands out from routine or everyday consciousness. In general, Heidegger's sense of the *clearing* and Jung's view of *consciousness* overlap as that mysterious aspect of being that enables both the world to "light up" and us to "see" it. Actual physical light offers an interesting analogy. In the same way that the *clearing* and *consciousness* can not be observed directly, but are what enable us to "see" the world, it is interesting that we cannot see light as distinct from the object being lit. Actual light is invisible, but in reflecting off of objects it enables us to see them.

Jung criticizes the traditional Cartesian view that "man is nothing but his consciousness," and here he does mean only the individual ego or the ontic individual. He states that individual consciousness is based on and surrounded by an indefinitely extended unconscious psyche."[32] Jung's view is that the human person's total identity is not merely their consciousness, and he even reverses the traditional perspective that consciousness belongs only to the ego by asking, "*Whose* consciousness?"! By this Jung suggests that it is the totality of psyche as the complex whole of ego and unconscious that becomes conscious in the field of consciousness. He goes on to say, "it is quite impossible to define the extent and the ultimate character of psychic existence. When we now speak of man we mean the indefinable whole of him, an ineffable totality, which can only be formulated symbolically."[33] Jung believes that the human person is not limited to the sum total of their mental contents, nor can the person be defined by rational explanations. By "symbol" Jung means "an indefinite expression with many meanings, pointing to something not easily defined and therefore not fully known."[34] A symbol is often an image

---

[32] Jung (1937) 140. References to the Collected Works (CW) cite the numbered paragraphs.
[33] Jung (1940) 140.
[34] Jung (1967) 180.

that can in part be consciously understood, but then finally points beyond itself to mystery. For Jung, one of the best symbols of the indefinite totality of the human person is the mandala. Jung also used the concept "self" to refer to this greater totality that constitutes the individual, and of which the ego is only a small part. I will explore this central archetype in the section on Jung's approach to the Christ.

Consciousness always has to do with something larger than the individual. In another context Jung suggests it is an unconscious "God" who becomes conscious through human consciousness.[35] Brooke states that, "the development of consciousness does not refer to a process outside of the world, but to a process in which the world itself comes into being in that human light called consciousness."[36] This does not mean that the world is created by consciousness, but rather that consciousness is that clearing, like Dasein, in which itself and the world are disclosed. Consciousness is a complex phenomenon that is conscious of itself, and conscious of that greater unconscious world from which it comes and upon which it depends.

The role of the ego as the agent of critical, rational thinking is crucial in the process of reflection and judgment that turns direct experience into knowledge and consciousness. But in most of his official writing Jung tends to emphasize the reality of the collective unconscious and the archetypes, in reaction to Cartesian and Enlightenment rational positivism, at the expense of the absolutely central and critical role of the ego in the overall system of his thought.

Jung's own method, along with the play of imagination, necessitates a critical stance toward the subject, both personal subjectivity as well as the deep ontological, archetypal structures of subjectivity. *It is the ego's recognition of the objective reality of the unconscious that establishes deep ontological subjectivity as a complex whole,*[37] as opposed to the conscious mental singularity of Cartesian subjectivity. It is actually the transformation of the ego's self-understanding that gives the objectivity of the unconscious its ontological status, i.e., reality. The relationship dynamic of this whole system, referred to as ego and unconscious, or ego and self, is dialectic. In my own appropriation of Jung's view of projection, the critical role

---

[35]This is one of the themes of *Answer To Job* (1952). For example see 740 and 746.
[36]Brooke (1991) 55.
[37]Kelly (1993) 80.

of the ego is vital to the positive role of projection in hermeneutic activity and historiography.

Consciousness is always consciousness of something, and so is always world related. Ontologically, "consciousness and world form a structural unity."[38] The identity that comes through consciousness is that of a world, as opposed to that of a Cartesian isolated subjectivity:

> As being-in-the-world, consciousness is the open clearing that gathers the world together. Its constitutive power is that such a world is gathered together in history, culture, and language, as well as through the peculiar twists of individual lives, and it is out of that gathered world-disclosure too that we come to understand ourselves as the persons we are.[39]

Heidegger states that the life of the individual is first of all the life of a world with the aphoristic statement, "Dasein *is* its world existingly."[40] Another way of putting this is that Heidegger perceives that "world" is a verb that "worlds," or is always "world-ing," and this "world-ing" is the "foundation" of our "be-ing."

As *being-in-the-world* Dasein and world form an ontological structural unity as a total web of interlocking and significant relationships of things, actions and others. Dasein's *world* is not made up of all the outer objects which are over and against Dasein; it is not the quantifiable world of geography. *World* is the web of significance and intentionality that constitutes Dasein.[41] The ontological structure of this intentionality is the *in-order-to*. The *in-order-to* is an embedded significance that is always *for-the-sake-of* Dasein. And *for-the-sake-of* is never an ego-centric *for-the-sake-of*; it is an unconscious intentionality related to a world of significance and meaning. Dasein's *world* is an unconscious world. As such it overlaps, phenomenologically, with Jung's concept of the collective unconscious. Heidegger states, "That wherein Dasein already understands itself in this way is always something with which it is primordially familiar. This familiarity with the world does not necessarily require that the relations which are constitutive for the world as world should be theoretically transparent."[42] The collective unconscious is that pre-reflective lived experience we all share. Before we become conscious individuals we

---

[38]Brooke (1991) 44.
[39]Brooke (1991) 43.
[40]Heidegger (1962) 416.
[41]Heidegger (1962) 92.
[42]Heidegger (1962) 119.

live life unconsciously, guided by common ontological, archetypal structures patterning living prior to any self-conscious thought.

When Heidegger raises the question of the meaning of being at the beginning of *Being and Time* his concern is that the philosophical tradition has forgotten the most fundamental reality of all, being itself. Even though being is the "most universal" concept, implicit in everything we approach and understand, it is still not a clear concept. "It is rather the darkest of all."[43] Being is of all concepts self-evident. We all understand "The sky *is* blue, and I *am* merry" without question. "The very fact that we already live in an understanding of Being and that the meaning of Being is still veiled in darkness proves that it is necessary in principle to raise this question again."[44] Being is indefinable and ambiguous. It is not a *thing* that can be clearly defined. These aspects of being, "most universal, yet "darkest of all," its indefinability, and its implicit understanding in our daily living, overlap with a phenomenological understanding of Jung's concept of the collective unconscious. Although Heidegger never uses the language of the unconscious and explicitly rejects the language of psychology in his analysis of Dasein, I do not believe it is a distortion of Heidegger's thought to roughly equate the terms ontological and unconscious if it is remembered that this is the shared *collective unconscious* and not the personal unconscious.

For Jung, the collective unconscious exists *a priori* to individual consciousness and personality. It determines who and what we *are* in general, our human being, before we become a self-conscious, individual subject. The collective unconscious is not a thing, or a place. Even the idea of it surrounding and permeating us, and that we are *in* it, is too thing-like. Like be-ing, the collective unconscious is a verb, a process, life itself. Clarke reminds us to avoid conceptualizing the collective unconscious as some kind of super or cosmic mind, which is another *thing*. The collective unconscious is our potential and disposition for typical human ways of being.[45]

The structures of the collective unconscious are the archetypes. They are comparable to Heidegger's *existentiale,* the primary, ontological structures, or modes of being, that make possible Dasein's abil-

---

[43] Heidegger (1962) 23.
[44] Heidegger (1962) 23.
[45] Clarke (1992) 117.

ity to be. The archetypes, as existential modes of being, are universal patterns of behavior and perception, such as mothering and fathering, for example. They are not simply echoes of Plato's ideal forms, or some other kind of abstracted metaphysical entity, although, as concepts, they do borrow from this idealistic tradition. "The archetype in itself is empty and purely formal, ...a possibility of representation which is given *a priori*."[46] The content of the archetype, its concrete particular expression, is determined first by history, culture and society, and secondarily by individuals. The archetype as a formal principle is for Jung a universal aspect of psyche (i.e., life) which guides typical ways of being human, but it is not an absolute, unchanging entity. "It persists throughout the ages and requires interpretation ever anew. The archetypes are the imperishable elements of the unconscious (of life), but they change their shape continually."[47] Jung insisted that the archetypes "are not inherited ideas but inherited possibilities."[48]

In Jung's early work there was a tendency not to distinguish between archetype and archetypal image. I believe this may have had something to do with the Cartesian subject-object problem in which the epistemological gulf between the subject and object had to be overcome. For example, if individuals are conceived of as isolated subjects then one is led to think in terms of an archetypal image of the Mother inside the child that has to get projected out onto the mother in order for the child to experience the mother, and likewise for the mother toward the child. On the other hand, realizing that psyche is a shared life, and archetypes are shared modes of being, it is more accurate to think that it is the child and the childlike that join with mothering to structure the relation of parenting. "Archetypes structure experience, they do not produce it."[49] Existence is the unified field in which archetypes structure relations, and images are the reflection of this world of experience. Brooke states,

> when archetypes are conceptually confused with images, or even thought to produce images, then experience and imagination are taken out of the world and located inside the subject, from which point meaningful relations become a function of 'projection'; they

---

[46]Jung (1968) 155.
[47]Jung (1968) 301.
[48]Clarke (1992) 123.
[49]Brooke (1991) 146.

lose sight of the human being's radical self-transcendence as a perpetually unfolding and self-transforming world.[50]

Phenomenologically images are not inside a Cartesian subject. Images reveal the lived-world of Dasein's immediate experience. The archetype is Dasein's way of *being-in-the-world*, not some thing located within a subject.[51] For example, the images of hero or victim reflect certain typical ways of experiencing oneself in relation with world. Because their archetypal aspect also means they are ways of personal being, they have an *inner* quality that is intimate and also private. But to say that much of the content of the psyche is images is not to say that images are inside a private, psychic capsule. Rather, life (i.e., psyche) uses images to reflect itself to itself. Mythological images then are images of the varied qualities of life and the varied ways of living. Their archetypal (i.e., existential) dimension means that all the subtle tones of emotion that mythological images arouse in us are what connect us via significance with our lived-world.

The archetypal field of being also structures our most mundane and ordinary experience. Archetypes are not only dramatic and big, such as the wise old man or wise old woman, the divine child, the king and queen, the lover, etc. Our typical relations with chairs, sidewalks, automobiles, computers, pencils, silverware, etc. are also archetypal. The archetype refers to those socially and culturally repetitive and shared ways of being we are all involved in with varying degrees of significance. For example, the archetype of the chair means we all implicitly know what a chair is and what its social and personal usefulness and significance is without thinking about it. The chair as archetype is a multidimensional cultural and unconscious "given" that determines in general how we will use and view chairs. What its archetypal character should emphasize however, is that its "givenness" is not absolute and eternal, but historically, culturally and socially embedded and therefore fluid and changeable.

Archetypes are fundamentally hermeneutic in that they *are* the "unconscious core of meaning" at the heart of all our relations. While the archetype is a meaning-structure, any specific interpretation is a human construction, and therefore finite and historical. The content of meaning is not eternal and absolute. "Every interpretation necessarily

---

[50]Brooke (1991) 147.
[51]Brooke (1991) 146-47.

remains an 'as-if.'"[52] The *as-if* of interpretation keeps every specific interpretation human, limited, temporary and open. Jung notes however, that traditionally, because of the archetype's "magnetic" force, its emotionally gripping power, any interpretation that gets close to the hidden core is usually proclaimed as the one and only absolute truth, and much blood is shed to maintain it. For Jung, the archetype would be what is at the heart of ideological dogmatism, or any passionately held –ism. And as we saw in chapter three, I would include the kind of "realism" that is associated with the being of narrative structure itself. The power of narrative to convince us of its "truth" is related to its archetypal dimension as a structure of our core being. Of course, as the archetype of the chair indicates, not every interpretation of an archetype is worth shedding blood over.

Jung's psychological hermeneutic taken phenomenologically re-veals the archetype as a metaphoric possibility of life. Such a psychological and hermeneutic understanding of the nature of archetypal structures can keep us connected to their meaning and aliveness, while also guard against the tendency to dogmatism. Of course, such talk as this can be glib if we forget the real power of the archetype to simply dominate situations against all good and reasonable intentions. Jung has referred to the situation in Nazi Germany to illustrate how com-pletely an archetypal wave can simply take over not just a good and reasonable individual, but whole societies or epochs.[53] This is why the conscious ego is so important in relation to the archetype. For Jung the archetype is a natural or divine force that is unconscious, and therefore amoral. It is consciousness, as the carrier of moral values, that takes a stand in relation to archetypal experiences, and does the work of integrating the archetypal values into ordinary existence. I will cover this topic in depth when I discuss the withdrawal of projections.

The archetype for Jung is also a historical concept. The arche-type gives psyche its living link with the past as a kind of existential thread of historical continuity running through the changing meanings given to specific mythological images. And it is each historical epoch's new interpretations that maintain the experiential contact with the archetype's meaning. For Jung it is religions that preserve the mythic (i.e., archetypal) images that maintain the vital link with the past, but it is the act of interpretation that keeps this heritage alive:

---

[52] Jung (1968) 265-66.
[53] Jung (1935) 371.

> The importance of hermeneutics should not be underestimated: it has a beneficial effect on the psyche by consciously linking the distant past, the ancestral heritage which is still alive in the unconscious, with the present, thus establishing the vitally important connection between a consciousness oriented to the present moment only and the historical psyche which extends over infinitely long periods of time.[54]

For Jung, the archetypes, as universal "psychic organs," that is, as basic existential structures of life, reach far back into the past, and serve as a kind of reservoir of accumulated human experience. The archetype also has purpose and an orientation to the future, in that it is a possibility of being and not a mere determinant from the past.[55] This sense of time that belongs to the archetype in general also makes it a kind of "historical organ" in that life itself has a basic "historical structure" that requires continual reinterpretation.

In summary, Jung's view of the structure of the psyche transforms the fundamental dualism inherent in the Cartesian metaphysical separation of subject and object (understood as individual and world) into an ontological unity. Jung's view of the psyche, as a unity of ego and unconscious, however, preserves the differentiation of subject and object that in itself is a major achievement of Cartesian ego consciousness. Within Jung's philosophical psychology, the Cartesian Model of epistemology that attempts to make rational knowledge the ground of being and truth is undermined by the realization that what counts as truth and knowledge is first determined by unconscious, emotion laden, archetypal images—what can also be called primary hermeneutic frameworks, or mythologies. To understand this further I will develop a phenomenology of how the unconscious and the archetype function in relation to the ego. For this I turn to Jung's concept of projection.

---

[54] Jung (1970) 474 fn 297.
[55] Jung (1968) 271-72.

The Structure of Projection

In this section my focus is on the ontological structure of projection in Jung's thought. In the next section I connect the structure of projection with the ontological structure of the hermeneutic circle in Heidegger's thought. Later in chapter six I will examine the process of withdrawing projections in relation to individuation and the differentiation of consciousness. My purpose in focusing on the deep structure of projection and the hermeneutic circle is to show that both projection and the hermeneutic circle are not methodological obstacles to be overcome, but rather that they describe a fundamental structure of being that makes consciousness and interpretation possible, and that these are the structures of being within which historiography operates.

Jung's understanding of projection is radically different from Freud's and the Freudian and Cartesian legacy that conditions our everyday understanding of the term. Psychoanalysis views projection as an ego defense mechanism whereby we falsely attribute personally unacceptable feelings or thoughts to another.[56] This view is useful in certain clinical situations, but it is not useful in conceptualizing the psyche because it views the psyche as a kind of internal "magic lantern"[57] or movie projector, literally projecting images from inside out onto the world.

Particularly with the concept of projection, Jung struggles with the Cartesian and Freudian framework. His own early, formal definition of projection states in part:

> Projection means the expulsion of a subjective content into an object; it is the opposite of introjection. Accordingly it is a process of dissimilation, by which a subjective content becomes alienated from the subject and is, so to speak, embodied in the object. The subject gets rid of painful, incompatible contents by projecting them, as also of positive values, which...are inaccessible to him.[58]

Much of Jung's discussion of projection has a Freudian ring, and therefore, has a psychologically reductive component. Especially in relation to religious experience or religious symbols, Jung's talk of projection can sound like personalistic psychologizing. Because of this, some Jungian psychologists are tempted to limit projection as a technical term to clinical manifestations, and drop it in relation to

---

[56]American Psychiatric Association (1994) 756.
[57]Bailey (1986) 72.
[58]Jung (1971) 783.

religious experiences. This thinking wants to limit the term *psyche* to the personally subjective in order to preserve the objective reality of transpersonal and religious experience. While this perspective seeks to limit the reductive tendency of psychologizing, its major flaw is in still separating ontologically, that is, substantially and spatially, the psyche and the transpersonal. Theologians are also drawn to make the same separation when engaging Jung's work.[59] However, Jung's contribution is precisely in establishing the fundamental ontological unity of personal psyche, objective psyche (the collective unconscious) and world, without psychological reduction.

Jung distinguishes between the personal unconscious and the collective unconscious. In general, the Freudian understanding of projection limits it to a function of the personal unconscious. I am attempting to understand projection in Jung's thought as a function of the collective unconscious, but there is always considerable influence back and forth between the personal and collective unconscious. The personal unconscious and the collective unconscious are not two separate compartments inside a psyche, or as Brooke noted, the collective unconscious is not just a "deeper basement."[60] They function as practical phenomenological terms to differentiate qualities of experience and being.

For Jung, projection is basically an involuntary happening. Jung says, "It is not the conscious subject but the unconscious which does the projecting. Hence one meets with projections, one does not make them."[61] Projections happen to us as the spontaneous and autonomous activity of the unconscious, that we need to remember is life itself, or our world. In another sense, we end up *in* projections, and the image of "falling in love" is a perfect description. Whatever we fall in love with, a person, an idea, a symbol, a text, a thing (car, house, money, etc.), it is something of the world that has become charged with our intense emotion and fantasy. This intense emotion can just as easily be hate or disgust. Whatever the emotion, the object has a strong quality of fascination. It is numinous and generally causes our behavior toward it to be compulsive—we must react to it, either positively or negatively.

---

[59]Brooke (1991) 76.
[60]Brooke (1991) 50.
[61]Jung (1951) 17.

When falling in love, the reality of the beloved as beloved, as god or goddess, is absolute and utterly self-evident. This is what I mean by the ontological reality of the archetype. It is a compelling experience that cannot be denied. Within such emotional experiences we know the world as alive and ourself as personally connected to this living world, in contrast to the Cartesian and materialist view that the world is dead and utterly other. Here I am referring to strongly emotional and, therefore, obvious projections as an example. However, I want to reiterate that most of the time the presence of the archetype is not a dramatic and emotional experience. We can speak of the archetype of the chair as just as ontologically real and compelling, but far more invisible than falling in love. And we can talk about our relationship to chair in terms of an unconscious projection in that we take its significance and usefulness for granted until a chair leg breaks.

The term *fantasy* is important in understanding Jung's view of projection and the unconscious in general. It belongs, along with emotion, to the dynamic and autonomous nature of the archetype. It is a natural form of life itself that manifests to consciousness as image. Jung defines fantasy as

> imaginative activity. Imagination is the reproductive or creative activity of the mind in general.... Fantasy as imaginative activity is...simply the direct expression of psychic life, of psychic energy which cannot appear in consciousness except in the form of images or contents....[62]

For Jung, fantasy, projection, dream and myth are direct expressions of the collective unconscious that always intermingle with the personal unconscious, as well as the consciousness, of the subject. It is proper to speak of fantasy and myth in this sense as objective manifestations of deep-subjectivity that is always world related. In traditional thinking fantasy and projection are private, intrapsychic phenomena. In Jung's view, fantasy, projection, myth and dream, are the ways we are unconsciously, and that means first of all, involved with our world. In this sense, fantasy is that primordial mode of being that relates us to the world in terms of images. Fantasy is not conscious. It is the "happening," the process, that we *are* in our world. Father, mother, daughter, son, student, teacher, rescuer, prisoner, poet, scientist, etc., are all archetypal images that are imbued with collective and personal meanings that give them their content as guiding stories,

---

[62]Jung (1971) 722.

or myths, of being human. More often than not we are not conscious of the fantasy or myth that guides our being. Again, such images are not first of all cognitive. They are primarily emotional, which means that our being this or that matters to us deeply and personally. The archetype is always image and emotion together. I can not be a father without caring about it, either embracing it or rejecting it.

Jung's concept of projection functions as a hermeneutic tool in relation to such emotionally gripping experience. To call such an experience a projection should not be to reduce it to some kind of unreal hallucination, nor a figment of one's own mind, and so dismiss it as a mere error of judgment or perception, although without a doubt, projections can get us in trouble with both judgment and perception. But to call an intense emotional experience a projection is to offer to the ego another perspective on the experience. It is an opportunity to struggle with the possibility that the qualities of the intensely charged, numinous object, are a call from an aspect of unconscious being wanting to become conscious in us.

Jung says that "Projections change the world into the replica of one's own unknown face."[63] The human face can be a symbol of both individuality and the particularity of consciousness. So, a projection makes an aspect of our world into intensely personal, and if I accept it as an aspect of my own unknown face, the experience challenges me to expand my sense of self, and to integrate something new, either positive or negative, into my own personality. A projection challenges the recipient, as a dream can, to a new level of responsibility toward oneself and the world. Accepting a projection as an aspect of "one's own unknown face" means it can be interpreted as a personal revelation of one's own potential for being that comes from an unknown source. The strong emotional component in projection, its numinosity and fascination, whether love or hate, signals the presence of an archetypal factor that has to do with our own being.

Jung comments on how difficult it is to get a critical perspective on numinous objects.[64] This is because a critical perspective usually involves some emotional distance, and in the presence of numinosity we are more often identified with the emotion associated with the object. The dimension of being that is involved in numinous experi-

---

[63] Jung (1951) 17.
[64] Jung (1952) 735.

ence is the collective unconscious where there is no separation, or differentiation, of subject and object—we are unconsciously identified with the emotion of the experience. The experience of fascination is most appropriately, and phenomenologically, put in terms of the fascination *having us*. In other words, the numinous thing seizes us, and we become the object of a larger subject. The intellect alone cannot disidentify from a projection:

> The recognition of something as a projection should never be understood as a purely intellectual process. Intellectual insight dissolves a projection only when it is ripe for dissolution. But when it is not, it is impossible to withdraw libido from it by an intellectual judgment or by an act of the will.[65]

The quality of unconscious identity that marks the psychological and archetypal structure of projection should help us understand part of the problem of deep-subjectivity for the ego. For example, to fall in love is to know without question that the other person is divine and ideal, and all their ordinariness and faults will just not be seen, or simply brushed aside or rationalized. Another example is to become unconsciously identified with an idea. If I know that a certain body of thought, say Jung's ideas, is *the absolute truth*, or that an idea like capitalism or socialism, theism or atheism, represents the absolute truth, then I am unconsciously identified with an archetypal aspect of being. No amount of rational argument, nor piles of "facts," will shake me loose from *the truth*. The problem is, that until something happens to challenge the identity at an emotional level, the identity is simply *the truth*. Until there is a critical crack in the conviction or certitude, the experience is not properly speaking, a projection. Jung puts it this way,

> Projection results from the archaic identity of subject and object, but is properly so called only when the need to dissolve the identity with the object has already arisen. This need arises when the identity becomes a disturbing factor, i.e., when the absence of the projected content is a hindrance to adaptation and its withdrawal into the subject has become desirable. ... The term projection therefore signifies a state of identity that has become noticeable, an object of criticism, whether it be the self-criticism of the subject or the objective criticism of another.[66]

An example of this state of affairs is the parent-child relationship. In general, the parent embodies such qualities of parent-

---

[65] Jung (1971) 421 fn 158.
[66] Jung (1971) 783.

ing and adulthood as nurturing, protecting, authority and independence. The child, on the other hand is, in general, protected, nurtured, obedient, taught and dependent. This is an unconscious identity that simply is, and has to be, the reality of this relationship, for both parent and child. But as the child grows into adulthood, the qualities the parent embodies should develop and emerge in the child as the child's own growing autonomy and adulthood. If the positive qualities of adulthood and parenting do not develop appropriately within the child, then it is correct to think of the child's own unconscious potential adulthood in terms of a projection onto the parent. The idea of withdrawing the projection is really a symbolic way of speaking, because the adult qualities of the parent are the model of the potential adulthood of the child that itself wants to be integrated and realized as the child's own unique adult personality. Obviously, if the child does not develop into an adult this is a serious hindrance to adapting to a larger world. At the point where the lack of adaptation is manifesting, usually in other relationships, but also in relation to oneself, it is time to speak of a projection. As such, a projection signals a break in what had been a seamless and unproblematic experience of reality, oneself, and one's relationships. The break, and arising problematic, then calls for a change in the personality through the integration of the particular contents of the projection. This is also spoken of as the differentiation of consciousness, which is an emergence from the original unconscious identity. Jung also speaks of this process of the development of consciousness as individuation.

As we will see later, Jung interprets the Christ in terms of a projection of the individual's own potential "christification," that is, the potential of the archetype of the self as the individual's own completeness and uniqueness.

A personal example of projection is my own relationship to the idea of history. My encounter with critical historiographical theory created something of a crisis for my uncritical assumptions about history. I had, without knowing it, Cartesian assumptions about the objective substantiality of historical—"what actually happened"—reportage, and a belief in the ability of historical critical method to establish facts with certainty. So, the *idea* of the historical Jesus provided a kind of unconscious security that I did not consciously know I relied upon. Now that I am convinced of the idea that history is a form of myth, and that the image of the historical Jesus is a form of myth, the qualities of security, substantiality and certainty that the idea of history was holding for me need to be integrated into my own personality. My unconscious identity with that particular idea of history is broken and no longer holds me. It is not unlike having the floor give way and suddenly finding myself suspended in air. I experienced, and can still feel, some vertigo and fear with this realization. The loss of a projection, the need to leave an unconscious state and become more conscious is, in varying degrees, a crisis for the ego, but it is a crisis of possibility, and not mere loss. And yet, the loss is real, and the "death" of fundamental aspects of one's supposed identity can be profoundly disturbing. On the other hand, it can also be profoundly liberating. I will discuss what it means to see the historical Jesus as a myth, and the withdrawal of that projection, in the next two chapters.

Jung relates the view of projection as "the archaic identity of subject and object" with Levy-Bruhl's *participation mystique,* a primary characteristic of primitive man's relationship with the environment. The idea here is that primitive people, and children, have a magical and mystical identification with their environment. Everything has power, is alive, has a kind of "consciousness," and is capable of independent action and communication. The word *primitive* also means *original*, and Jung's comments on the "primitive" psyche, regardless of their anthropological validity, reflect the archetypal situation we all inhabit. This state is not limited to so-called primitives or children. Our relationship with our most unconscious assumptions about reality have a magical and mystical quality of their own because they *are* our life, they are what is *real* for us, as was my original idea about history.

The existential structure of collective identity may be found in part in what Heidegger calls *Mitdasein*. This could count as an ontological description of projection as unconscious identity. Ontologically, Dasein is not differentiated from other Daseins as an individual subject. Dasein's "world is always the one that I share with Others. The world of Dasein is a *with-world [Mitwelt]*. Being-in is *Being-with* Others. Their Being-in-themselves within-the-world is *Dasein-with [Mitdasein]*." The Others of this *with-world* are "those from whom, for the most part, one does *not* distinguish oneself—those among whom one is too."[67] By "too" Heidegger means "the same." All

---

[67]Heidegger (1962) 155.

Dasein's have the same existential structure, and at this level there are no individual differences, no differentiation of consciousness.

This basic structure of *Dasein-with* is that unconscious identity which Jung claims for the being of the collective unconscious. According to the theory of projection, a self-conscious "I" is not possible until some disturbance breaks open the *with-world* of Dasein, and then comes the possibility of distinguishing oneself from the collective identity. Jung has noted that the ego and consciousness themselves are first projected unconsciously, that is, they are first experienced as potentials seemingly external to the subject, and are only gradually integrated into individuals. Jung points to the creation story in Genesis as an example of the projection of the emergence of consciousness. The emergence of consciousness, which is what a creation story symbolizes for Jung, is told as an objective event in which the active subject is Elohim and not the ego. In this same context, Jung also notes that "Illumination and inspiration, which in reality are sudden expansions of consciousness, still seem to have, even for us, a subject that is not the ego."[68]

The most extended statement of Jung's transformed view of projection is found in his essay *Archaic Man*. Jung finds himself confronted with a radically different view of the psyche and his understanding of projection by taking the primitive view of life seriously. For him the primitive mana theory (we could say "primitive ontology") undermines his own tendency to a Freudian view of projection (note especially the second paragraph):

> According to this theory [mana], beauty moves *us*, and it is not we who create beauty. A certain person *is* a devil, we have not projected our own evil on him and in this way made a devil out of him. There are people—mana personalities—who are impressive in their own right and in no way thanks to our imagination. The mana theory maintains that there is something like a widely distributed power in the external world that produces all those extraordinary effects. Everything that exists acts, otherwise it would not *be*. ... Being is a field of force.

> It is then not my imagination or my awe that makes the medicine-man a sorcerer; on the contrary, he *is* a sorcerer and projects his magical powers on me. Spirits are not hallucinations of my mind, but appear to me of their own volition. Although such statements are

---

[68]Jung (1970) 129 fn 67.

logical derivatives of the mana idea, we hesitate to accept them and begin to look around for a comfortable theory of psychic projection. The question is nothing less than this: Does the psychic in general—the soul or spirit or the unconscious—originate in *us*, or is the psyche, in the early stages of conscious evolution, actually outside us in the form of arbitrary powers with intentions of their own, and does it gradually take its place within us in the course of psychic development?

Were the split-off "souls"—or dissociated psychic contents, as we would call them—ever parts of the psyches of individuals, or were they from the beginning psychic entities existing in themselves according to the primitive view as ghosts, ancestral spirits, and the like? Were they only by degrees embodied in man in the course of development, so that they gradually constituted in him that world which we now call the psyche?

The idea of a complex building-up of the psyche is expressed on a primitive level in a variety of forms, for instance in the widespread belief in possession, the incarnation of ancestral spirits, the immigration of souls, and so forth. … When in the course of our own development we feel ourselves achieving a unified personality out of a multitude of contradictory tendencies, we experience something like a complex growing-together of the psyche.[69]

With this perspective Jung grants the otherness of the collective unconscious an objective otherness that is *sui generis*. He does not try to reduce it to a creation of personal subjectivity with a "comfortable theory of psychic projection." If we are *in* the psyche, then what is unconscious is experienced *as if* it is *outside* of us, but according to this "primitive" view, it has not originated inside us. As we are identified with our center of consciousness, the ego, we experience what is unconscious as objective and external to ourself. The spatial sense of a projection is metaphorical, and not a literal distance. The "distance" involved here is existential, a quality of being, and not a location in space. Again Jung says,

The word "projection" is not really appropriate, for nothing has been cast out of the psyche; rather, the psyche has attained its present complexity by a series of acts of introjection.[70]

Jung is speaking here of a historical and cultural development, but this is also true of psychological development. We know the ego

---

[69]Jung (1931) 139-41.
[70]Jung (1968) 54.

develops over time and is not a full-blown given at birth. Young children's literature is almost exclusively devoted to talking animals, those indirect personifications, i.e., projections, of the unconscious and dispersed personality that want to gradually coalesce into a consistent ego consciousness and identity. In these cases it is clear we are not dealing with something that has been repressed and rejected, but with unconscious aspects of personhood that have not yet been gathered as an integrated personality, which is a form of achieved consciousness.

Jung experienced the ontological reversal of the ordinary understanding of projection through two dreams he reports in *Memories, Dreams and Reflections*. In one dream, a UFO, flying over his house, came directly at him. It looked like "...a lens with a metallic extension which led to a box—a magic lantern. At a distance of sixty or seventy yards it stood still in the air, pointing straight at me. I awoke with a feeling of astonishment. Still half in the dream, the thought passed through my head: 'We always think that the UFOs are projections of ours. Now it turns out that we are their projections. I am projected by the magic lantern as C. G. Jung. But who manipulates the apparatus?'"

In the other dream Jung is hiking through a hilly area and comes upon a small chapel. Inside he is surprised to find no Christian symbols, but rather a beautiful flower arrangement and a Yogi sitting before the altar in deep meditation. "When I looked at him more closely, I realized that he had my face. I started in profound fright, and awoke with the thought: 'Aha, so he is the one who is meditating me. He has a dream, and I am it.'" Jung recalls these two dreams within the context of a discussion about the relationship between eternal man (the self) and earthly man (the ego). Jung sees the Yogi as his "unconscious prenatal wholeness," and says, "Like the magic lantern, the yogi's meditation 'projects' my empirical reality." The self of "C. G. Jung" projects the ego of C. G. Jung, and not vice versa. Jung goes on,

> The aim of both these dreams is to effect a reversal of the relationship between ego-consciousness and the unconscious, and to represent the unconscious as the generator of the empirical personality. This reversal suggests that in the opinion of the "other side," our unconscious existence is the real one and our conscious world a kind of illusion, an apparent reality constructed for a specific purpose....[71]

---

[71] Jung (1962) 323-24.

This echoes Heidegger's ontological reversal of the Cartesian legacy's complete separation of ego and world, and the ascendancy of rational thought as the arbiter of reality. Heidegger reverses this picture by showing the secondary and derivative nature of the personal subject (ego), and the utter, fundamental priority of being in general. In psychology, the use of the negative *un-* to refer to the un-conscious, in opposition to the conscious, betrays our Cartesian bias for the priority of consciousness, and influences us to view the unconscious as a derivative of the conscious. In Jung's view the opposite is true. The unconscious is not a negation of the conscious, although it is our cultural common sense tendency to view it this way. Rather, what we call consciousness is a kind of negation of what we call the un-conscious. Unconscious is primary, and consciousness is derived from what has been unconscious. But as derived, it is also achieved. The phenomenon of consciousness, in Jung's view, is an achievement requiring great effort on the part of humankind and the individual. In fact, in Jung's cosmology, it is consciousness that gives the human person ultimate value and meaning. For Jung, the individual is the only possible carrier of consciousness, and consciousness is the fundamental desire of the cosmos.

The concept of projection in Freud's hands was used incorrectly to reductively explain cultural phenomena such as animism and religion. This approach merely perpetuates the tendency of rational thought to control and dominate all of reality. For Jung the idea of projection is more complex, and in fact, respects the otherness of the unconscious and of numinous experience in any form. Projection, understood as the manifestation of a need for consciousness, is more of a hermeneutic perspective than an explanatory one. And while the ego has a crucial and prominent role, it has more to do with moral responsibility toward the self and emerging consciousness, than control and dominance. Jung's view of projection points to an *a priori*, unconscious understanding of reality that seeks consciousness. This idea, that unconscious understanding seeks to become conscious understanding, brings us to the hermeneutic circle in general and Heidegger's ontological analysis of it, as the fundamental constituting structure of Dasein, in particular.

The Hermeneutic Circle

In order to set the stage for Heidegger's ontological view of the hermeneutic circle I will begin with introductory comments about hermeneutics in general and the idea of the hermeneutic circle in the philosophy of Schleiermacher and Dilthey, two important fore-runners of Heidegger.

Historically and conventionally, hermeneutics has been understood in terms of those methods and rules utilized by an interpreter in the process of interpretation. In this sense hermeneutics refers to the intellectual tools brought to a text by an interpreter. To anticipate, Heidegger's ontological analysis of Dasein (i.e., existence) shows that there is a pre-cognitive hermeneutic understanding that is a constitutive structure of human being in general. In this sense, "hermeneutics" does not refer to tools used by an interpreter, but to that fundamental aspect of the interpreter's being which makes it possible to interpret at all. Within Heidegger's perspective, our first interest is not how to interpret, but rather, what is the basic condition that makes interpretation possible.

The word *hermeneutics* first appeared in English in the seventeenth and eighteenth centuries in reference to biblical interpretation. A distinction was also made between exegesis (the actual commentary on biblical texts) and hermeneutics (the rules, methods and theory guiding the commentary). After the Reformation, hermeneutic manuals were in great supply. They were especially important in Protestant circles because the clergy could not depend on the authority of the Church to decide questions of interpretation.[72] In this context the word *hermeneutics* was specifically limited to biblical exegesis. When the term *hermeneutics* was applied to the interpretation of other texts, these were invariably difficult and obscure, and so *hermeneutics* tended to mean a specialized interpretation needed to get at "hidden" meaning.[73] While the use of the English word *hermeneutics* is relatively recent, interpretation and theory of interpretation have been in practice since antiquity. Today the word is widely used with regard to theory of interpretation, whatever the field, law, philology, aesthetics, literature, theology, etc.

---

[72]Palmer (1969) 34.
[73]Palmer (1969) 35.

Our word *hermeneutics* derives from the Greek verb *hermeneuein* and the noun *hermeneia.* They mean simply "to interpret" and "interpretation." "The Greek word *hermeios* referred to the priest at the Delphic oracle."[74] The Greek understanding of interpretation meant making what was unintelligible intelligible. The pronouncements of the Delphic oracle were not understandable and required an interpreter. The Greek god Hermes is generally understood, and accepted informally, as the source of the Greek words which seem so obviously related to him. Whether or not this is an accurate etymology seems to be undecided. Hermes is the messenger-god and the messenger of the gods. Hermes crosses boundaries, and travels between the worlds of gods and humans, Olympus, earth and Hades. He is also credited with the discovery of language and writing, a culture god, and with this he makes understanding possible for humans. If not etymologically, he is phenomenologically, definitely related to *hermeneia.*

Heidegger also makes this connection when he says the Greek word *hermeneus* "is referable to the name of the god Hermes by a playful thinking that is more compelling than the rigor of science. Hermes is the divine messenger. He brings the message of destiny; *hermeneuein* is that exposition which brings tidings because it can listen to a message."[75] This "message" is from the gods, and the Hermes' function brings it near, makes it familiar and understandable. The process of interpretation makes something unknown known, something incomprehensible comprehensible, something foreign familiar. For the Greeks this process was associated with a god. From Jung's archetypal perspective on mythology this means that interpretation has an irreducible archetypal basis.

In its conventional meaning hermeneutics refers to the *tools or methods* used by the interpreter. The guiding assumption for *explanation* is that the correct tools and the correct usage of the tools will yield the *one correct, true meaning* of the text. The first appreciation of the *hermeneutic circle* was as one of these methodological criteria of correct interpretation. Martin Luther's approach to scripture implicitly employed the hermeneutic circle. Against the Catholic view of the infallibility of Church tradition as the final decider of biblical meaning, Luther stated Scripture can be understood from itself alone. The meaning of any one text can be understood, along with a knowledge of ancient languages and the inspiration of faith, *in the light*

---

[74]Palmer (1969) 13.
[75]Heidegger (1971) 29.

of the Scripture as a whole. For Luther, the whole of Scripture has a self-contained harmony, and this harmony between the part and the whole is self-sufficient in a final determination of understanding and meaning.[76] This relationship of mutually conditioned understanding between a part and its whole context is the basic structure of the hermeneutic circle.

The concept of the *hermeneutic circle* tries to express the paradox on which human understanding is based. In order to understand something it must be in a larger context that gives it meaning. But the larger context gets much of its structure and meaning from the parts that make it up. We usually grasp the meaning of a sentence without attending to the individual words one at a time. But the overall meaning is created, in part, by the mutual relationship between the sentence as a whole and the individual words as parts. If a sentence does not make sense we may back up and examine individual words. Or, we can go on to get the larger context of the sentence, the paragraph, or chapter, etc. We need to continually do both, focus on the part or enlarge the whole, as we move around the circle. Each larger context can modify our understanding of the parts, and a part can modify our understanding of the whole. The shape of a circle is itself significant. It does not matter where one enters the circle, but that one understands the movement around the circle. In moving around the circle one comes to a point opposite to where one entered, as well as encountering many other different angles of perspective on the entry point. Eventually one returns to the beginning point with a larger and deeper perspective on the original beginning. This circular process continues *ad infinitum.*

The problem for philosophy is, how do we understand something before we understand it. The hermeneutic circle suggests we do have a certain *a priori* understanding which is implicit before we have understanding which is explicit. Palmer, in his discussion of Schleiermacher and the hermeneutic circle says, "To operate at all, the hermeneutical circle assumes an element of intuition."[77] The intuition has an implicit grasp of the nature of the whole which enables us to approach and begin to understand the individual parts. As our knowledge of the individual parts grows, so then does our grasp of the

---

[76]Connolly (1988) 7.
[77]Palmer (1969) 87.

whole change and grow. The understanding with which we grasp the whole is always partial and indistinct, and our initial understanding of individual parts is also partial. This partialness fills itself out and grows more and more complete as the dialogue between whole and part becomes more and more explicit and distinct in our understanding. The *hermeneutic unending spiral* might be a more apt image as hermeneutic understanding is an ongoing process of the unfolding of clarity out of unclarity that occurs over time through unfolding levels or stages. But as an image, the circle has an enduring and universal quality that the spiral lacks. It is helpful to think of the process of learning a foreign language or a musical instrument. Throughout these learning experiences we continually find that the fragmented knowledge we so painstakingly build suddenly clicks into an intelligible and wonderful whole. From a psychological point of view this dynamic circular hermeneutic structure is analogous to the developmental, unfolding relationship between the unconscious and conscious components of the personality.

Friedrich Schleiermacher (1768–1834) is considered the father of modern hermeneutics, with its focus on the art of understanding in general.[78] Aware of the various special "hermeneutics" of his time, each field requiring its own mode of interpretation, he went to work to develop a general theory of understanding.

There are two main, interlocking, aspects to Schleiermacher's hermeneutic theory, the grammatical and the psychological. The grammatical is knowledge of language and its rules, and the psychological is knowledge of the author's thought processes. What is to be interpreted, a text, exists in the context of the totality of the language and the totality of the author's thoughts, and understanding must include these two areas and how they influence each other.[79] Schleiermacher insisted these two areas, the grammatical and the psychological interpretations, were equal. One was not to be more important than the other. The act of understanding is dependent on their mutual interdependence. "Complete knowledge always involves an apparent circle, that each part can be understood only out of the whole to which it belongs, and vice versa."[80]

The *hermeneutic circle* is, for Schleiermacher, the way understanding is structured, and how it progresses. The language and history

---

[78]Palmer (1969) 97.
[79]Schleiermacher (1988) 74.
[80]Schleiermacher (1988) 84.

of an author's age form the whole of which their writings form a part. The more we know about the author and the author's historical setting the more complete our interpretation will be. Schleiermacher makes it clear understanding increases the more times we read a text, and with the more we know of the historical period and language of the text. The aim, in Schleiermacher's well known words, is "To understand the text at first as well as and then even better than its author." He knows this hermeneutical task is "infinite," both with regard to the grammatical and the psychological interpretations. Because the task is "infinite," in that it requires us to see more and more of the whole context in the part statement we are interpreting, the hermeneutic process, in Schleiermacher's view, is as much an "art" requiring "inspiration" as it is objective science.[81]

For Schleiermacher the hermeneutic circle is a way to conceptualize the process of intellectual understanding in its task of collecting more and more objects of knowledge in building the interpretive reconstruction of meaning of a given statement. It is not an ontological structure of being as it will become for Heidegger. Schleiermacher's use of psychology is similarly limited, through no fault of his own. He is simply using the concepts and meanings of his historical time.

The psychological, in Schleiermacher's theory, refers to the *inner mental* process of the author who wrote the text being interpreted. The point is to understand and grasp the individuality and style, the unique genius, of the author. It is not a psychoanalysis of unconscious motivations, but a positive attempt to enter into the inner thought process of the author, and understand this in the context of the author's whole life and time. Palmer notes how Schleiermacher tended to separate the inner mental thought process from the outer linguistic expression, and to idealize the inner mental process in relation to the outer, limited, written expression.[82] Schleiermacher's hermeneutics, in his later thought, aimed to get behind the mere words, to the true thought processes of the author. In earlier thinking he emphasized the fully contingent nature of thought and being on language. This earlier view was closer to the historical view of understanding which emerges later in Heidegger and especially in Gadamer.

---

[81]Schleiermacher (1988) 83.
[82]Palmer (1969) 93.

Schleiermacher does not make self-understanding an explicit component of his hermeneutics. His concern is with correct and "precise" understanding of the object out there, the text and its author. But, divining the individuality of the author, through Schleiermacher's "divinatory method" (an intuitive process), is based on the presupposition "that each person contains a minimum of everyone else, and so divination is aroused by comparison with oneself."[83] Again, this statement, while it is not intended as a "fundamental ontology" or a theory of a "collective unconscious," points out that, for the "divinatory method" to work, every individual must contain some common ground of shared humanness.

Schleiermacher developed his hermeneutic theory within the historical context of Cartesian metaphysics and its complete ontological separation of subject and object. Within this world-view subjects and objects do not share a common ground of being and are fully separate. Subjects are also quite separate from other subjects. This deep separateness at the heart of human self-understanding has plagued philosophers trying to grasp how it is possible to have knowledge of something from which we are supposedly so completely separated. Schleiermacher's "divinatory method" can be seen as an attempt to overcome this profoundly felt separateness.

Wilhelm Dilthey (1833–1911) is the other major figure in hermeneutics before Heidegger, and in the words of Palmer, may be "regarded as the father of the contemporary hermeneutical 'problematic.'"[84] This "problematic" is the view that all understanding and self-understanding is conditioned and determined by history, in so far as history is specific time and specific place, and is characterized by process, motion and change. This *historical* view of human understanding challenges traditional metaphysical views that absolute, eternal and unchanging truths are at the heart of being.

The radical historicality of understanding and self-understanding, introduced by Dilthey, means that from within a historical view of understanding we can never get outside of our own particular historical vantage point in order to achieve an atemporal, absolute, objective point of view. We *are* our history. The focus here is on the *historical nature* of being and meaning, and the hermeneutical nature of history. This historicality of human expressions, and our under-

---

[83]Schleiermacher (1988) 96.
[84]Palmer (1969) 123.

standing of them, is not some thing that simply attaches to human being—it constitutes human being.

Dilthey is known for making hermeneutics the foundation of the *Geisteswissenschaften*, the science of human expressions, i.e., the humanities and social sciences. He wanted to distinguish the methods appropriate to the human sciences from those of the natural sciences. The reductionistic and mechanistic conceptions of the natural sciences were encroaching on the human sciences. Dilthey knew the materialistic orientation of the natural sciences could not do justice to the historical nature of the human sciences. The key concepts in Dilthey's hermeneutic approach are *meaning* and *understanding*, as opposed to a concept like *power*, and its role in the cause and effect explanations of natural science. Understanding and meaning grasp lived experience by interpreting "expressions of life," all those cultural objects, such as, art, language, law, etc., which Dilthey called the "objectifications of the spirit of man."[85]

Dilthey sought to establish "objectively valid knowledge" in the human studies, which shows his own tendency to incorporate scientific conceptions of knowledge, even though this is what he was trying to escape.[86] True to his own theory, Dilthey did not escape his own historicality. However, he did set the stage for modern hermeneutic phenomenology and its deep problematics for understanding.

With Dilthey, the hermeneutic circle takes on a significant historical dimension. Now the hermeneutic circle refers to how meaning and understanding change and develop through time and through repeated interpretations. It is the understanding which grasps the meaning of the mutual and reciprocal relationships between the parts and the whole of whatever is being understood, whether it is a text or a life. Palmer, talking of Dilthey and the hermeneutic circle states, "Meaning is historical: it has changed with time; it is a matter of relationship, always related to a perspective from which events are seen."[87]

Dilthey refers to what is commonly understood by everyone, that which is the common context for understanding in general, as "objective mind." It is the medium within which self-understanding and understanding of others takes place. "Objective mind" is the sum total

---

[85]Palmer (1969) 103, 112.
[86]Palmer (1969) 106.
[87]Palmer (1969) 119.

of all those unconscious, taken for granted, assumptions we all live within. Both Heidegger and Jung deepen our understanding of "objective mind" with their views, respectively, of the existential structures of being and the archetypes of the collective unconscious.

The understanding of the meaning of an individual life always takes place within the hermeneutic circle. The first *whole* of self-understanding and identity is an *a priori*, unconscious given that is far greater than the individual person. It begins to take shape unconsciously during childhood within the family and the larger culture. Throughout life, events can influence and change our self-understanding and bring new understanding of the meaning of the whole of our life. Our life experiences, which are the parts of our life, are also brought into the meaning of the whole. Context influences interpretation, and interpretation influences context.

Dilthey states, "Behind life itself our thinking cannot go."[88] *Life* for Dilthey is the foundation and context of experience which hermeneutics grasps indirectly by interpreting its cultural objectifications. Life happens immediately and directly, and is unmediated by thought or reflection. Meaning is the result of our relationships with the cultural objects which are 'expressions of life.' Meaning is created within the hermeneutic circle, which is the interaction between the individual and their cultural context, what Dilthey called the objectified *Geist*, or "spirit." The individual and the objectified spirit act on each other as the *hermeneutic circle* generating historically understood meaning. Understanding occurs only within a context that is already understood. And meaning is created only within a context that is already meaningful. There is no neutral, objective starting point for interpretation. All interpretation begins within an already existing, and more or less influential, interpretive point of view.[89]

As we have seen, Dilthey's understanding of *Life* overlaps with Heidegger's understanding of Dasein and Jung's understanding of psyche. *Life*, as a kind of unconscious web of experience, is the common medium of all beings. If there is a beginning to the hermeneutic circle this is it. An unconscious world of experiences prior to any distinctions or reflections made by self-conscious thought. Dilthey is the one who opens up the hermeneutic problematic of our needing to become aware of just how thoroughly and deeply our interpretations and meanings are contextual and historical. For Schleier-

---

[88]Palmer (1969) 99.
[89]Palmer (1969) 120-21.

macher the hermeneutic circle is more of a methodological tool in working with a text, although its broader implications are implicit in his thinking. With Dilthey the hermeneutic circle becomes a deeper problem, for not only understanding is involved, but self-understanding is thoroughly implicated. The act of understanding cannot be achieved through a psychological intuition into an author or an object. The problem now becomes finding the "viable modes of interaction" between oneself and the cultural objects we interpret.[90] I suggest that Jung's conception of projection, understood ontologically in relation to the hermeneutic circle, can function as one of these "modes of interaction." A deeper understanding of the hermeneutic circle as constitutive of existence (Dasein) occurs with Heidegger.

Heidegger notes that Dasein is in itself a circular way of being when he states,

> The 'circle' in understanding belongs to the structure of meaning, and the latter phenomenon is rooted in the existential constitution of Dasein—that is, in the understanding which interprets. An entity for which, as Being-in-the-world, its Being is itself an issue, has, ontologically, a circular structure.[91]

Heidegger, in pointing out a circular relationship between *understanding* and *interpretation*, is not referring to the methodological process outlined by Schleiermacher above. Heidegger is describing one of the existential structures of Dasein that constitutes Dasein as the clearing in which the world can show up as such. He notes the paradox of the circle of interpretation when he says, "Any interpretation which is to contribute understanding, must already have understood what is to be interpreted."[92] But he then goes on to say that,

> What is decisive is not to get out of the circle but to come into it in the right way. This circle of understanding is not an orbit in which any random kind of knowledge may move; it is the expression of the existential *fore-structure* of Dasein itself. It is not to be reduced to the level of a vicious circle, or even of a circle which is merely tolerated. In the circle is hidden a positive possibility of the most primordial kind of knowing.[93]

---

[90]Palmer (1969) 121.
[91]Heidegger (1962) 195.
[92]Heidegger (1962) 194.
[93]Heidegger (1962) 195.

Understanding for Heidegger, is an ontological existentiale, and as such, it is that shared unconscious ability to be a human being. A double reminder here, that one, Heidegger did not use the language of psychology, and two, that at this level of his ontological analysis of Dasein, by unconscious I mean Jung's "collective unconscious." *Understanding* at this level is not the conscious, cognitive under-standing of a concept, thing or situation—this *understanding* is not a matter of thought which would be an ontic process. Thought processes, like explanations and assertions, are derivatives of ontological under-standing. This original and innate *understanding* is *Being as existing.* It refers to that sense of understanding as competence and being able to manage something that comes from long years of practice and experience, as in "I understand how to drive a car." But ontological *understanding* is not to be identified first with any particular ontic doing. In the same way that an oak tree *understands* how to be an oak tree, or a fish a fish, so Dasein *understands* how to exist—it is not at first a matter of learning something. Existential *understanding* is Dasein's *potentiality-for-Being.*[94] *Understanding* simply means we know how to be a human being without thinking about it. We *understand* unconsciously how to be, and this relationship with the world is not based on discursive and rational thought, but is first of all emotional and imaginative.

In Heidegger's view, *understanding* is dynamic and presses itself forward into possibilities. It is our *possibility* to be human, and as such characterizes an aspect of our freedom. This is because "...the understanding has in itself the existential structure which we call *projection.*"[95] The German word for projection here is *Entwurf.* Although it bears no direct connection with psychological projection, later I will suggest a relationship between the structure of possibility and Jung's view of psychological projection. Heidegger's *projection* retains a strong sense of its root meaning as 'throwing.' "Projection, in throwing, throws before itself the possibility as possibility, and lets it *be* as such."[96] An essential aspect of Dasein's being is to always project itself as possibilities.

Dasein, as projected possibility, is also always tied to specific contexts. We do not choose our gender, our social class, our family, our culture. We are *thrown* into these contexts. Dasein's *da*, its *there,*

[94]Heidegger (1962) 183.
[95]Heidegger (1962) 185.
[96]Heidegger (1962) 185.

is its *thrownness*. This is "…meant to suggest the facticity of its being delivered over."[97] The specific, limited givens are the *there* of our possibilities for being. Dasein, as *thrown projection*, is ontologically constituted as this paradox of being both determined and free. Dasein's factual, limited existence is the only place wherein possibility is possible. Dasein, as projected possibility, is always 'more' than it is at any time. In its potentiality-for-Being, Dasein always is *not yet.*[98]

The circle in understanding is not a vicious, one-dimensional circle, as it is in logic, because it is not limited to the ontic or ego dimension. The hermeneutic circle gives expression to the phenomenological unity that ontic-ontological, and ego-unconscious, are as that pre-conscious totality called Dasein or psyche. The hermeneutic circle in this sense can also refer to the always indefinite wholeness of existence. This totality that we are is also a world of involvements and significance. Heidegger sees that ontological *understanding* is constituted by this totality of tacit involvements and assumptions in which we are always already immersed before we interpret. This preconscious background in which all everyday interpretation is based Heidegger refers to as the *fore-structure* of *understanding*.

The *fore-structure* of understanding encompasses all the tacit presuppositions and prejudices which influence and ground interpretation. Before we make interpretations we always already have a totality of involvements called Being-in-the-world, ("fore-having"); we already have a point of view, ("fore-sight"); we already have concepts which decide how things will be conceived, ("fore-conception").[99] These unconscious fore-structures are emotional. We have a stake in them and they matter to us personally. They represent strong desires, needs and commitments we are usually not even aware of until they are challenged or obstructed. It is Jung who helps us understand that these unconscious fore-structures are involved in what gets projected (and here I mean the psychological projection that is our experience of the collective unconscious) in interpretive activity such as historiography. And it is the interpretive activity that can bring the unconscious understanding to consciousness. Two cultural examples of the *fore-structure* of *understanding* that I am dealing with in this work would

---

[97]Heidegger (1962) 174.
[98]Heidegger (1962) 186.
[99]Heidegger (1962) 191.

be on the one hand Cartesian metaphysics and its epistemology, and on the other the traditional Christian myth of Christ. The totality of presuppositions which guide all interpretation Heidegger calls the "hermeneutical Situation."[100] As *thrown* we are already immersed in totalities of *understood* meanings. This is equivalent to saying we are always immersed in an unconscious psyche that guides consciousness. At one point, Jung speaks of the self as "an archetype that invariably expresses a situation within which the ego is contained."[101] Heidegger sees that Dasein, as Being-in-the-world, is unconsciously, already-understood being.

Interpretation takes understanding and makes it explicit *as something*. We understand how to use a flat surface to write on, and we simultaneously know it *as a table*. Interpretation is understanding's own possibility to develop itself. As interpretation, understanding becomes itself. Interpretation "…is the working-out of possibilities projected in understanding."[102] The structure of interpretation, the *as* structure, seeing *something as something*, which enables understanding to develop itself, is not at first necessarily conscious. But it is this linkage through the *as* structure that makes it possible for unconscious *understanding* to become conscious as interpretation. Ontological possibilities show up as ontic phenomena through interpretation. Interpretation takes what is already unconsciously given as the hermeneutical situation, the fore-structure of our being, and works it out as existence.

For Heidegger *meaning* belongs to the fundamental being of Dasein. Meaning is not something added on as an extra. Meaning is the context in which understanding interpretation becomes conscious, the further development of understanding through interpretation to explicit awareness:

> Meaning is that wherein the intelligibility of something maintains itself. That which can be Articulated in a disclosure by which we understand, we call "meaning". The *concept of meaning* embraces the formal existential framework of what necessarily belongs to that which an understanding interpretation Articulates.[103]

Disclosure makes visible, and *articulation* here is associated with the way the joints of a skeleton articulate the individual bones into a mean-

---

[100]Heidegger (1962) 275.
[101]Jung (1951) 257.
[102]Heidegger (1962) 189.
[103]Heidegger (1962) 193.

ingful whole. Meaning is the structure, or framework, of awareness: "...'meaning' must be conceived as the formal-existential framework of the disclosedness which belongs to understanding."[104]

Narrative structure can serve as an example of both this "framework" of meaning and intelligibility, as well as the hermeneutic circle. We have seen Dilthey say that the "meaning" of life is always known in terms of beginnings and ends, origins and purposes and this is the basic structure of narrative. The structure of narrative, its beginning, middle and end, is a skeletal "existential framework" that maintains the intelligibility of story in general, and the intelligibility of anything called a "fact." We also saw Munz make this basic point as well in chapter three with his discussion of the *Sinngebild* as the basic mini-narrative that constructed every so-called fact.

The ontological-existential structure of *understanding* and *meaning* confirms our discovery in chapter three that every historiographical "fact" is an interpretation that takes place within an *a priori* totality of meaningful involvements and traditional assumptions. In order to make any interpretation and call anything a "fact" we must already be a "fore-having" (being-in-the-world), a "fore-sight" (be a point of view), and a "fore-conception" (be determined by ready made concepts). This allows us to say that facts are actually created by ever changing historical understanding, that historical knowledge is created by historical knowledge, and, in short, that history creates history. The relationship between narrative (whole) and "fact" (part) is dialectic— they help create each other and mutually influence their shared meanings. When we understand that this view of Dasein is not any kind of solipsism we are in effect saying that human being *creates* its own ever changing knowledge, understood in the light of Heidegger's assertion that "In the circle is hidden a positive possibility of the most primordial kind of knowing." This view that knowledge is *created* and changes, stands in strong contrast with the original hope of positivism to *discover* unchanging, universal true knowledge.

The structure of narrative also illustrates the dynamic relationships of the hermeneutic circle between the whole and the parts. The narrative as a whole is related to every part ("fact"), or sub-plot, and every sub-plot is related to the total plot. Every part, every fact, has a meaningful relationship to every other part through their rela-

---

[104]Heidegger (1962) 193.

tionship with the structural meaning of the whole. The whole narrative derives meaning from the parts, and the parts derive meaning from the whole. Overall this is an ongoing and complex interweaving of part meanings and larger meanings and ever expanding or deepening inter- pretations. The continuity and coherence that is the wholeness of the narrative structure itself is a pre-conscious experience of *understand- ing* that grounds all the possibilities that are projected as interpre- tations. Without the meaningful structure of narrative the "facts" are just one damn thing after another—a meaningless string of beads.

The unity and wholeness of narrative also relates it to the structure of the archetype of the self. Jung understands the self-ego relationship as that between whole and part. He states that

> The ego is thus related to the self as part to whole. To that extent the self is supraordinate. Moreover, the self is felt empirically not as subject but as object, and this by reason of its unconscious component, which can only come to consciousness indirectly, by way of projection.[105]

The self is the central organizing principle of the psyche and includes the history of the psyche as well as its future possibilities. Jung also sees in mandala symbolism a representation of the phenomenological structure of the self—a center, boundedness, inclusiveness, symmetry, as well as an ineffable and mysterious quality. It is not surprising that narrative shares these same characteristics. And, I would also say that *understanding* and *meaning*, as formal ontological structures of being, are also basic structures of what Jung calls the archetype of the self.

These associations allow me to suggest that narrative itself is an archetypal image of the self, and therefore, it does not seem unwarranted to say that narrative is a god-image. Narrative as god- image is suggestive about narrative's power to persuade and convince, and hold us in thrall to its story. The ability of master narratives to hold us unconsciously and unquestioningly in their meanings is also a witness to the power of myth (and, I might add, the myth of history in particular). This ontological perspective means that we *are* our stories and story, and every story is by no means always in our best interests. Stories, or myths, are also not simplistically good or evil, but complex mixtures of both. To be able to evaluate stories is crucial and this requires a way to get a purchase on them, to get some distance on them, in order to take a critical and evaluating look at them. But this is

---

[105] Jung (1968) 315.

easier said than done when the story is really unconscious and also shared by an entire culture. This brings up my theme of the crucial value of the differentiation of consciousness. This, in part, entails the withdrawal of projections, in order to emerge from an unconscious identity with their imagery that otherwise determines who we are and how we are in the world.

Let us remember however that we can never become conscious of all of our assumptions or projections. The hermeneutic circle, like the collective unconscious, is of indefinite extent. It will always expand or deepen beyond our capacity to make it completely explicit. The contextual *whole* that any one thing is a *part* of can itself become a part in a larger *whole*. Narrative contexts can always expand and deepen. For example, Christian scripture is a part of the whole of world religious literature; religious literature is a part of the whole of world literature; world literature is a part of the whole of world cultural expressions; and finally, existing cultural expressions are a part of the whole of all future potential cultural expressions. As Guignon notes, speaking in the light of Heidegger's ontological view of the hermeneutic circle, the attempt to make explicit the larger context within which any interpretation takes place generates a new context that "itself remains largely tacit and unclarified." He goes on to express the seemingly infinite and finally ungraspable nature of the hermeneutic circle this way,

> All our interpretations take place within a hermeneutic circle in which things are discovered only in terms of a pre-understanding of the whole. We can constantly strive to move toward deeper and fuller clarity about this background of pre-understanding, but we can never reach a point where all assumptions have been made explicit. For this reason the Cartesian ideal of finding a horizonless vantage point is an illusion. All inquiry, justification, and grounding are contextualized within the framework of our unfolding horizon of pre-understanding.[106]

This is another way of saying that the reality of the collective unconscious will always remain beyond our conscious grasp—life will always remain dense and opaque, and fundamentally unknowable in any final sense. This brings to mind the analogue of the medieval idea of God as "a circle whose centre is everywhere and the circumference

---

[106]Guignon (1983) 178.

nowhere" and the idea that "God is an infinite sphere."[107] It was also understood by some of the Renaissance practioners of the occult sciences like alchemy that God was the "circle" of prior knowledge which alone could bestow understanding on the adept. Jung cites Dorn (seventeenth century) as saying, "It is not possible for any mortal to understand this art [alchemy] unless he is previously enlightened by the divine light."[108]

To return to Heidegger's terms that describe the hermeneutic circle, it is important to repeat that Heidegger's presentation of these terms, *understanding, interpretation* and *meaning*, has nothing to do at first with cognitive, intellectual functions. He is describing the structures and processes of pre-cognitive being and existence. At the level of understanding as an *existentiale* the as-structure functions implicitly and automatically amidst the web of significant relations that are Being-in-the-world. We neither think explicitly about the everyday things we use, nor do we think explicitly about how we are getting along or who we are, when everything is going smoothly, uninterrupted by breakdowns or contradictions. Existence as such is unconscious existence. Existential understanding and meaning, because they are outside the field of consciousness, are, in Jung's view, projected as myths. They are not properly called projections until their status as *the truth,* and *the absolutely real,* is disturbed and brought into question.

In my view, it is Heidegger's abstraction, "the fore-structure of *understanding,*" that manifests as those myths and fantasies that guide being human in a world of involvements that matter to us. The hermeneutic foundation that is *understanding*, that makes interpretation possible, is also the mythological foundation of being. Archetypal *understanding* manifests to us in terms of the images of myth and fantasy, and myth and fantasy can be understood as pre-reflective interpretations of primordial *understanding*. The idea of "projection" signals that moment when what is already "known" unconsciously, a particular fantasy or myth with which we are unconsciously identified, needs a new conscious interpretation in order to emerge and embody as a new form of consciousness. All this may be said to be the existential expression of Hermes, the messenger who circulates between worlds. In this we see the structure of deep-subjectivity, the ontological nature of the reflection at the bottom of the well, and the source of the multiple images of Jesus. It is in the reflection at the bottom of the well, those

---

[107]Cited in Jung (1948) 229 fn 6.
[108]Jung (1967a) 443.

multiple images of Jesus, that we have the possibility of discovering fantasies of the self (that is, images of God) that desire consciousness and incarnation.

It is time to turn to Jung's interpretation of the Christ in the light of our phenomenological understanding of his hermeneutic psychological-archetypal method.

Jung's Interpretation of the Christ

In my view, Jung's interpretation of the Christ is important to a study of historical critical method and the quest for the historical Jesus because, from a phenomenological perspective, Jung's approach to the Christ, and the historical critical method's approach to the Gospel texts, have fundamentally the same purpose: the critical differentiation of consciousness in relation to the Christian myth for the sake of continuing incarnation. And while Jung's psychological-archetypal approach to the Christ and Crossan's historical critical approach to Jesus seem, methodologically, to be miles apart, their basic phenomenological similarity lies in the critical, reflective and hermeneutic stance each takes toward the Christ myth. I believe Jung's work realizes the potential of this stance with his new interpretation of the Christ myth through his psychological-archetypal method that is self-consciously existential and hermeneutic. Crossan, and historical critical method in general, falls short of this potential, because the historical myth used to reinterpret the Christ myth does not realize itself self-consciously as an existential, hermeneutic phenomenology of being that functions to differentiate consciousness for the sake of continuing incarnation. Historical critical methodology, when under the influence of positivism, is in a state of unconscious identity with the numinosity of material reality, that is, historical reality. As such, it harbors no doubts about the reality of the historical truth it seeks. Furthermore, the varied historical myths of Jesus (those historical critical treatments of the Jesus Christ traditions attempting to reconstruct the historic Jesus), as I read them, are projecting the Christ myth and the problem of consciousness onto the historic Jesus. This is what makes the image of Jesus fascinating in the first place. In chapter six I will suggest that the failure of historical critical method to realize its traditional aim, the recovery of the historic Jesus, can be transformed for a new purpose, namely, the ongoing work of withdrawing the projection of the self from Jesus for ongoing incarnation.

In this section I will look at Jung's approach to the Christ myth. In the next chapter I will look at Jung's ideas about the historic Jesus. Jung's approach to the Christ occurs most explicitly in four major works, "A Psychological Approach to the Dogma of the Trinity" (1948), "Transformation Symbolism in the Mass" (1954), *Aion* (1951), and "Answer To Job" (1952). My focus is primarily on *Aion* and "Answer To Job," and I am interested in the following two themes in his treatment of the Christ: (1) Jung's critical interpretation of the Christ in terms of the archetype and phenomenology of the self, and, (2) Jung's interpretation of the self as an archetype that develops historically in relation to the development of consciousness, and is related to the meaning of time itself. A third theme, Jung's contribution to the differentiation of myth and history in relation to the figure of Jesus Christ, will be explored in chapter five.

The complete title of Jung's major book on the self and the Christ is, *Aion: Researches into the phenomenology of the self.* The term *aion* (aeon) itself is significant. It not only means an unspecified vast stretch of time in the past or future (the eternal), or a specific great eon, but it also means, "a power emanating from the supreme deity, with its share in the creation and government of the universe."[109] The frontpiece illustration in *Aion* is a photograph of a second to third century Roman statue of the Mithraic god Aion, Mithras himself as the god of time, which is an image of the meaning of time.[110] These associations suggest that the term *aion* combines our ideas of time and being, and that time is here viewed as the dynamic manifestation of

---

[109] Chambers 20th Century Dictionary (1983) 17.

[110] This image is extraordinary and worthy of extended contemplation. It is comprised of a standing human male body with a lion's head, huge wings on its back, entwined by a large serpent from head to toe, with the serpent's head jutting over the forehead of the lion. The figure's body is covered with astrological symbols, and in each hand he holds a (now broken) key. He stands on a round orb with his mouth open. It is interesting that this image is never mentioned in the text of Aion. Jung's comments on it can be found in CW 5 (1967) 425. There, among other things in reference to this time symbol he says "Time is thus defined by the rising and setting sun, by the death and renewal of libido, the dawning and extinction of consciousness." Jung interprets this mythological symbol as expressing the meaning of time in terms of the transformations of the creative force, the libido or life force. To discuss this image further would take me too far afield, but I imagine that its inclusion at the beginning of Aion is hardly incidental.

being as becoming: an emanating power that creates and orders. Jung tells us in his Foreword that he wants, "with the help of Christian, Gnostic, and alchemical symbols of the self, to throw light on the change of psychic situation within the 'Christian aeon.'"[111] With his phenomenological and comparative method Jung is undertaking a psychological-archetypal interpretation of the Christian meaning of time, or, in other words, the Christian myth of history, and its preoccupation with the beginning and end of time. Jung's own interpretation of the meaning of time, or history, is in terms of an evolutionary relationship between ego and self.

Traditionally, Jung's particular historical perspective would be viewed within the context of the history of ideas. This is valid up to a point, but for Jung an idea is never merely the product of the intellect. For Jung, the self and the Christ are no mere intellectual ideas. Behind, or within, the idea, Jung always sees a power, a god, or, in his preferred language, an archetype. For this reason I emphasize that Jung's approach to the Christ is not idealist, but phenomenological. Jung's epistemology in this instance takes as his starting facts the thoughts and ideas (or, symbols) of Christian theology and myth, along with Jewish, Gnostic and alchemical thought, and combines it with his archetypal interpretation of human experience. In other words, Jung's epistemology begins with historic interpretations as facts (in this case, ideas about the Christ) and continues with his own reinterpretation. Jung does not try to establish positivist facts about the historic person of Jesus. This distinction is important for the differentiation of history and myth in relation to the person of Jesus.

In general, when Jung writes about Jesus Christ he usually distinguishes between the Christ of myth and the Jesus of history, but he also, at times, shares in the common tendency to use the words *Jesus* and *Christ* interchangeably. In the light of historical critical consciousness and the quest for the historical Jesus, the conceptual differentiation between the Christ of myth and the Jesus of history is critical for my purposes. I believe the continuing uncritical and interchangeable use of the terms *Christ* and *Jesus* leads to confusion about the relationship between history and myth in relation to the figure of Jesus, as well as confusion about history and myth in general. This is especially important in terms of the distinction I am making between

---

[111] Jung (1951) ix.

the historic Jesus and the christological interpretation of Jesus as the Christ, which is the myth of Christ. The distinction I make between the *historic* Jesus (the actual man) and the *historical* Jesus (the stories we tell about the historic Jesus using the terminologies of history) is also relevant here because the story of the *historical* Jesus is also mythic in structure. I believe the term myth can function in this double way without confusion because I distinguish between the *historic* Jesus, the *historical* myth of Jesus and the theological myth of the Christ. I will use the name *Jesus* to refer broadly to the Jesus of history (both the *historic* and the *historical* Jesus), and the term *Christ* to refer to the Christ of myth. For my purposes, and following Jung's own usage, the "Christ of myth" is interchangeable with the Christ of faith, the theological Christ and the metaphysical Christ.

With regard to the self and the Christ, Jung puts the problem this way, "Is the self a symbol of Christ, or is Christ a symbol of the self?"[112] Jung affirms the latter. The archetype of the self is the greater reality that gives rise to its own interpretation through the Christ symbol. Jung's psychological-archetypal approach to the Christ is phenomenological-empirical in that he correlates the varied descriptions of the Christ with specific descriptions of human experience. Jung is interested in the experiential meaning of the Christ. He is not interested in it as an abstract metaphysical or theological principle. For Jung the Christ is not ontologically transcendent, outside of human experience. What does transcend the human epistemologically is the archetype of the self. It cannot be known directly, but its effects, its phenomena, are experienced, and can be interpreted. The self is both a phenomenological and epistemological term in that "the spontaneous symbols of the self, or of wholeness, cannot in practice be distinguished from a God-image."[113]

Jung states explicitly that the term "unconscious" is an epistemological concept,[114] and not a psychologically reductive and explanatory concept. As an epistemological concept it merely asserts that there are limits to what we can know directly about the origin, meaning and purpose of our experience and the phenomena of life in general. As an epistemological limit, along with his phenomenological approach, Jung is able to speak interchangeably about the unconscious and myth without psychological reduction:

---

[112]Jung (1951) 122.

[113]Jung (1951) 73.

[114]Jung (1977) 208.

I prefer the term "the unconscious," knowing that I might equally well speak of "God" or "daimon" if I wished to express myself in mythic language. When I do use such mythic language, I am aware that "mana," "daimon," and "God" are synonyms for the unconscious—that is to say, we know just as much or just as little about them as about the latter.[115]

For Jung, the transcendent nature of the contents of the unconscious does not mean an ontological transcendence (that is, a substantial and spatial separation), but an epistemological limit that does not separate ontologically the knower and the unknown.

Jung finds that the metaphysical and theological descriptions of the Christ, and the fact that the Christ image occupies "the centre of the Christian mandala,"[116] correlate the Christ image with other religious and mythological symbols of ultimate completeness and totality. Jung links the mandala structure in general with the god-image,[117] and then links the mandalas in the dreams, visions and active imaginations of modern people with the experience of "God" by way of a new interpretation: "A modern mandala is an involuntary confession of a peculiar mental condition. There is no deity in the mandala, nor is there any submission or reconciliation to a deity. The place of the deity seems to be taken by the wholeness of man."[118] The "wholeness of man" is an existential interpretation of god-images based on their descriptive similarity with that special human experience Jung called completeness or wholeness. For Jung, this means that "Christ exemplifies the archetype of the self."[119] The self as an archetype is an existential possibility for human being that is first of all unconscious.

The phenomenology of the self links both mythological and theological descriptions of divine imagery with the psychological descriptions of the experience of "wholeness." The self is the possibility of wholeness or completeness for the human person. But the term "wholeness" is problematic because it does not mean an idealized and achievable perfect balance of all the aspects of oneself as some kind of humanistic superperson. The self, as the "goal" of individuation, points to our "wholeness" as the deepening of the one-sided conscious per-

---

[115] Jung (1961) 336-37.
[116] Jung (1951) 69-73. And see "Concerning Mandala Symbolism" (1968) 355-384.
[117] Jung (1940) 136-38.
[118] Jung (1940) 139. Also, "A Study in the Process of Individuation" (1968) 290–354.
[119] Jung (1951) 70.

sonality through an on-going relationship with the unconscious. For Jung, "unconscious processes are compensatory to a definite conscious situation."[120] The self in this way serves as a correcting and regulating factor of the psyche, responding to the conscious personality. Jung sees the compensatory function of the self at work not only in the individual but also in larger historical and social situations. As "goal" the self is never realized as a static completion, but expresses the purposive intentionality of life that is lived and always remains open-ended. Jung contrasted "wholeness" and "perfection" because perfection is a cultural and ego ideal while wholeness includes imperfection, what the ideal excludes. "The individual may strive after perfection...but must suffer from the opposite of his intentions for the sake of his completeness."[121] The striving for perfection based on cultural and religious models is an ideal imposed on the personality from without. The self, however, is an ontological intentionality of life (i.e., psyche) itself over which the ego has no direct control. The choice available to the ego in relation to the self is to cooperate or not cooperate with the primordial desire for individual completeness:

> Whatever man's wholeness or the self, may mean *per se*, empirically it is an image of the goal of life spontaneously produced by the unconscious, irrespective of the wishes and fears of the conscious mind. It stands for the goal of the total man, for the realization of his wholeness and individuality with or without the consent of his will. The dynamic of this process is instinct, which ensures that everything which belongs to an individual's life shall enter into it, whether he consents or not, or is conscious of what is happening to him or not.[122]

Wholeness or totality is not a universal ideal that is the same for everyone. "Wholeness" is always specific and unique to the individual. The goal is that one become one-self as much as one can. In this sense the idea of wholeness can be misleading. It has more to do with an individual specificity that develops as a result of the relationship between the ego and the unconscious (life). The individualizing tendency of the self has to do with its drive for consciousness. For Jung, one's own uniqueness is a God-given sacred task. This natural process can be conscious (you can cooperate with it) or unconscious (it can just happen to you). Jung called this process individuation.

---

[120]Jung (1951) 320.
[121]Jung (1951) 123.
[122]Jung (1952) 745.

Jung says of the self that, "it is completely outside the personal sphere, and appears, if at all, only as a religious mythologem...."[123] The unconscious and its archetypal structures cannot be observed directly by personal consciousness. They are not "things" anywhere, but the background ways of being human that we are. As the process of being human they are also the potential of being human, and so represent the future possibilities of being human. As unconscious they can only appear to consciousness indirectly via the projected form of a symbol. The invisible reality of being reveals itself as images, which in their turn, are reflections of both our current experience of ourself and the world, and our potential for being-in-the-world. Jung says of the self,

> I usually describe the supraordinate personality as the "self," thus making a sharp distinction between the ego, which, as is well known, extends only as far as the conscious mind, and the *whole* of the personality, which includes the unconscious as well as the conscious component. The ego is thus related to the self as part to whole. To that extent the self is supraordinate. Moreover, the self is felt empirically not as subject but as object, and this by reason of its unconscious component, which can only come to consciousness indirectly, by way of projection.[124]

This formulation should make it clear again that the interpretation of the Christ as a projection of the self is not a psychologically reductive explanation. It is rather an existential interpretation that sees in the Christ a symbol, or fantasy, of a potential of the conscious personality that comes from being itself, or as Jung would say, from the objective psyche (his other term for the collective unconscious). The felt objective otherness of the projected symbols of the self, as religious symbols and god-images among others, is a result not of their ontologically separate otherness, but of their unconsciousness. Among the projected symbols of the self I would include the narrative structure of historical discourse, by which I mean that narrative structure is an expression of the self. As such it is an innate component of psyche (life), but as projected symbol it has a taken for granted absoluteness that we are unconsciously, and thus we forget it is an image that requires criticism and interpretation.

---

[123]Jung (1951) 57.
[124]Jung (1968) 315.

The ego and the self are clearly distinguished, and this differentiation is crucial for the critical dialogue between them that Jung views as necessary if these two aspects of psyche are to have a positive influence on each other. Jung maintains a critical perspective on both the conscious and the unconscious aspects of psyche, by maintaining an open-ended dialogue between the conscious and the unconscious. This dialogue represents a general phenomenology of the relationship between ego and archetype. In the following citation this dialogue is put in terms of the anima and animus as personifications of the collective unconscious:

> Though the effects of anima and animus can be made conscious, they themselves are factors transcending consciousness and beyond the reach of perception and volition. Hence they remain autonomous despite the integration of their contents, and for this reason they should be borne constantly in mind. This is extremely important from the therapeutic standpoint, because constant observation pays the unconscious a tribute that more or less guarantees its co-operation.[125]

The idea that "contents of the collective unconscious" can be integrated by the conscious personality is a profound hermeneutic and ontological shift in the fundamental understanding of the relationship between human and divine. What is unconscious wants consciousness, and strives to be integrated by consciousness. Yet consciousness has to strive against the desire to sink back into unconsciousness:

> …the conscious mind is always in danger of becoming one-sided, of keeping to well-worn paths and getting stuck in blind alleys. The complementary and compensating function of the unconscious ensures that these dangers…can in some measure be avoided.[126]

The unconscious can function as a critic of the conscious standpoint, but this requires a particular attitude on the part of the ego. The ego needs to observe unconscious manifestations and processes (projections, dreams, fantasies, emotions, ideas and behavior), give them significant importance, i.e., ontological value, while preserving its own boundaries. When the ego lacks an appropriate critical attitude toward the realities of the unconscious, inflation results as the ego is assimilated to the contents of the unconscious. Jung realizes that,

> the increase in self-knowledge resulting from the withdrawal of impersonal projections—in other words, the integration of the

---

[125] Jung (1951) 40.
[126] Jung (1951) 40.

contents of the collective unconscious—exerts a specific influence on the ego-personality. To the extent that the integrated contents are *parts of the self,* we can expect this influence to be considerable. Their assimilation augments not only the area of the field of consciousness but also the importance of the ego, especially when, as usually happens, the ego lacks any critical approach to the unconscious. In that case it is easily overpowered and becomes identical with the contents that have been assimilated.[127]

Jung's phenomenology of the relations between ego and collective unconscious can also serve as an interpretive phenomenology of the relations between person and God, as well as the relations between individual and world, all of which constitute a complex living whole that is self-regulating and self-developing.

I will utilize Jung's distinction between the ego and the self as a model to help clarify a distinction between history and myth in understanding the person of Jesus and the symbol of Jesus Christ (this distinction is developed further in chapter five). The ego can represent the ordinary, empirical person, the actual historic individual, who is finite and limited. The conscious aspect of the person is by definition limited, narrow and imperfect, and in need of constant feedback from both the unconscious and from others, in order to correct and expand it. The person named Jesus, in order to be imagined as a realistic, historic person, needs to be thought of in such prosaic terms. The term history itself can refer to prosaic life in general. The ego is the location of concrete, everyday existence, in its limited particularity and imperfection. In Jung's view the ego has a critical function in relation to the self, for sometimes the ego needs to tell the self about certain aspects of reality. In the following quotation Jung is speaking about the self and ego during one of his seminars on Nietzsche's *Zarathustra*:

> It [the self] is not only our best friend, but also our worst enemy; because it doesn't see, it is as if not conscious of time and space conditions. We must say to the self, "Now don't be blind; for heaven's sake be reasonable. I shall do my best to find a place for you in this world, but you don't know the conditions. You don't know what military service means or tax collectors or reputations. You have no idea of life in time and space. So if you want me to do something for you, if you want me to help you to manifest, you must

---

[127]Jung (1951) 43.

be reasonable and wait. You should not storm at me. If you kill me, where are your feet?" That is what *I* (the ego) am.[128]

From this perspective the ego sees things the self cannot see, while at other times, the self sees things the ego cannot see. They need each other for the creation of consciousness, but like any relationship, it is messy and imperfect, and requires a lot of work.

The other aspect of the phenomenology of the self that gives Jung a critical perspective on the Christian image of the Christ is the shadow. Jung includes evil in his view of the self in contrast to the sinlessness of Jesus Christ and the God who is only the greatest good. In its original historical context Jung believes the Christ was an image of wholeness for its time: "There can be no doubt that the original Christian conception of the *imago Dei* embodied in Christ meant an all-embracing totality that even includes the animal side of man." What constitutes a symbol of "wholeness" is relative to the historical cultural context and its particular needs. But today, "the Christ-symbol lacks wholeness in the modern psychological sense, since it does not include the dark side of things but specifically excludes it in the form of a Luciferian opponent."[129] As Jung also notes, this religious division between light and dark, good and evil, resulted in a deep, ontological split:

> The psychological concept of the self, in part derived from our knowledge of the whole man, but for the rest depicting itself spontaneously in the products of the unconscious as an archetypal quaternity bound together by inner antinomies, cannot omit the shadow that belongs to the light figure, for without it this figure lacks body and humanity. In the empirical self, light and shadow form a paradoxical unity. In the Christian concept, on the other hand, the archetype is hopelessly split into two irreconcilable halves, leading ultimately to a metaphysical dualism....[130]

Jung frequently refers to the phrase "omne bonum a Deo, omne malum ab homine"[131] (all good belongs to God, all evil belongs to humankind) as characterizing this state of affairs that so radically separated the divine and humankind in terms of good and evil. To pursue Jung's long and vehement rejection of the Christian view of evil as a *privatio boni* would take us too far afield. What matters here

---

[128]Jung (1988b) 978.
[129]Jung (1951) 74.
[130]Jung (1951) 76.
[131]Jung (1951) 74.

is that Jung's inclusion of the shadow, or evil, in the structure of the self is an important aspect of his view of the completeness, or wholeness, of the person and of being. In this way the self is not a one-sided ideal that accentuates one aspect of being but a complex of opposites that comprise an unconscious totality. The shadow lends a thickness and density to the prosaic reality of the individual. The reality of the shadow balances, or corrects, the natural tendency to idealize our own self-image and the image of any great personality.

Jung's interpretation of the Christ as one historical manifestation of the archetype of the self that stands in historical relationship with other symbols of the self, involves him in a new interpretation of time through a reinterpretation of the Jewish-Christian understanding of the meaning of history (that is, the Jewish-Christian myth of history). Jung's developmental view of individuation is not limited to the individual, but is seen as a possibility of history in general. It is this larger view that I will now take up in relation to Jung's *Answer To Job*.

In *Answer To Job* Jung takes the view that the Jewish and Christian symbols of God, Messiah, Christ, Satan, Son of Man, Holy Spirit and the Virgin Mary participate in a mythological drama that develops over time, a historical-psychological development in which his interpretation participates, that he interprets as "the differentiation of consciousness."[132] Jung discusses these symbolic figures as if they were real entities. But Jung does not believe this is an exercise in mere anthropomorphism because he understands the symbolic figures as expressions of the archetypes that have both an autonomy of their own relative to the ego, and appear to the ego *as if* they were definite personalities. The *as if* aspect Jung understands as the fantasy images spontaneously produced by the collective unconscious in communicating with consciousness.

Jung starts his narrative of the development of consciousness with the book of *Job*. Briefly, and at risk of an extreme condensation, in the book of *Job*, as Jung reads it, Yahweh is exposed as an amoral, ambivalent, brutal, unconscious power. The human Job turns out to be the morally superior being because, in spite of all that he has suffered at the hands of Yahweh, by knowing and asserting his own innocence, he is able to *see* the terrible duality of Yahweh, his injustice and justice, and still call upon Yahweh's justice for aid. As Jung states,

---

[132] Jung (1952) 758.

This is perhaps the greatest thing about Job, that, faced with this difficulty, he does not doubt the unity of God. He clearly sees that God is at odds with himself—so totally at odds that he, Job, is quite certain of finding in God a helper and an "advocate" against God. As certain as he is of the evil in Yahweh, he is equally certain of the good. ... Yahweh is not split but is an *antinomy*—a totality of inner opposites—and this is the indispensable condition for his tremend-ous dynamism, his omniscience and omnipotence. Because of this knowledge Job holds on to his intention of "defending his ways to his face," i.e., of making this point of view clear to him, since notwithstanding his wrath, Yahweh is also man's advocate *against himself* when man puts forth his complaint.[133]

Jung understands the symbol of Yahweh in terms of the collective unconscious, that is, as a complex dynamism of opposing forces that lacks a key ingredient, namely self-reflection, or consciousness. In Jung's view, this is why God has always been so jealously interested in humankind. Totally lacking in self-insight (which corresponds with the self's ignorance of the ego), Yahweh "can only convince himself he exists through his relation to an object." And Jung later says, "Existence is only real when it is conscious to somebody. That is why the Creator needs conscious man even though, from sheer unconsciousness, he would like to prevent him from becoming conscious."[134] This tension in the Creation between unconscious and conscious establishes a dynamic and creative instability that tips back and forth between the two.

Jung believes that Job's real achievement is to have seen and registered Yahweh's dual nature. "Such a revelation, whether it reached man's consciousness or not, could not fail to have far reaching consequences."[135] Jung states that "Whoever knows God has an effect on him." Job saw and knew "the unconscious split in [God's] nature. God was now known, and this knowledge went on working not only in Yahweh but in man too."[136] Job's knowledge changed God's nature, in Jung's view, thus paving the way for Christ's incarnation.

Over the intervening centuries between Job and Christ, Jung sees in the successive appearance of the Son of Man in the visions and dreams of Ezekiel, Daniel and Enoch, the progressive movement of God drawing nearer to humankind. In Jung's view, the writer of *Job's*

---

[133] Jung (1952) 567.

[134] Jung (1952) 574, 575.

[135] Jung (1952) 608.

[136] Jung (1952) 617, 623.

sense of Job's moral superiority to God, Job's greater moral consciousness of God's amoral and split unconsciousness, set up an imbalance between God and humankind that Jung describes as a disturbance in the unconscious. God, disturbed by the unconscious knowledge of itself, wants to make this knowledge more conscious and thereby become more moral, as well as expiate the wrong done to Job.

Christ is the answer to this need. In Christ, according to Jung, God incarnates its all-good aspect, its complete love of humankind, through the self-sacrifice of the crucifixion. Christ as God's son is sacrificed to God's evil, and in so doing establishes the divine status of human consciousness, in that God became a human being. This Incarnation is an idealized manifestation of God's goodness. As Jung understands it,

> The unconscious wants to flow into consciousness in order to reach the light, but at the same time it continually thwarts itself, because it would rather remain unconscious. That is to say, God wants to become man, but not quite. The conflict in his nature is so great that the incarnation can only be bought by an expiatory self-sacrifice offered up to the wrath of God's dark side.[137]

For Jung, consciousness develops as a result of suffering the intense emotional conflict of opposing forces and values within the individual. The inertia of unconsciousness requires the energy and heat of emotional conflict to be overcome. This is why Jung believes the passion of Christ is the appropriate vehicle for the Incarnation, and why the struggle within the individual with competing emotional values yields the incarnation of consciousness.

But Jung views this Incarnation as incomplete. The sinlessness of Jesus Christ means that God has not yet become completely human. For Jung this is prognostic. He believes that, "At first, God incarnated his good side in order, as we may suppose, to create the most durable basis for a later assimilation of the other side."[138]

For Jung, the Job-Christ drama symbolizes a developing consciousness, but it is not yet a realized consciousness because it remains in the projected form of a mythic drama. Its consummation as the Second Coming is still in the future, a potential that is still unconscious.

---

[137]Jung (1952) 740.
[138]Jung (1952) 741.

The Christian insistence on the full and complete historical embodiment of God in Christ is a crucial aspect of the myth, even though Christ manifests as an ideal mortal rather than an ordinary mortal. But at least in the symbol of Christ the ontological unity of God and person is affirmed and preserved, albeit in unconscious, projected form. Jung then interprets this symbol of ontological unity in terms of the relationship between self and ego, and applies it archetypally and existentially, historically and psychologically, to all persons. The myth of the historical Incarnation, in the light of Jung's hermeneutic of projection, has the possibility of becoming a historic actuality, and therefore more complete, as the process of individuation in individuals. Jung sees in the sending of the Holy Spirit the continuing incarnation and the desire of God to become completely human: "From the promise of the Paraclete we may conclude that God wants to become *wholly* man; in other words, to reproduce himself in his own dark creature (man not redeemed from original sin)."[139]

But for Jung this continuing incarnation now needs the sinful and guilty human within which to realize itself. For the shadow of the person and the shadow of God overlap, and the coming to consciousness of the one brings the other to consciousness also. For Jung, the historic opposition was between God and man, infinite and finite, good and evil. But today, the opposition is within God itself, that is, the collective unconscious, and these opposites can only be united in the consciousness of the human person. Therefore, in Jung's view, God, as the collective unconscious that wants to become conscious, that is, human,

> has chosen, through the Holy Ghost, the creaturely man filled with darkness—the natural man who is tainted with original sin and who learnt the divine arts and sciences from the fallen angels. The guilty man is eminently suitable and is therefore chosen to become the vessel for the continuing incarnation, not the guiltless one who holds aloof from the world and refuses to pay his tribute to life, for in him the dark God would find no room.

> Since the Apocalypse we now know again that God is not only to be loved, but also to be feared. He fills us with evil as well as with good, otherwise he would not need to be feared; and because he wants to become man, the uniting of his antinomy must take place in man. This involves man in a new responsibility. He can no longer wriggle out of it on the pleas of his littleness and nothingness, for the dark God has slipped the atom bomb and chemical weapons into

---

[139]Jung (1952) 741.

his hands and given him the power to empty out the apocalyptic vials of wrath on his fellow creatures. Since he has been granted an almost godlike power, he can no longer remain blind and unconscious. He must know something of God's nature and of metaphysical processes if he is to understand himself and thereby achieve gnosis of the Divine.[140]

Jung's interpretation of the Christ drama in psychological-archetypal terms is a new myth of the meaning of life and of history, a new "mask on the face of time," that gives human consciousness a cosmic significance. This is not the triumphal dominance of rational intellect that Western humanity has equated with its cosmic significance. This is a moral consciousness of good *and* evil that includes the willingness to suffer the reality of one's own evil, knowing that this is also God's problem, and so mitigate its devastating power. This consciousness knows its ordinary limitations and is aware, through experience, of the dangers of inflation.

As Jung says, his view in *Answer To Job* of "the development of symbolic entities corresponds to a process of differentiation of human consciousness."[141] The differentiation of consciousness is the emergence of individual consciousness out of, and in relation to, that unconscious identity with projections that constitute our lived world. It is the withdrawal of projections in the differentiation of consciousness that brings our world to consciousness. Here we return to the structure of the hermeneutic circle. Heidegger's view of the hermeneutic circle states that we *interpret* (make clearer) what we already *understand* indistinctly and vaguely. The withdrawal of projections and the differentiation of consciousness means that we bring to consciousness what we already "know" unconsciously. I understand Heidegger's statement, "In the circle is hidden a positive possibility of the most primordial kind of knowing," as equivalent to gnosis of the divine, or the consciousness of "God" Jung is talking about.

Jung raises another problem though that is brought about by the differentiation of consciousness. For Christianity, Christ is the one and only God-man. Yet as Jung says, "the indwelling of the Holy Ghost, the third Divine Person, in man, brings about a Christification of many, and the question then arises whether these many are all complete God-

---

[140] Jung (1952) 746, 747.
[141] Jung (1952) 758.

men."[142] In other words, the ordinary person who consciously indi-
viduates is a christ. This gives the unique and prosaic individual life an
ultimate value, over and against the traditional, singular and ideal type
of Christ. But if everyone is to think they are a God-man what kind of
conflicts and inflation will this lead to? This is a serious concern because working at consciousness necessarily exposes one to these dangers. It is ironic that the attempt to become conscious can also result in
unconscious inflation. This is why it is well to remember, in Jung's
words, that

> the enlightened person remains what he is, and is never more than
> his own limited ego before the One who dwells within him, whose
> form has no knowable boundaries, who encompasses him on all
> sides, fathomless as the abysms of the earth and vast as the sky.[143]

Summary

This chapter has explored two major themes in Jung's work that
bear on the quest for the historical Jesus.

The first is that the intent of Jung's psychology is most fully
realized in terms of a philosophy of life understood in the light of
Heidegger's hermeneutic phenomenology. This perspective establishes
the foundation of epistemology (knowledge) not in rational and clear
methods, but in *primordial understanding* and fantasy (as the imaginal
language of the unconscious). It is through fantasy that the world first
grasps us, and it is through fantasy (images) that we first grasp the
world. Heidegger's *primordial understanding* is at odds with how we
usually grasp the word "understanding." *Primordial understanding*
refers to shared general, vague and mostly unconscious perspectives
and points of view, but these are what we must start with in order to
build clearer interpretations. This ontological insight affirms, along
with critical historiography, that all historical knowledge is fundamentally hermeneutic, and can only be, in the final analysis, a hermeneutics
of meaning. This means that there are no such things as absolute facts,
and even "facts" that everyone might agree on are embedded, as
interpretations, in *a priori* and culturally accepted structures of meaning. Rather than *facts* it is more appropriate to speak in terms of ever

---

[142] Jung (1952) 758.
[143] Jung (1952) 758.

changing *historical images* that take their meaning from that larger image of time, the historical narrative, itself, always changeable.

The second is that the Christ, interpreted as a symbol of the archetype of the self, is understood in mythic terms, and as such, is differentiated from history in that the Christ is not a historic person. Jung's differentiation between ego and self lets us see Jesus as an ordinary empirical person, and the Christ as the symbol of an unconscious projected content, the self, that ultimately wants consciousness in humanity. The Christ, as archetypal symbol, is interpreted as a mythic expression of an ongoing historical, individuation process.

Within the context of these realizations, I suggest that the quest for the historical Jesus is best understood and undertaken, not as a quest for the historic Jesus, nor a quest for a historical understanding of a plausible Jesus, but as the evolving differentiation of consciousness in relation to the projection of the self. Jung's concern for the problem of evil in God suggests that the critical exploration of a historically and psychologically plausible Jesus (which, while not the goal itself, is the essential exercise for the differentiation of consciousness) should include "imagination for evil"[144] regarding the problem of Jesus' own shadow. This humanizes and embodies Jesus fully along with the rest of us, relativizes his idealized importance, and increases the value of the unique individual life and individual consciousness. Thus the quest for a historically and psychologically plausible Jesus involves the full use of the myths of historical and psychological realism in the exercise of hermeneutic imagination, rather than being oriented toward trying to establish objective and absolute, historic facts.

Questions remaining have to do with how the quest for the historical Jesus functions in the withdrawal of projections and the differentiation of consciousness. What is the meaning and nature of the *historical image* of Jesus as *image* we are seeking? What effect does the image of the historical Jesus have on the psyche and life? What happens when psychological realism is not included with historical realism? How can the qualities of the image of the historical Jesus be evaluated, and how do we handle the inescapable presence of the unconscious and archetypal factors that influence our image of the historical Jesus? I will address these questions in the next two chapters.

---

[144] Jung (1957) 572.

CHAPTER FIVE

MULTIPLE IMAGES OF JESUS
IN CROSSAN AND JUNG

Introduction

This chapter will examine the *images* of Jesus in the work of Jung and Crossan. This approach to the image of Jesus will serve as a model of a working hypothesis for evaluating historical images of Jesus and why I think it is important to do so.

I will approach the question of the image of the historical Jesus, not from the perspective of the historic truth of the image, but in terms of a critical phenomenology of the relationship between history and myth that draws on specific aspects of Jung's understanding of the relationship between the ego and the collective unconscious, or the self. Because I believe there are no epistemological grounds on which to either establish the one correct depiction of the original historic Jesus, or to determine whether one depiction is more correct than another, I propose a phenomenological approach to the *historical image* of Jesus. In fact, *the historic Jesus* occupies a similar transcendent position epistemologically in relation to our consciousness as does God, or the archetype—we can only know an *image* of God, or an *image* of the archetype, or an *image* of the historical Jesus, and we can never know in terms of direct observation the actual reality. Therefore, I believe that phenomenological criteria are more adequate to the epistemological situation. Such phenomenological criteria should include psychological, historical and mythical factors in evaluating *images* of the historical Jesus, rather than trying to establish the correct historic Jesus. In this context, by "mythical" I mean a phenomenology of transpersonal factors that are not reducible to historical or personal psychological dynamics. The difficulty in developing psychological and historical approaches to Jesus is that the problem of God and the Christ either get overlooked, are explained reductively, or, tacit images of God or Christ are utilized, or intrude, uncritically. In what follows I will suggest one possible phenomenology of the history-myth relationship utilizing Jung's description of the ego-self relationship. This model will work as a guide for my discussion of the Jesus-images held by Jung and Crossan.

In what follows I will not pursue the problem of whether or not the conventional mythic themes in the Gospel portrayals of Jesus associated with the supernatural and the miraculous are actual historic events. By this I mean that the historical awareness typical of historical positivism precludes certain Gospel themes, such as the virginal conception of Mary, the resurrection of Jesus, walking on water, turning water into wine, etc., from being historic events. This problem area engages larger philosophical issues involving conflicting narratives or worldviews that from the perspective of historical positivism are simple, but from the perspective of "history as myth" are much more complex. For my purposes, the question of what is symbolic metaphor and what is historic event in the gospel portrayals of Jesus, and the philosophical basis on which such distinctions are made, does not have to be pursued here. It must be noted however, that both Crossan and Jung assume the modern view of reality that rules out the virginal conception, etc., as historic events, and approach these Gospel themes as metaphor and symbol.

A Working Phenomenology of History and Myth

This chapter explores phenomenological criteria that may help detect subtle "mythic" elements in historical and psychological descriptions (images) of the person of Jesus. This phenomenology of history-myth draws on aspects of Jung's phenomenology of the ego-unconscious relationship. It will focus on the tendency to *idealize*, that is, exaggerate and de-humanize, the historical and psychological image of Jesus. Jung's phenomenology of the ego-unconscious relationship is a phenomenology of ordinary humanness in relation to religious images and their transpersonal reality. This criteria has to be a matter of degree, because as we have seen, every historical and psychological description must make use of generalizations, which are unavoidably idealizations, to some extent. The criteria used here to help identify the idealizing tendency in relation to Jesus are drawn from Jung's understanding of how the unconscious can exert an idealizing influence on consciousness. The criteria will include (1) the linguistic usage of superlatives and hyperbole in descriptions of Jesus, (2) the tendency to emphasize only positive traits and remove ambiguity, and, following from these first two, (3) the absence of any critical questions about the value of Jesus' perceived message and actions.

I draw on Bernstein's idea of the prosaic for a contrast with the idealizing tendency. The idea of prosaics includes an ethical insistence that finitude and ambiguity, i.e., sideshadowing, are what constitute the realistic understanding of human life and historicity. The prosaic and the ideal cannot function as either-or polarities in evaluating images of Jesus. They represent a continuum on which all images of Jesus must be drawn, and as such are relative criteria of evaluation.

The explicit use of superlatives is easy to detect. They are ultimate and absolute descriptions, and appear in such phrases as "Jesus the *most* obedient man," "the man of the *greatest* love," "the *most* conscious man," or, "the *most highly* developed human who ever lived," etc. Many attempts to describe the human Jesus turn into descriptions of a human Christ, that is, an image of an idealized human being, with no real limitations, failings, idiosyncrasies or ambiguities. For example, Jungian oriented psychotherapists, like J. Sanford (1970), E. Howes and H. Wolff, who have attempted psychological-historical descriptions of Jesus and who know about the reality of the shadow, inevitably idealize Jesus' positive attributes and pay mere lip service to his shadow. Or, if aspects of his shadow are imagined then the consciousness with which he handles his shadow is idealized, thus negating the unmanageable reality of the shadow. Of course, evil, or the shadow, can also be mythologized and idealized, as the conventional Catholic image of Satan, and the contemporary image of Hitler, demonstrate. My concern is not just with the tendency to idealize Jesus' goodness, but the tendency to idealize any of his human traits, that, by the definition of a phenomenological realism of the human, must always be conceived of in terms of limitation, particularity, imperfection and ambiguity, i.e., the prosaic.

It is Jung's phenomenology of the collective unconscious and the self that is helpful in developing a psychological phenomenology of myth and history. From Jung's perspective, the collective unconscious and the self are the source of the mythologizing and idealizing tendency. For Jung, the term "mythic" itself is at times a synonym for the grandiose, pompous and hyperbolic manner with which the unconscious often speaks.[1] There is an absolute quality that attaches to communications from, or experience of, the self, or any archetype, and this is its emotional and numinous aspect. For Jung, the expressions of absoluteness and ultimacy that characterize mythic speech is "characteristic of the language of love," and occurs whenever "speech is heightened by emotion."[2] Who of us has never felt, after falling in love with someone either near, or from afar, "You are *the most* beautiful person in the world," or, gripped by a wonderful idea, "this is *the greatest* truth humankind has ever known"? And even if we know intellectually that the experience is a projection and we could add those qualifying words *to me*, the emotional or numinous component is still felt as if it is absolute. Most often, the emotional intensity of the archetype that is the source of the absoluteness of an image or idea is not consciously felt. One can be gripped passionately and compulsively by an image or idea and not consciously feel the emotion. In this condition, one simply *is* the emotion, and this is the state of being in a projection, which is an unconscious identification with the emotional dimension of being. By definition, to consciously feel the emotion would be to begin to dis-identify from the unconscious emotion, and begin the process of integrating the meaning and possibility of the projection. This is also a way of converting emotion into feeling. Emotion is the unconscious archetypal force that leads to acting out and compulsion. Feeling, in Jung's view, is a conscious human valuation toward something or someone. Contrast, for example, the *emotion* of falling in love, and the *feeling* of love in a long-term relationship. This is a step in the withdrawal of projections that will be discussed in more detail in chapter six.

It is my view that it is impossible to approach the historic Jesus without the self, through the symbol or image of the Christ, influencing

---

[1]Jung (1967) 62.
[2]Jung (1967) 65.

us in some way. Throughout this discussion the term "Christ" means the divine Christ of the Christian tradition that is our heritage today. Although the term Christ in the gospels means "messiah" as "the anointed one," and as a first-century Jewish concept does not mean divinity, the Christ concept of the gospels does stand in continuity with the Christ concept of the Christian tradition. And from Jung's archetypal perspective, the self is a factor in both concepts although defined differently in their particular historical contexts. The fact that Jesus has been the Christ in Christian tradition for two-thousand years cannot be dismissed by an intellectual claim that one is focusing on purely historical research and has no religious or theological agenda. The historic fact of the theological (mythical) interpretation of Jesus as the Christ is not a mere intellectual idea, but an aspect of the core identity of our collective being. It is this archetypal aspect of the Jesus-Christ connection that is our inescapable collective "hermeneutical situation" that makes Jesus interesting at all in the first place. It is in this sense that I mean that the influence of the "Christ," in terms of the presence of an unconscious archetype, is inescapable for anyone who approaches Jesus. This factor must be accounted for in dealing with images of the historical Jesus. When one becomes conscious of the unconscious influence, the unconscious influence can change and become integrated into consciousness. Here I will explore Jung's description of the ego-self relationship and my appropriation of the concepts of history and myth as phenomenological terms.

The distinction between ego and self began early in Jung's life during his childhood. In *Memories, Dreams, Reflections* (1961) he describes the experience, between the approximate years of seven and nine, of sitting on a stone, and thinking,

> Am I the one who is sitting on the stone, or am I the stone on which *he* is sitting. This question always perplexed me, and I would stand up, wondering who was what now. ... But there was no doubt whatsoever that this stone stood in some secret relationship to me.[3]

The stone became a source of calm and reassurance. He, as himself, "the schoolboy of 1890," was a passing phenomenon of turbulence, inner conflict, doubt and emotion. The stone, as the Other that he also was, was timeless, secure, self-contained, consistent and imperishable.

---

[3] Jung, (1961) 20.

In looking back on his childhood, Jung speaks of these two dimensions of himself in terms of "personality No. 1 and personality No. 2." No. 1 was the ordinary limited schoolboy, or the man with a family and work, who lived temporarily (the finite human life span) in a specific town at a specific time. Personality No. 2 is the stone, or the self, that eternal, boundless reality that extends deep into the past and far into the future. And Jung says,

> The play and counterplay between personalities No. 1 and No. 2, which has run through my whole life, has nothing to do with a "split" or dissociation in the ordinary medical sense. On the contrary, it is played out in every individual. In my life No. 2 has been of prime importance, and I have always tried to make room for anything that wanted to come to me from within. He is a typical figure, but he is perceived only by the very few. Most people's conscious understanding is not sufficient to realize that he is also what they are.[4]

Jung sees personality No. 2, the self, as ubiquitous and as typical as personality No. 1, the ego. Every person is composed of these two dimensions of psyche (life), one conscious and one unconscious.

The reality of the self is also paradoxical. On the one hand it is the eternal dimension of the personality, and yet, as an archetype of individuality and unique personality, it is also extreme limitation, which is the ego's self-awareness. For Jung, *consciousness*, that is consciousness of one's completeness, or what I will call deep-consciousness, does not belong only to the ego, but is a function of a relationship between ego and self, as in the following:

> The feeling for the infinite, however, can be attained only if we are bounded to the utmost. The greatest limitation for man is the "self"; it is manifested in the experience: "I am *only* that!" Only consciousness of our narrow confinement in the self forms the link to the limitlessness of the unconscious. In such awareness we experience ourselves concurrently as limited and eternal, as both the one and the other. In knowing ourselves to be unique in our personal combination—that is, ultimately limited—we possess also the capacity for becoming conscious of the infinite. But only then![5]

Such "becoming conscious of the infinite" from the perspective of self-aware limitation implies a conscious differentiation between ego and self that is a kind of double-awareness, or deep-consciousness. Deep-

---

[4]Jung, (1961) 45.
[5]Jung (1961) 325.

consciousness, because it is aware of being simultaneously finite-infinite, or ego-self, is in principle less prone, but not immune, to inflation and projection. Deep-consciousness in this sense knows that it is constituted by both conscious and unconscious dimensions. This is the same as knowing that one is constituted by both a subjective sense of self that is more or less the ego, the I, and an objective sense of self that is a world, that is social, cultural, historical *and* a mysteriously vast and eternal unknown.

Jung's phenomenological clarity about the difference between the empirical and limited person (symbolized for my purposes by the ego) and the archetype (in this case, the self) in relation to Jesus Christ make available critical psychological and hermeneutic tools with which to talk about the problem of history and myth in relation to the quest for the historical Jesus. As he struggles to write *Aion* he describes to Father Victor White his discovery of the Christ as archetypal symbol,

> In spite of everything, I felt forced to write on blindly, not seeing at all what I was driving at. Only after I had written about 25 pages in folio, it began to dawn on me that Christ—not the man but the divine being—was my secret goal. It came to me as a shock as I felt utterly unequal to such a task. ... My further writing led me to the archetype of the God-man....[6]

Jung is gripped by the enormous quality of the Christ as "divine being" and archetypal symbol. When Jung says "divine being" he is not making a traditional theological or metaphysical reference, but a symbolic reference to the vastness of the archetypal reality. Jung's distinction between Jesus the man and the Christ as archetypal symbol enables him, in principle, to avoid conflating ego and archetype when he talks about either Jesus or Christ.

With regard to the figure of Jesus Christ Jung's categories provide a greater clarity of differentiation between *Jesus* and *Christ* than is generally possible within both Christianity in general and the quest for the historical Jesus in particular. I have not found in either psychological or historical approaches to Jesus the person an adequate appreciation of history (as empirical reality) and myth (as archetypal reality) as equal realities, nor an appreciation of the necessity to

---

[6]Jung (1973) 19 Dec 1947.

differentiate between history and myth. Rather, I find either confusion of one with the other, or reduction of one to the other. In general, psychological approaches tend to idealize the personality of Jesus and so re-mythologize him unwittingly, forgetting that superlatives and hyperbole are the language of myth and theology. Historical approaches tend to reduce mythic or theological formulations to historical forces that, while they transcend the individual, are still fundamentally materialistic if they give all their interpretive power to factors that are only sociological, political, economic, etc. Or, the historical approach to Jesus relies on the traditional modernist split between history and theology. In this case there are two problems. First, the historical approach relies unwittingly on Cartesian positivist epistemology and continues the misleading pursuit of the original historic Jesus, and two, theology continues its interpretation of the historic Jesus as a separate enterprise.

My working phenomenological definitions of history and myth are as follows. By history I mean the reality of the past, and life itself, in its arbitrary, contingent, daily ordinariness. This is the unpredictable, irreducible complexity and imperfection of real life. For history in this sense I draw on Bernstein's concepts of the "prosaic" and "quotidian" as the "ideal" description of daily, historic life. This is the reality of the *historic* in contrast to *history* which is a story about the *historic*. But *history* as a story, or myth, or narrative, about the *historic* cannot help but "idealize" the *historic* to some extent. However, the word *history* remains ambiguous because it also refers to the reality of the past as such. By myth I mean those universal and eternal archetypal images and metaphors that have to do with the experience, structure and interpretation of meaning at many levels, and in our case is what structures the narratives of *history*. And in Jung's sense "myth" refers to those spontaneous, autonomous and irreducible powers, the archetypes themselves, of the collective unconscious. However, it is important to remember that myth, as archetypal mode of being, does not only manifest as cultural artifacts, but also and primarily as historic and psychological reality, that is, the behavior, attitudes and thoughts of people.

I believe Jung's distinction between the archetype and the archetypal image is useful because it helps us to understand the ambiguity of the word myth. Myth in my usage refers to both archetype and archetypal image. This is the same ambiguity that holds for the word history. The word history refers to the real past as well as the historical image of the past. In this way, both the archetype as such and the historic as such share the same epistemological status—neither can be directly observed by us. We "know" both the unconscious and the historic through traces and images.

Within a phenomenological understanding of history and myth informed by Jung's view of the ego-self the name *Jesus* can refer to the historic, limited and ordinary, i.e., empirical, human person who lived and died two-thousand years ago, and in theory is not ontologically inferior to the *Christ*. The term *Christ* refers to the mythological symbol giving expression to the archetype of the self, or the archetype of the God-man, and is not ontologically superior to Jesus. The archetype of the self and its mythological symbols should not be confused, or conflated, with the empirical, historic person of Jesus, if our aim is to preserve a historical and psychological realism while at the same time preserving the ontological status of myth. The Christian tradition in general, as the myth of the historical Incarnation of Jesus Christ, conjoins and identifies Jesus and Christ. In the light of my phenomenology of history and myth this identity can lead to confusion about myth and history when talking about the historic Jesus. In general, my phenomenology of history and myth is a differentiation between two orders of being that includes the differentiation between ego and self (or, collective unconscious), as well as a differentiation between Jesus and Christ. This phenomenological differentiation is dependent on Jung's distinction between personality No. 1 as the historic identity of the individual, and personality No. 2 as the mythic "identity" of the individual. This phenomenological view of history-myth in terms of the ego-self relationship is also dependent on the view that the differentiation of consciousness has a historical and moral value as continuing incarnation.

One other consideration before I begin examining the particular Jesus-images of Jung and Crossan. Because I am interested in the relationship between the problem of method and the problem of multiple images of Jesus I am interested in this chapter in whether there is any relationship between Jung's and Crossan's methods and their images of Jesus. In the light of my analysis of Crossan's methods and Jung's methods I will anticipate the following. I would expect to find in Crossan's image of Jesus some kind of split or dichotomy related in some way to the split I see in Crossan's method between fact and interpretation, the split between his traditional positivist episte-mology and hermeneutics. In Jung's image of Jesus I would expect to find a figure more or less integrated as to history and myth, and in-terested in consciousness. And because Jung is at times contradictory, I would also expect to find contradictory images of Jesus, but not split images. The warning I give here is not only that we find what we look for, but that as we saw in Batdorf's examination of method and image in chapter one, there is no necessary correlation between method and image. Knowing this, I understand method not merely as a particular technique, but as representative of a larger theory or worldview that informs it. In this sense it is reasonable to expect that the theory on which any method depends will influence the image of Jesus.

C. G. Jung's Images of Jesus

Jung never turned any systematic or significant attention to the Jesus of history. Most often his comments about the man Jesus occur spontaneously in other contexts, such as *Answer To Job,* the Nietzsche *Zarathustra* seminars, and his letters. And because Jung did not systematically distinguish the terms Jesus and Christ, and often used the term Christ to refer to the historic man (which only reflects general practice), it is not always clear whether Jung is referring to the historic man, or the Christ figure of Christianity. Sometimes the context will help determine the referent, and at other times it does not. His ideas about Jesus are entirely sketchy, and by and large, purely speculative. Also, he is at turns diffident and bold in how he expresses his views about Jesus the man. But whether or not Jung's thoughts about Jesus are historic truth is not my focus. I am interested in his attitude toward this man, and how his image of Jesus functions in terms of this problem of a phenomenology of history and myth.

I will not undertake a chronological review of Jung's ideas about Jesus, but I will begin with the first glimpse we get of Jung's thinking in this area, which includes his early thoughts about biblical scholarship. This is a lecture he gave to fellow students in 1899, when he was 23, titled, "Thoughts on the interpretation of Christianity, with reference to the theory of Albrecht Ritschl."[7]

---

[7]Jung (1983) 89-118.

This student talk has some of the quality of a romantic polemic. Here Jung attacks what he sees as the dry and rational historicist thinking characteristic of academia in general, and in this case, of theological and biblical scholarship in particular. Fed up with the aridity of Enlightenment anthropology he wants to return humankind to its rightful place within a vast and unpredictable mysterious and mythological cosmos. In spite of its somewhat grandiose tone, this paper actually lays out in brief the outline of his life work (I am sure, at the time, unknown to him). Here he is struggling with the personal conflict between the rational prejudices of scientific materialism and the spiritual and mythical sensibility he also felt so strongly.

Jung's argument is with the normative concept of "normal man," developed by post-Renaissance philosophy, that became the tacit epistemological yardstick used everywhere by scholars to judge and control the results of thought. It particularly angers him when it becomes the yardstick by which to determine the historical personality of "Christ." Although Jung never makes the explicit connection in this talk, it is clear that this "normal man" is representative of Enlightenment anthropology, the direct result of Enlightenment (or, Cartesian) epistemology. The clear and distinct, rational and conscious idea is the only normative reality against which everything else is judged. What Jung attacks as Ritschl's epistemology is Cartesian epistemology in general. This Enlightenment epistemology determines what counts as valid and real knowledge. Only the contents of the conscious mind, derived from conscious sensory experience, are valid epistemologically, and count as real knowledge. Anything else, emotion, intuition, feeling, mystery, that could be a source of legitimate knowing, is thereby diminished, relegated to the merely personal, and seen as unreal.

It is this rational historicism, this yardstick of the "normal man," that makes the image of the historical Jesus it produces so repugnant to Jung. At this early stage it is not quite clear to what extent Jung distinguishes between the historical man Jesus and the mythic drama of the Christ hero. It seems that "history" in this context stands for the dry, rational discourse devoid of mystery and meaning that Jung sees is common to academia. Jung pens a satirical view of critical scholarship:

> Modern people no longer acknowledge the New Testament accounts to be absolutely reliable, but only relatively reliable. Armed with this judgment, critical scholarship lays hold of the person of Christ, snips

a bit off here and another bit off there, and begins—sometimes covertly and sometimes overtly, blatantly, and with a brutal naivete—to measure him by the standard of the normal man. After he has been distilled through all the artful and capricious mechanisms of the critics' laboratory, the figure of the historical Jesus emerges at the other end.[8]

Apparently the depiction of his human personality is intended to present us with a clearly-defined image.[9]

Indeed, they are willing to concede three-quarters of the personality of Christ—his faith in miracles, his prophetic powers, and his consciousness of his own divinity.[10]

Clearly Jung is not happy with critical biblical scholarship (later we will see that he was never happy with Bultmann's demythologizing project). For Jung the attempt at a "clearly-defined image of Jesus' human personality" leaves much to be desired. What is really important to Jung is the mythic prowess of the Christ. This is one of those places where it is impossible to tell whether or not Jung thinks he is referring to the historic man Jesus, with regard to miracles, prophecy and divinity, or whether he means the Christ personage of the Gospels.

The above citations might be a partial expression of Jung's own view of the historic Jesus. However, while it contrasts sharply with the "normal man" of the philosophers and theologians, it is a good example of the dilemma of distinguishing between historical (prosaic) description and mythical (ideal) description. Today we can read it as naive to the degree that Jung posits Jesus as a giant of a man who transcended his own history and historic conditions. Two sentences illustrate Jung's overblown depiction of Jesus, the Great Man (although he uses the plural third person, he is clearly including Jesus):

They *are* their own idea, untrammeled and absolute among the minds of their age, and not susceptible to historical analysis, for they experience the products of history not as conditions of their being but rather as the object of their activity, and as their link with the world. They have not evolved from any historical foundation, but know that in their inmost natures they are free of all contingency,

---

[8]Jung (1983) 247.

[9]Jung (1983) 251; italics added.

[10]Jung (1983) 284.

and have come only in order to erect on the foundation of history the edifice of their own ideas.[11]

This is a romantic and idealistic image, and it tells us more about Jung's argument with Ritschl's theology and Cartesian anthropology than it does about Jesus. The mythical hyperbole is glaring: "not evolved from any historical foundation" and "free of all contingency" are only two obvious examples. The hyperbole tells us this is not a realistic description of a real person, but rather an emotional and metaphoric description of a type. To take this description too literally would probably do injustice to Jung's rhetorical intent. Throughout this talk Jung expresses amazement at the lack of "sensibility" and "feeling" with which the typical scholar undertakes his work, and the intellectual aridity of the epistemology that cuts human being off absolutely from direct personal experience of "the mystery of a metaphysical world...."[12] Again, it is not possible to know whether Jung is intending to describe the actual man Jesus, or whether he is expressing an interpretation of the significance of the man. Using my criteria of the idealizing tendency places this description in the realm of myth rather than history. When Jung makes comments about the person of Jesus later in his life they reflect a more prosaic perspective.

Jung's criticism of Bultmann's demythologizing approach to the Gospels also leads to some of his opinions about the man Jesus. In a letter he says, "Bultmann's attempt at demythologization is a consequence of Protestant rationalism and leads to the progressive impoverishment of symbolism." As we have seen, Jung believes that myth and symbol, as expressions of the deep structures of life itself, are essential and necessary for a meaningful life. Without them life is empty. In the same letter Jung declares that "demythologizing" is "hybris!". He then comments that "Christ was no doubt a moral philosopher—what else remains of him if he is not a mythologem?"[13] Clearly, here Jung means the historic Jesus, and this simple description of the man is more prosaic than ideal. Take away the myth and the historic Jesus is quite ordinary, but also uninteresting because Jung means "only" a moral philosopher. Jung addresses this issue again in

---

[11]Jung (1983) 243.

[12]Jung (1983) 288.

[13]Jung (1975) 17 March 1951.

Answer to Job where he clearly distinguishes between the mythic drama of Christ the God-man and the historic person of Jesus.

Jung first describes what he believes is the impossibility of writing a biography or history of Jesus from the Gospel accounts (although he continually uses the term Christ):

> Seen from a distance of nearly two thousand years, it is uncommonly difficult to reconstruct a biographical picture of Christ from the traditions that have been preserved. Not a single text is extant which would fulfil even the minimum modern requirements for writing a history. The historically verifiable facts are extremely scanty, and the little biographically valid material that exists is not sufficient for us to create out of it a consistent career or an even remotely probable character. Certain theologians have discovered the main reason for this in the fact that Christ's biography and psychology cannot be separated from eschatology. Eschatology means in effect that Christ is God and man at the same time and that he therefore suffers a divine as well as a human fate. The two natures interpenetrate so thoroughly that any attempt to separate them mutilates both. The divine overshadows the human, and the human being is scarcely graspable as an empirical personality. ... The commonplace is so interwoven with the miraculous and the mythical that we can never be sure of our facts. ... The synoptic gospels are...unsatisfactory as they have more the character of propaganda than of biography."[14]

If we read Jesus for Christ, and mythology for eschatology, I believe this paragraph is clear about the degree to which Jung views the historic personality of Jesus as absorbed and obliterated by mythological elements (in another context he says "smothered by metaphysical conceptions"[15]). This expresses Jung's basic view of the impossibility of extracting anything meaningful about the person of Jesus from the Gospel material, and although he does deviate from this at points, in general this perspective also makes it clear that Jung's opinions about the historic personality of Jesus are speculation.

Jung again expresses his lament over demythologizing and his view of what kind of Jesus remains after the myth is stripped away:

> How, then, can one possibly "demythologize" the figure of Christ? A rationalistic attempt of that sort would soak all the mystery out of his personality, and what remained would no longer be the birth and tragic fate of a God in time, but, historically speaking, a badly authenticated religious teacher, a Jewish reformer who was hellenistically interpreted and misunderstood—a kind of Pythagoras,

---

[14]Jung (1952) 645.

[15]Jung (1948) 228.

maybe, or, if you like, a Buddha or a Mohammed, but certainly not a son of God or a God incarnate.[16]

In another context Jung refers to Jesus' similarity to historic figures like Socrates or Appollonius of Tyana.[17] Jung's view of Jesus as prominent teacher or reformer positions Jesus in the past as a figure in history, and though very generalized, it is a prosaic perspective.

The above citation is from a paragraph that begins with what I consider to be a prosaic speculation on Jesus' character:

> Besides his love of mankind a certain irascibility is noticeable in Christ's character, and, as is often the case with people of emotional temperament, a manifest lack of self-reflection. There is no evidence that Christ ever wondered about himself, or that he ever confronted himself.

This is a prosaic and critical perspective on Jesus' personality that is all too human. Of course it is impossible to prove, but neither is it created out of thin air, although Jung is not citing texts to support his suppositions. The value I find in such a view is that it prompts concrete thinking about the possible real personality of Jesus against what seems to be the natural mythic tendency to idealize the personality of Jesus. However, Jung continues with an interesting transition that is at first confusing because he seems to shift into myth. He suggests that Jesus did confront himself in one critical instance:

> To this rule there is only one significant exception—the despairing cry from the Cross: "My God, My God, why hast thou forsaken me?" Here his human nature attains divinity; at that moment God experiences what it means to be a mortal man and drinks to the dregs what he made his faithful servant Job suffer. Here is given the *answer to Job*, and, clearly, this supreme moment is as divine as it is human, as "eschatological" as it is "psychological" [read mythological for eschatological]. And at this moment, too, where one can feel the human being so absolutely, the divine myth is present in full force. And both mean one and the same thing.[18]

What has happened here? First we are reading about Jesus' lack of self-knowledge, and then we are reading that his humanity has

---

[16]Jung (1952) 647.

[17]Jung (1948) 228.

[18]Jung (1952) 647; italics added.

attained divinity. (At this point Crossan cannot help Jung because Crossan has rejected the words from the cross as historic.) But Jung finds in these all too human sounding words a profound self-consciousness on Jesus' part of both his own failure and suffering, *as well as* the evil and destructive nature of God. I believe this confusing shift occurs because we suddenly find ourselves reading Jung's own myth (interpretation) of the Jesus Christ myth. In Jung's view, the dark and unconscious God that he finds in the book of *Job,* becomes conscious of its own darkness through, and as, the human consciousness of Jesus. It seems that Jung has moved from a speculative comment about Jesus' lack of self-knowledge to his own myth (interpretation) of the Christian myth. This is the critical moment in his own interpretation because here is the phrase that is the title of this essay, "the answer to Job."

The problem for us as readers is that the whole essay, *Answer to Job,* is Jung's interpretation (myth) of the Judeo-Christian myth, and it moves almost seamlessly back and forth between the mythic language of the Christian tradition and the language of his own psychological interpretation. Because the question of historicity with regard to Jesus is finally always undecidable, the question as to whether these words from the cross are historic is not the relevant question. The relevant question is whether this image of Jesus is prosaic or ideal.

In my view, Jung's interpretation of Jesus' consciousness on the cross is both prosaic and ideal. To read it this way means that it is not a superlative ideal, but a limited ideal image of prosaic human consciousness recognizing a dark aspect of God that has not been noticed, according to Jung, for a long time. This kind of human consciousness of the unconsciousness of the divine is a possibility, to the degree appropriate to the individual, for anyone who takes the trouble in their own finite existence. This is the meaning of individuation, making the unconscious God conscious. What makes this image of Jesus ideal is that it is a symbol of human consciousness and we cannot know if it was ever actual consciousness. What makes this image of Jesus prosaic is the definition of human consciousness as limited, particular and imperfect. Another aspect that contributes to this image's prosaic quality is that this image does not present Jesus' consciousness as inflated or grandiose, but rather as a horrified and suffering awareness of a dark dimension of reality. And while we can never know whether or not this was Jesus' actual consciousness (and again, this is not the point) we do know it is Jung's consciousness because this is his interpretation. However, because of the psycho-logical and historical realism of such an interpretation it is tempting to retroject it back onto the historic Jesus without realizing this is what we are doing.

Sorting out Jung's understanding of the differentiation between history and myth in relation to Jesus in *Answer to Job* is difficult at times as the following example demonstrates. Jung notes that other scholars also recognize the great difficulty of determining the historic facts of Jesus, and therefore conclude "that Christ was nothing but a myth, in this case no more than a fiction." Jung then counters this "nothing but" conclusion with the argument that myth "consists of facts that are continually repeated and can be observed over and over again." By this he means archetypal patterns of human behavior, but he also means the idea of fate, and that humans can have mythic fates just as well as the Greek heroes. He then goes on to say,

> The fact that the life of Christ is largely myth does absolutely nothing to disprove its factual truth—quite the contrary. I would even go so far as to say that the mythical character of a life is just what expresses its universal human validity. It is perfectly possible, psychologically, for the unconscious or an archetype to take com-plete possession of a man and to determine his fate down to the smallest detail. At the same time objective, non-psychic parallel phe-nomena can occur which also represent the archetype. It not only seems so, it simply is so, that the archetype fulfills itself not only psychically in the individual, but objectively outside the individual [i.e., what Jung in another place refers to as the synchronistic phenomena that accompanied Christ's life]. My own conjecture is that Christ was such a personality. The life of Christ is just what it had to be if it is the life of a god and a man at the same time. It is a *symbolum*, a bringing together of heterogeneous natures, rather as if Job and Yahweh were combined in a single personality. Yahweh's intention to become man, which resulted from his collision with Job, is fulfilled in Christ's life and suffering.[19]

Does Jung mean to say here that the Gospel portrayal of the life of Jesus could be historic actuality? Is Jesus to be seen as a mere puppet of an archetypal pattern? My guess is that Jung is confusing somewhat the narrative realism of the Gospel accounts, especially the passion narratives, with his own deep understanding of the reality of

---

[19]Jung (1952) 648.

archetypal factors to determine human behavior, for good or ill. On the other hand, I think Jung's own interpretive position on Jewish-Christian mythology, his view of "Yahweh's intention to become man," is what leads to this kind of confusion of the mythic account of Christ in the Gospels with a possible literal life of Jesus. At the same time, this does not mean that Jung is taking every mythic theme in the Gospels literally or concretely.

However, this picture of Jesus as a man completely possessed by an archetype and whose fate has been predetermined is hardly con-genial to anyone who wants to give Jesus the benefit of the doubt and a modicum of consciousness. Jung is writing this material at the end of his own long life, and his autobiography tells us he viewed his life under the auspices of fate and archetypal factors, but whether he would consider his own life as lived out within the "complete possession" of an archetype is another matter. This statement by Jung about Jesus could be a suggestive but not literal statement in the light of his own personal experience, or it could be a statement that presents a highly problematic psychological view of Jesus.

Psychologically, unless one is using the word "possession" metaphorically or loosely, rather than clinically, to be possessed by an archetype, with little or no personal ego consciousness, would be considered a psychotic, or near psychotic, condition (although, to be sure, the idea of possession is generally not a modern understanding of psychological disorders, and the word possession is not used in the American Psychiatric Association's *Diagnostic and Statistical Manual of Mental Disorders*). But this is what Jung has in mind when, putting it indirectly, he says that if we look at certain of Christ's statements in the light of psychology, deprived of their mythical context because of demythologizing, they can only be read personalistically. As he puts it,

> what sort of conclusion are we bound to arrive at if a statement like "I am the way, and the truth, and the life; no one comes to the Fa-ther, but by me" [Jn 14:6] is reduced to personal psychology? Obviously the same conclusion as that reached by Jesus' relatives when, in their ignorance of eschatology, they said, "He is beside himself." (Mk 3:21)[20]

Naturally, today, anyone who spoke in such terms as "I am the way" or "I am Christ," and could not differentiate between their per-sonal sense of I and their mythical thoughts, would be demonstrating a

---

[20]Jung (1952) 647.

thought disorder associated with schizophrenia. Such a person is, to varying degrees, mentally incapacitated, and if need be, is institution-alized. This may or may not be what Jung means by "archetypal pos-session" in the case of Jesus; nevertheless, such an image challenges conventional idealized Christian imagery of Jesus. This, however, is exactly what Jung is doing throughout *Answer to Job*, challenging conventional Christian images of God and Christ.

However, if we expect Jung to be consistent with regard to his image of Jesus we will be disappointed. In one of the Nietzsche semi-nars Jung said,

> Even if the man Jesus existed at all, the story of his life is not historical. It is clearly mythology, like the mythology of Attis, or Adonis, or Mithras; that was all syncretistically put together into the figure of *Christus*.[21]

And, in a letter we find Jung saying,

> I cannot prove the identity of an historical personage with a psychological archetype. That is why I stop after establishing the fact that in the Occident this archetype [the self], or this "God-image," is seen in Christ [meaning Jesus]....[22]

In another letter Jung guesses that "Jesus Christ was probably a definite human person, yet highly enveloped in archetypal projections, more so than other historical figures like Buddha, Confucius, Lao-tse, Pythagoras, etc."[23] In these instances Jung is clearly not conflating the archetype of the self, the myth of Christ, with the historic person Jesus, although he continues to use the term Christ to refer to Jesus.

Yet the problem of how Jung saw Jesus related to the self is not easily solved. He took a similar but different perspective from the above comment about being possessed by an archetype in the following citations from a letter,

> The existing statements about Christ are, in part, about an empirical man, but for the other and greater part about a mythological God-man. Out of these different statements you can reconstruct a personality who, as an empirical man, was identical with the traditional Son of Man type, as presented in the then widely read

---

[21] Jung (1988a) 208.

[22] Jung (1975) 29 June 1955.

[23] Jung (1975) 25 October 1955.

Book of Enoch. Wherever such identities occur, characteristic archetypal effects appear, that is, *numinosity* and *synchronistic phenomena*, hence tales of miracles are inseparable from the Christ figure. The former [numinosity] explains the irresistible suggestive power of his personality, for only the one who is "gripped" has a "gripping" effect on others; the latter [synchronistic phenomena] occur chiefly in the field of force of an archetype, and because of their aspatial and atemporal character, are acausal, i.e., "miracles."

In consequence of the predominance of the archetype the personality that is "gripped" is in direct contact with the *mundus archetypus*, and his life or biography is only a brief episode in the eternal course of things or in the eternal revolution of "divine" images.

Anyone who is gripped by the archetype of the Anthropos [a symbolic figure Jung takes as equivalent to the Son of Man as expressions of the self] lives the God-man—one can very well say that he *is* a God-man.

This description of Christ satisfies me because it permits a non-contradictory presentation of the paradoxical interplay of his human and divine existence, his empirical character and his mythological being.[24]

But in this same letter Jung goes on to say "the archetype *per se*...must be strictly distinguished from the archetypal idea or mythologem...." So when Jung says that Jesus, gripped by the archetype of the God-man, *is* a God-man, he does not mean that Jesus is identical with a metaphysical Christ. The God-man is a metaphor for the archetypal pattern Jung believes Jesus lived out as his personal limited historic existence. Nevertheless we are still stuck with the question about the nature of the relationship of Jesus' ego to the archetype. Jung's description, in these instances at any rate, with its emphasis on the vastness of the *mundus archetypus*, certainly diminishes, if it does not obliterate, the role of Jesus as conscious ego. In another context Jung states that it is impossible to know the answer to this question. He says, "Whether [Jesus] lit the light with his own strength, or whether he was the victim of the universal longing for light and broke down under it, are questions which, for lack of reliable information, only faith can decide."[25]

On the other hand, Jung does have a picture of Jesus as conscious of his shadow. In a long letter to Victor White, in which he

---

[24]Jung (1975) 30 August 1951.

[25]Jung (1948) 228.

chides White for "mixing up the idea of Christ being human and being divine," Jung discusses the difference between Christ as divine and Christ (that is, Jesus) as human:

> Inasmuch as he is divine, he is the self, yet only its white half. Inasmuch as he is human, he has never lost his shadow completely, but seems to have been conscious of it. How could he say otherwise: "Do not call me good..."? [Mk 10:18, Mt 19:17, Lk 18:19] It is also reasonable to believe that as a human he was not wholly conscious of it, and inasmuch as he was unconscious he projected it indubitably. The split through his self made him as a human being as good as possible, although he was unable to reach the degree of perfection his white self already possessed.

Jung continues with a distinction between divine and human that is similar to the phenomenological distinction I draw between history and myth in terms of the prosaic and the ideal:

> Christ as understood by the Church is to me a spiritual, i.e., mythological being; even his humanity is divine as it is generated by the celestial Father and exempt from original sin. When I speak of him as a human being, I mean its few traces we can gather from the gospels. It is not enough for the reconstruction of an empirical character. Moreover even if we could reconstruct an individual personality, it would not fulfil the role of redeemer and God-man who is identical with the "all-knowing" self. Since the individual human being is characterized by a selection of tendencies and qualities, it is a specification and not a wholeness, i.e., it cannot be individual without incompleteness and restriction, whereas the Christ of the doctrine is perfect, complete, whole and therefore not individual at all, but a collective mythologem, viz. an archetype.[26]

Whether or not Jung thinks Jesus' character can be reconstructed from the evidence, he does have some speculations to make about the incompleteness of his life. Picking up from Nietzsche's comment that Christ died too young, Jung says

> I always regret that Christ only reached the age of thirty-three, because I would like to know what he would have been at fifty or thereabouts, having had a wife and half a dozen children. I wonder what his teaching would have been then. I have an idea that certain things would have been quite different. Since the normal human life lasts more than thirty-three years, and since most people do marry and propagate themselves and are on the battlefield of life or even

---

[26]Jung (1975) 10 April 1954, 164-65.

the burial grounds, they surely must have different views of life from
people who never are fully born into the darkness of existence.[27]

Here Jung speculates aloud about the premature death of Jesus.
Jung sees, in this instance, that Jesus' life, although certainly the one
he had to live, was a very partial life from Jung's own perspective.
Jesus lived

> the life of a philosophical tramp who really has the idealistic purpose
> of teaching a new saving truth, who recognizes no other respon-
> sibility. You see, he had no profession and no human connections
> which were valid to him. He separated himself from his family, was
> the lord of his disciples, who had to follow him while he had to
> follow no one, being under no obligations. This is an exceedingly
> simple situation, tragically simple, which is so rare that one cannot
> assume that the teaching coming from such a life can be possible or
> applicable to an entirely different type of life.[28]

Not only does Jung see Jesus as an unemployed, homeless philosopher
with no ordinary earthly responsibilities, but he also sees him holding
eschatological beliefs quite literally when, in comparing our modern
view of life with Jesus' supposed beliefs, he says, "We don't believe
that the life of the earth will soon be finished, that the kingdom of
heaven is to come, and that the legions of angels will fall upon the
earth so that its power will be finished."[29] Jung is making these
comments about Jesus in the context of his discussion of Nietzsche's
critique of Christianity. So, not only is Jung saying that the Christian
myth as myth is not understandable and meaningful to scientifically
minded moderns, but also that the historic Jesus' life was so different
and so partial that the teachings coming out of such a life could not be
relevant to our contemporary problems. Therefore, what we need is a
new interpretation of the Christ myth that will be meaningful to us, and
Jung offers the myth of individuation.

Jung's image of Jesus also sees him belonging "to the lowest
stratum of the people," and that he "was an illegitimate child and Mary
was an immoral woman." He emphasizes that the prostitutes, and the
adulterous woman Jesus speaks of, were just that, and he refers to the
social milieu and life of Jesus as "a poor miserable thing, in no way
respectable." Jung is emphasizing this impoverished and seamier

---

[27] Jung (1988a) 507.

[28] Jung (1988b) 780.

[29] Jung (1988b) 780.

aspect of Jesus in stark contrast to his comment that "we paint everything with gold." Jung also refers to Jesus as a "criminal" because he was a creative individual who went his own way in relation to the tradition and the law. Jung believes any truly creative individual is a criminal in the eyes of the establishment, and that Jesus was a criminal in the eyes of the Jews and was executed.[30]

In this last regard, Jung refers more than once, with obvious admiration, to the statement attributed to Jesus at Luke 6:4b (found in Codex Bezae): Jesus says to a man he sees working on the Sabbath, "Man, if indeed you know what you are doing, you are blessed; but if you do not know, you are cursed and a transgressor of the law." Jung interprets this as more than a simple warning specific to the Sabbath. In Jung's eyes this represents an ethical standard in which "the moral criterion is *consciousness*, and not law or convention." Ordinary goodness is commendable but not enough. Jung understands Jesus as saying that "to act unconsciously is evil."[31] In reference to this passage in another context Jung suggests a contemporary parallel, trying to emphasize the shocking and radical nature of such a view, when he says this would be like saying to a murderer today, "If you *know* that you are a murderer, you are blessed."[32] Jung sees Jesus teaching a way of consciousness that will engender terrible moral conflicts between the conventional belief that it is good to respect and obey the law and tradition, and bad to go against it. Another value may emerge that leads one to consciously break tradition, and thereby stand out from the crowd and suffer the consequences. Jung sees Jesus teaching such an alternative revolution that goes against the tradition.

This same theme is apparent in another context where Jung is discussing separating ego consciousness from the psychical background of the collective unconscious, and changing from the condition of ego as passive witness to ego as agent. This is psychological language for taking an individual moral stand that puts one in conflict with one's tradition, which is one's psychical background. He says this about Jesus,

---

[30]Jung (1988a) 267.

[31]Jung (1952) 696.

[32]Jung (1988b) 1325.

Christ himself gave ruthless advice. What did he say to the young man when he wanted to bury his father? "Let the dead bury the dead." [Mt 8:22] And what did he say to his own mother when she reminded him that the wine was nearly gone and he must do something about it? "Woman, what have I to do with thee?" [Jn 2:4] She is completely swept aside. Now think of a Jewish boy sweeping his mother out of the way! That is unheard of. You see, those are symbolic gestures, hints as to Christ's attitude toward the detachment from the past.[33]

I would tend to assume that Jung imagines Jesus had the kind of consciousness himself that he is admonishing others to adopt. And yet we have seen that Jung holds contradictory ideas about the extent of Jesus' consciousness about his own actions. However, another indicator for Jung that Jesus taught a counter-establishment morality is the parable of the unjust steward (Lk 16:1-9).[34] Because I will comment on Crossan's handling of this parable later I cite it here in full.[35]

He also said to the disciples, "There was a rich man who had a steward, and charges were brought to him that this man was wasting his goods. [2] And he called him and said to him, 'What is this that I hear about you? Turn in the account of your stewardship, for you can no longer be steward.' [3] And the steward said to himself, 'What shall I do, since my master is taking the stewardship away from me? I am not strong enough to dig, and I am ashamed to beg. [4] I have decided what to do, so that people may receive me into their houses when I am put out of the stewardship.' [5] So, summoning his master's debtors one by one, he said to the first, 'How much do you owe my master?' [6] He said, 'A hundred measures of oil.' And he said to him, 'Take your bill, and sit down quickly and write fifty.' [7] Then he said to another, 'And how much do you owe?' He said, 'A hundred measures of wheat.' He said to him, 'Take your bill, and write eighty.' [8] The master commended the dishonest steward for his prudence; for the sons of this world are wiser in their own generation than the sons of light. [9] And I tell you, make friends for yourselves by means of unrighteous mammon, so that when it fails they may receive you into the eternal habitations."

According to Crossan, the story that Jesus told stops with verse 7. In Crossan's analysis the next verses are explanations that attempt to soften the blunt and shocking nature of the story. Jung views this story as teaching the same morality of consciousness as the above noted-

---

[33] Jung (1988b) 940.

[34] Jung (1952) 696.

[35] All scripture quotations are from the Revised Standard Version.

statement from Codex Bezae. What is important in this story is not conventional good and bad behavior, but the active consciousness one brings to one's circumstances. It is the consciousness of one's motivation that makes the moral difference.

These teachings led Jung to believe that Jesus had knowledge of the mystery teachings of his time and had received a Gnostic initiation. He says that "it is more than probable that Christ received a Gnostic initiation and possessed a rather profound understanding of the human soul and the peculiarities of spiritual development."[36]

At the same time Jung wants "Christ" to have been an ordinary human being (and not just an omnipotent and omniscient God), who was confronted by his shadow, what Jung thought of as "*his* devil, the power devil."[37] Jung suggests that the man Jesus' central problem had to do with the desire for power over others. He refers to Jesus as a "spiritual sort of dictator."[38] In the following extemporaneous remarks Jung delivered at a dinner, he develops this psychological view of Jesus further:

> Jesus, you know, was a boy born of an unmarried mother. Such a boy is called illegitimate, and there is a prejudice which puts him at a great disadvantage. He suffers from a terrible feeling of inferiority for which he is certain to have to compensate. Hence the temptation of Jesus in the wilderness, in which the kingdom was offered to him. Here he met his worst enemy, the power devil; but he was able to see that, and to refuse. He said, "My kingdom is not of this world." But "kingdom" it was, all the same. And you remember that strange incident, the triumphal entry into Jerusalem. The utter failure came at the Crucifixion in the tragic words, "My God, my God, why hast thou forsaken me?" If you want to understand the full tragedy of those words you must realize what they meant: Christ saw that his whole life, devoted to the truth according to his best conviction, had been a terrible illusion. He had lived it to the full absolutely sincerely, he had made his honest experiment, but it was nevertheless a compensation. On the Cross his mission deserted him. But because he had lived so fully and devotedly he won through to the Resurrection body.[39]

---

[36] Jung (1988b) 788, 1031-32.

[37] Jung (1988a) 721.

[38] Jung (1988b) 1525.

[39] Jung (1977) 98.

First a word about this particular text of Jung's. Here Jung conflates a statement from the Gospel of John, "My kingdom is not of this world" (Jn 19:36—in the Revised Standard Version the word is actually *kingship*, which would give stronger support to Jung's argument), actually spoken to Pilate during Jesus' trial, with the Temptation narratives that are found only in the Gospels of Matthew and Luke (Mt 4:1–11; Lk 4:1–13); the Gospel of John has no Temptation of Jesus in the wilderness. This is not unusual for Jung, especially when he is speaking, but it also reveals his general attitude toward the biblical material about Jesus. For Jung the New Testament as a whole is the *Corpus Christianum* and it must be accepted as a whole or not at all, if we are going to understand Christianity. For Jung the *Corpus Christianum* is One Gospel and everything in it is related to everything else, and he treats it as such. Jung never undertakes the kind of literary textual analysis that we find Crossan devoted to in his work.

Is this psychological view of Jesus reigning as a spiritual king in compensation of an inferiority complex a simplistic reduction? Only if it is meant to explain everything. It is more likely an attempt by Jung to humanize the figure of Jesus and realize that he very well could have had a serious problem with power with which he struggled. It could also be an attempt by Jung to shock his listener's Christian assumptions about Jesus. But it is also important for Jung to imagine Jesus as a limited human being who struggled with his own imperfections. Then he is a useful model for us. If he is only the sinless and glorified Christ, then we can only feel inferior in relation to such an image and are not helped at all. Jung brings a kind of critical psychological prosaics to the Christian image of Christ in an attempt to build a psychological and archetypal bridge between the traditional Christ image and the prosaic lives of the rest of us.

If there is a summation of Jung's basic attitude toward the problem of Jesus and the Christian texts about Jesus as well as the person of Jesus, it appears in two letters to Upton Sinclair in response to Sinclair's book, *A Personal Jesus*.[40] At first Jung states that although he himself has tried to form an idea of Jesus' personality he finds such a task to be impossible because the New Testament data has too little history and too much myth. As he put it,

> I have repeatedly, i.e., at different phases of my life, tried to realize what kind of personality—explaining the *whole effect* of its exis-

---

[40] Jung (1975) 3 November 1952; 24 November 1952.

tence—could be reconstructed from the scanty historical evidence offered by the New Testament. Having had a good deal of psychological experience, I should have been sufficiently equipped for such a task, but in the end I came to the conclusion that, owing on the one hand to the paucity of historical data, and on the other to the abundance of mythological admixtures, I was unable to reconstruct a personal character free from rather fatal contradictions.[41]

And he does not like the result of Sinclair's attempt. Jung accuses Sinclair of being too selective, of simply choosing the texts which support the image of Jesus he is portraying—"a rationally understandable teacher of fine morals and a devout believer in a good Father-God." While this may appeal to a modern American, Jung complains that this image tells us nothing about why "the Gospels [should] be stuffed with miracle stories and He Himself saddled with esoteric and eschatological statements, showing Him in the role of a Son-God and cosmological saviour." At first it seems as if Jung expects that any reconstructed image of the person of Jesus should be able to explain the "*whole effect* of its existence." Does this mean that Jung thinks that a single historic person could be the sole agent of the phenomena of Christianity? No, he certainly does not. A careful reading of these letters reveals that the issue is not really about an adequate portrayal of the historic Jesus of Nazareth, but rather, an adequate, to Jung, understanding of the whole of the New Testament portrayal of Jesus Christ. The conflict in this letter is between what Jung perceives to be a reductive rationalistic attempt, implicit in Sinclair's presentation, to portray a *reasonable* image of Jesus, and Jung's attempt to understand the whole of the New Testament witness to Jesus Christ, what he calls the *Corpus Christianum*, with a perspective that certainly includes rationality, but that does not dismiss nor ignore the profoundly mysterious mythological imagery that permeates the texts. Jung believes that if we cannot come to an understanding of what the New Testament means by presenting Jesus as a God-Man, then we are unable to understand anything at all about the New Testament.

But Jung also seems to believe that a full range of texts are "authentic" with regard to Jesus in the following:

---

[41] Jung (1975) 3 November 1952, 87-88.

> ...you exclude too many authentic statements for no other reason
> than that they do not fit in with your premises, for instance,
> predestination and esoterism, which cannot be excluded for textual
> reasons. They cannot be dismissed as mere interpolations. There is
> also incontestable textual evidence for the fact that Jesus foresaw his
> tragic end. Moreover, you exclude practically the whole overwhelm-
> ing amount of eschatology, the authenticity of which is undeniable
> whether it offends our reason or not.[42]

Jung's phrases "textual reasons," "textual evidence," and "undeniable
authenticity" tell us nothing about the criteria he uses to arrive at these
judgments. Perhaps it is simply that these subjects appear as statements
attributed to Jesus. How does Jung know which statements attributed
to Jesus are historically authentic, that is, derive from the historic
Jesus? I do not think that Jung believes the "I am" statements of the
Gospel of John go back to the historical Jesus. As seen above, if we
attribute the Johannine "I am" statements to the personal Jesus then we
come to the conclusion that he was "mad." On the other hand, Jung
also seems to believe that Jesus was identified with the archetypal
image of the Son of Man, or Anthropos, and that his tragic fate reflects
the transformational process this archetypal symbol represents.

Yet, Jung also says, "If Jesus had indeed been nothing but a
great teacher hopelessly mistaken in His messianic expectations, we
should be at a complete loss in understanding His historical effect,
which is so clearly visible in the New Testament."[43] So, even though
Jung does see Jesus under the influence of eschatological literature, it
is not the mere biography that will explain the total phenomena. Jung
finally concludes that,

> What we call "Jesus Christ" is—I am afraid—much less a biographi-
> cal problem than a social, i.e., collective, phenomenon, created by
> the coincidence of an ill-defined yet remarkable personality with a
> highly peculiar *Zeitgeist* that has its own no less remarkable
> psychology.[44]

For Jung the answer to this larger problem is found in the "history and
comparative psychology of symbols," and it is precisely such a
psychological-archetypal understanding of the *Zeitgeist*, the time, that
Jung undertook in *Aion*.

---

[42] Jung (1975) 3 November 1952, 88.

[43] Jung (1975) 3 November 1952, 89.

[44] Jung (1975) 3 November 1952, 90.

Sinclair wrote back to Jung and challenged him to write his own book about his personal Jesus. In his explanation as to why he cannot write such a book we get as much of a glimpse as we ever get of Jung's personal feeling about the actual Jesus:

> *I have a certain picture of a personal Jesus.* It has been dimly suggested to me through certain New Testament data. Yet the strongest impression came to me from the Linceul de Turin, the Saint Suaire [the Shroud of Turin]. Its stern and august countenance has confirmed my formerly vague expectations. I am, as a matter of fact, so profoundly impressed by the superiority of this extraordinary personality that I would not dare to reconstruct its psychology. I am not at all sure that my mental capacity would be up to such a task. That is why I must personally refrain from a biographical attempt.[45]

Here is an interesting problem. It appears that Jung is accepting the myth of the Shroud of Turin as if it were historic. That is, that this shroud with the image of a man on it, apparently the corpse of a man who had been crucified, was the original burial shroud used by Joseph of Arimathea to wrap the body of Jesus. It states in a footnote to this letter that "in Catholic tradition, the image of Christ's face and body was sweated out and imprinted on the shroud." This note also states that "Jung kept a copy of the face in his study, behind a curtain." The myth-history problem of the Shroud is compounded by the fairly recent dating of it to the middle ages. Whether or not Jung's critical reason has deserted him in relation to the Shroud is beside the point, although that is how it seems to me. It is not unlike thinking that, at last!, we have a "photograph" of Jesus of Nazareth, and he looks just like what I thought he would look like. I wonder if Jung would say, even if he thought the Shroud was art, or the impression of some other historic figure, that, at any rate, this is how I think Jesus should look. Whatever the case, the fact that Jung kept a copy of the face, concealed behind a curtain, in his office should tell us a great deal about Jung's veneration of the historic person of Jesus of Nazareth.

Jung's attitude toward the problem of history in general, and in relation to Jesus in particular, becomes clearer when he suggests to Sinclair that he has already written everything he can and could write about the "*documentary phenomenon of Christ* and its psychological reconstruction." He goes on to say,

---

[45] Jung (1975) 24 November 1952.

People mostly don't understand my empirical standpoint: I am dealing with psychic phenomena and I am not at all concerned with the naive and, as a rule, unanswerable question whether a thing is historically, i.e., concretely, true or not. It is enough that it has been said and believed. Probably most history is made from opinions, the motives of which are factually quite questionable; that is, the psyche is a factor in history as powerful as it is unknown.[46]

I understand Jung here as saying that the question of whether we can ever know what happened in the past is, in the final analysis, undecidable. I also hear him saying that history as the real past is created by the will and ideas of the people of the past, and that the motives of the agents of history can never be "photographed"—the role of the psyche in history is both central and finally unknowable in that the specific motives of the people of the past can never be determined. But what we can do is interpret the repository of psychic phenomena, and it seems Jung believes that his work with the symbolic expressions of the psyche are as close to history as we can expect to get.

In another letter, Jung makes what is again a brief and general hint that adds to the "stern and august" qualities he associates with Jesus when he says, "I am quite in sympathy with a much darker and harsher image of the man Jesus" than the dogmatic and traditional view of Christ.[47] While these final qualities Jung sees in Jesus are generalities and do not tell us much about Jesus, they contrast sharply with the conventional Christian image of a light, sinless, all-loving, caring, spiritual Jesus. How much do these anti-Christian qualities Jung sees in Jesus reflect Jung himself? Is Jung only seeing himself reflected in Jesus, or is he seeing more? And where on the prosaic-ideal continuum would I place Jung's image(s) of the historic Jesus?

Summary of Jung's Images of Jesus

Jung presents several contradictory images of the historic Jesus. One image is not unlike Albert Schweitzer's failed eschatological visionary. Another is the youthful, irresponsible, wandering, philosophical tramp who has little, if anything, to say to people living in twentieth-century Europe and North America. Jung also continued to

---

[46]Jung (1975) 24 November 1952, 97.
[47]Jung (1975) 17 February 1954, 156.

see Jesus as a man seized by the archetypal image of the Son of Man, or Anthropos, who lives out his tragic life with little insight into his own fate. Then again, Jung can see Jesus as the Gnostic initiate who gathers up the wisdom of the ancient near east, teaching a morality of counter-tradition consciousness that gets him into trouble and executed. And a more psychological view is that, because of his illegitimate birth, he suffers an inferiority complex for which his spiritual "kingship" is a compensation. On the other hand, he struggles with his "power devil" and is conscious, to some extent, of his shadow. By and large these are prosaic images of Jesus. And they are perhaps pushed in this direction by Jung's own strong and angry criticism of Christianity. As a psychologist Jung is very familiar with the rough and imperfect reality of human nature and he expresses these characteristics naturally and realistically. It is Jung's psychological-archetypal realism, applied to Jesus, that fleshes out his prosaic humanness.

Jung is not interested in the historic Jesus for his own sake. In Jung's view the "historical" Jesus equates to the rationally explained Jesus, and this is a poor, if not totally inadequate way to understand both the man Jesus and the Christian phenomenon of the mythological Christ. And this perspective did not change in Jung from age 23 until his death at 86. For Jung, any understanding of the man Jesus must include both "Personality No. 1 and Personality No. 2." Jesus was a remarkable person who was fated to suffer at the hands of God, or in Jung's language, suffer the struggle with the overwhelming archetypal dynamics of the Son of Man. It seems that for Jung the image of Christ's suffering reflects some real, similar suffering of the historic Jesus. But to say this is to say no more than that, as a prototype of individuation, Christ and his suffering reflects the suffering of anyone who suffers their own individuation. In the idea of individuation, myth and history meet existentially and in individual consciousness. And in Jung's view, self-realization is a form of incarnation.

Jung's image of Jesus has an ideal aspect, but I believe it is a prosaic ideal. Throughout all these images the one consistent ideal is that Jesus lived his own unique life to the full. Jung does believe that Jesus fulfilled the destiny of his own unique individuality, risked his particular life completely, and whether consciously or unconsciously does not seem to matter. According to Jung, this is the ideal way of living one's own life and Jesus can be a model of this if he is going to model anything. Jung's view is that "[Christ] took himself with exemplary seriousness and lived his life to the bitter end, regardless of human convention and in opposition to his own lawful tradition, as the worst heretic in the eyes of the Jews and a madman in the eyes of his family."[48] For the contemporary Western person who is no longer unconsciously contained in the Christian myth, Jung believes that the *conscious* fulfillment of one's own individuation is the modern meaning of continuing incarnation. As Jung puts it, "in every feature Christ's life is a prototype of individuation and hence cannot be imitated: *one can only live one's own life totally in the same way with all the consequences this entails.*"[49]

John Dominic Crossan's Images of Jesus

The vast majority of Crossan's work, in contrast to Jung's focus on the same traditions, is systematically concerned with "the historical Jesus" in clear distinction from "the confessional Christ."[50] For Crossan, the confessional Christ is both the heavenly Christ and Lord of dogmatic Christianity and the Jesus Christ figure presented in both canonical and extracanonical gospels. In *In Parables* Crossan draws the distinction in terms of the difference between the form and content of Jesus' words, as determined by his use of the criteria of dissimilarity and literary analysis, and the "usage of the primitive church" found in the gospels. For Crossan, the gospel traditions as we have them, are creative interpretations by early Christians of the significance of Jesus. In this regard the gospels are distortions of the original Jesus of Nazareth. It is as if, in looking at Jesus through the gospels, we are looking down through the surface of a body of water—Jesus is at the bottom, but badly distorted by refraction. Crossan believes that historical critical methods can counter and correct the refraction and restore the original image. Crossan views the refracting process as the result of a natural and inevitable hermeneutic process that expresses itself in terms of "mythology," with which he equates "ideology, theology, or propaganda."[51] In terms of my distinction between the

---

[48]Jung (1975) 3 July 1952, 76.

[49]Jung (1975) 3 July 1952, 77.

[50]Crossan (1994) xi.

[51]Crossan (1994) 4.

prosaic and the ideal, Crossan's own conception of the difference between the historical Jesus and the confessional Christ would, in theory, place the historical Jesus clearly, and without ambiguity, in the prosaic. Keeping this distinction between the prosaic and ideal in mind, I will examine the images of Jesus in *In Parables*, *Raid on the Articulate* and *The Historical Jesus* in turn.

The Image of Jesus in *In Parables: The Challenge of the Historical Jesus*

In *In Parables* Crossan overtly equates the term "historical Jesus" with the language of Jesus. In this context the term "Jesus" equates to Crossan's "reconstructed parabolic complex." Crossan also establishes an identity between Jesus' experience of God and the experience engendered by the parable in the hearer. Therefore, hearing and experiencing the parable is equivalent to experiencing the immediate presence of God as Crossan believes Jesus knew God.[52] It follows then, that in *In Parables*, the language Crossan uses to describe the parables and their effect is also a description of Jesus and his effect, or at least his intent.

In his demonstration of the criteria of dissimilarity early in the book he uses the scene where the Pharisees request a sign from Jesus (Mk 8:11–12; Lk 11:29–32; Mt 12:38–41). The Pharisees seek a sign from heaven to test Jesus. And Jesus' response is reported in verse 12 as, "And he sighed deeply in his spirit, and said, "Why does this generation seek a sign? Truly, I say to you, no sign shall be given to this generation." Crossan determines that the Markan version is original to Jesus, and describes Jesus' words as an "absolute and unconditional denial of the request," as well as a "radical" and "sworn" denial of the request for a sign.[53] Crossan establishes Jesus' attitude toward traditional Jewish interests in signs, and similar early Christian interests, in extreme terms: absolute, radical, unconditional, and denial. This sets the tone for how Crossan understands the equation of God and parable in Jesus' message as "permanent eschatology": "the per-

---

[52]Crossan (1973) 22.

[53]Crossan (1973) 6.

manent presence of God as the one who *challenges* world and *shatters* its complacency repeatedly."[54] This interpretive perspective is existential in that "world" is not the physical world, but the world of society and tradition.

In this book Jesus and God emerge as iconoclastic and anarchic figures. God's radical presence in the parables of Jesus functions to "shatter" and "reverse" our conventional expectations about our past and our future. The shattering of conventional assumptions is to lead to action or response, but the nature of this action and response is never spelled out, and as we will see, this is intentional.

Crossan establishes linkages between the parables, the kingdom of God, eschatology and time. For Crossan, Jesus told the parables in order to convey an immediate experience of the kingdom of God. The kingdom of God, in Crossan's approach, is so intertwined with the idea of eschatology, and therefore the problem of time, that he develops an understanding of Jesus' view of time based on the parables. Crossan does this by first defining time, not as linear, measured, chronological time, but in terms of the concept of "authentic and primordial time" derived from Heidegger.

Crossan says that "human time and human history arise from response to Being which comes always out of the unexpected and the unforeseen, which destroys one's planned projections of a *future* by asserting in its place the *advent* of Being.[55] In Crossan's view "God" and "Being" are synonyms for that which is "permanent eschatology." Therefore, for Crossan, the parables do not describe, nor derive from, Jesus' history or historical situation. They are not timeless truths, nor are they examples illustrating another teaching. For Crossan, the parables of Jesus "express and...contain the temporality of Jesus' experience of God; they proclaim and they establish the historicity of Jesus' response to the Kingdom."[56] This view depends on redefining the conventional linear view of time as "past-present-future," to a view of time as the "ontological simultaneity of three modes in advent-reversal-action."[57] The advent is the presence of God that shatters and reverses the conventional view of both world and self-understanding that is constituted by our personal and collective memory of the past

---

[54]Crossan (1973) 26; italics added.

[55]Crossan (1973) 31.

[56]Crossan (1973) 32.

[57]Crossan (1973) 31.

and our goals for the future. This advent and reversal leads to action-response as the present, the historical moment. For Crossan, the parables are not what got Jesus executed, but they express the "ontological ground" from which Jesus spoke and acted in ways that led to his crucifixion. Echoing Heidegger, Crossan says, "Parable is the house of God."[58] Crossan's view of the parables gives expression to his core image of the historical Jesus.

Crossan views Jesus' fundamental critique of the various religious options available to his contemporaries not in terms of the Law, but as a critique of an "idolatry of time." Crossan puts it as follows,

> The one who plans, projects, and programs a future, even and especially if one covers the denial of finitude by calling it God's future disclosed or disclosable to oneself, is in idolatry against the sovereign freedom of God's advent to create one's time and establish one's historicity. This is the central challenge of Jesus. ... It is the view of time as man's future that Jesus opposed in the name of time as God's present, not as eternity beyond us but as advent within us. Jesus simply took the third commandment seriously: keep time holy![59]

Jesus' understanding of the threefold temporal nature of the kingdom is, according to Crossan, "its *advent* as gift of God, its *reversal* of the recipient's world, and its empowering to life and *action*."[60]

The advent of the kingdom is described in terms of "surprise," "gift," and "graciousness," as the inevitable and unpredictable nature of life itself, but whose agent is always God.[61] These terms however remain more formal than specific and it is not clear what they mean in relation to concrete lives in specific historical and social situations. It appears that Crossan believes Jesus intends to leave proscription of any kind out of the picture when he says that Jesus' parables seek "to help others into their own experience of the Kingdom and to draw from that experience their own way of life."[62] In other words, in this view, the

---

[58] Crossan (1973) 32, 33. Heidegger's phrase is "Language is the house of being," found in his essay "Letter on Humanism" (1977) 193 (Frank A. Capuzzi & J. Glenn Gray, Trans.).

[59] Crossan (1973) 35.

[60] Crossan (1973) 36.

[61] Crossan (1973) 50-51.

[62] Crossan (1973) 52.

experience of the kingdom and the resulting way of life is highly individual, and by implication, anarchistic.

Crossan continues in this direction when he links the form of Jesus' parables and proverbs to the structure of paradox. He says that if "the original intention of the historical Jesus toward his own milieu" was to shatter its world, to shatter its tacit assumptions about the meaning of time and life and God's purposes, then "his language is sharpened necessarily into paradox, for paradox is to language as eschaton is to world." And Crossan adds, "Paradox is the form of eschaton." In Crossan's eyes, Jesus is the one who "announces God as the shatterer of world, as the one of permanent eschatology...."[63] Paradox, as literary structure, is one way, according to Crossan, that Jesus makes God present to others.

Although Crossan examines many parables, I want to refer to only one because it occupies a significant paradigmatic position, and it is the same parable Jung finds so significant, the Unjust Steward. Found at Luke 16:1-12, it is cited in full at page 273 above. Crossan views verse 8a as an unnecessary addition because the mere telling of the steward's shrewd actions in the parable's context is commendation enough. It, and the other verses that follow it, are later attempts to deal with the blunt and shocking moral offense of verses 1-7.

In Crossan's understanding, metaphor and paradox are never explained by the original creator. They are simply asserted because it is the experience they engender that is important. It is the literary critic who explains the poem, never the poet. It is the biblical commentator who explains the parable, never the parable teller, and Crossan is self-conscious of this paradox when he wonders aloud "what the maker of parables must think of the maker of comments."[64] The relationship Crossan establishes between Jesus and parable is like the relationship between comedian and joke. The hearer either gets it (and laughs) or does not get it. It cannot be explained. So with the parables. You either get it, and respond, and are thereby in the kingdom, or you do not. And if you do "get it" you are left to your own devices as to what to do about it.

With the parable of the Unjust Steward the shattering Crossan refers to is stark and abrupt. The "good" model in this story is a deceptive, dishonest, cheat who does not even mend his ways on being

---

[63] Crossan (1973) 76.

[64] Crossan (1973) xv.

caught. In fact, the very deceptiveness that got him in trouble in the first place is being highlighted. The moral Crossan draws from this is that

> like a wise and prudent servant calculating what he must do in the critical reckoning to which his master summons him, one must be ready and willing to respond in life and action to the eschatological advent of God. But, unfortunately, the eschatological advent of God will always be precisely that for which wise and prudent readiness is impossible because it shatters also our wisdom and our prudence.[65]

In another context, but in a similar vein, Crossan also states, "God also shatters our understanding of graciousness and that is the most difficult of all to accept."[66]

According to Crossan, Jesus' purpose is to challenge those around him, through the parables, with an "absolute" call to life and action within the kingdom, and an equally absolute lack of specified detail about what that life and action should be.[67] This Jesus of the parables Crossan presents is an interesting iconoclastic absolutist. It is as if Jesus has become, in Crossan's interpretation, an iconoclastic principle devoid of flesh and blood and human feeling. Certainly Crossan does not intend to present a complete image of Jesus, but nevertheless, the image given is of a Jesus going around smashing core values and identity seemingly without any awareness or care about what happens afterwards.

I realize Crossan's focus in this book is on the original literary form and content of Jesus' parables and so his attention to this literary theme is limited, as well as his attention to the person of Jesus. Still, he claims to be uncovering the original voice of the historic Jesus. And while his focus is on the paradoxical structure of the parable itself as the eschatological advent of God, he offers no exploration of what kind of life events count as the eschatological advent of God, nor does he explore the psychological and social ramifications for the person who is the object of God's shattering activity. Without this dimension of specific human actuality and application the historical Jesus of linguistic paradox remains disturbingly abstract, and therefore ideal and theo-

---

[65]Crossan (1973) 119-20.

[66]Crossan (1973) 115.

[67]Crossan (1973) 83.

logical. The prosaic potential of this image of Jesus, that I believe has genuine and rich possibilities, is never realized.

What kind of human experience does the language of "radical and absolute shattering" refer to? It is one thing to use it meta-phorically in a literary and theological analysis, but psychologically this is the language of overwhelming trauma. For example, would Crossan accept an equation between "God is permanent eschatology" and "God is a trauma"?[68] Would Crossan find in the robbery, the rape, the devastating fire or flood, the speeding drunk driver who kills a child, the "gracious gift of God's advent"?

Mogenson, a Jungian psychologist, defines trauma as "an event which transcends our capacity to experience it. Compared to the finite nature of the traumatized soul, the traumatic event seems infinite, all-powerful, and wholly other."[69] The traumatic events of violence that shatter our world once, or continue chronically, may become, and "may be God images if, like God, they create us in their image, after their likeness."[70] For example, the shell-shocked soldier relives the trau-matic event compulsively without ever integrating it. The abused child becomes an abusing adult. It is interesting to note that Crossan never uses the world "violence" in relation to God's shattering of our worlds. And neither is Jesus, or his intent, characterized as violent, even thought the word "shatter" is used constantly.

The general picture of Jesus in this book is of a teacher who presents a difficult and challenging truth about God as "permanent eschatology," as the shatterer of our conventions and the gift of new life. However, the image of Jesus as person tends more toward the ideal than the prosaic. I believe this is the case because the entire discussion of the historical Jesus seems to be controlled by a back-ground theology that remains suspended above ground in literary and theological abstractions. Crossan states that the paradoxical "feature of Jesus' language will reappear later restated as that of the Christ: the proclaimer of God in paradox will be proclaimed as the Paradox of God."[71] This statement sounds like a reasonable historical perspective in relation to Crossan's claim to have uncovered Jesus' original para-doxical parables. But, in fact, Crossan, as a twentieth-century Christ-

---

[68]This is the title of Mogenson's book that I draw from in what follows.

[69]Mogenson (1989) 1-2.

[70]Mogenson (1989) 8.

[71]Crossan (1973) 78.

ian, begins with the theological Christ as Paradox of God, and reads back into the parables of the historical Jesus an existential interpretation of this particular theological Christ. (And this is what we have seen Jung do too. He interprets the Christ as a symbol of individuation, an existential and psychological interpretation, and then suggests that Jesus also lived out his own individuation process.)

Crossan's descriptions of Jesus in this book seem exaggerated and verge on the hyperbolic. The kingdom and God seem to stand, in Crossan's depiction of Jesus' teaching, in absolute contradiction to convention and tradition. There does not seem to be any ambiguity about Jesus' own person, nor any ambiguity in his relationships with others, with society or his own religious tradition. Jesus appears to be completely free of any social and historical constraints and limitations. And while Crossan's Jesus here is a human Jesus in contrast to a "confessional" or heavenly Christ, the depiction of his teaching remains generally one-sided and unproblematic, and therefore idealized.

Comparing Crossan's depiction of Jesus' teaching with Jung's view of the psyche points to other interesting possibilities. Structurally, Crossan's literary and theological descriptions of the function of Jesus' parables share a striking phenomenological similarity with Jung's view of the psyche and its dialectic relationship between conscious and unconscious that parallels Crossan's view of the relationship between God and human. One function of the unconscious, in Jung's view, is to compensate the one-sided and limited nature of consciousness. Dreams often help in this process, offering images that can expand the conscious viewpoint. This work involves becoming conscious of the shadow, and this has a "shattering" effect on the persona, when we understand the persona as that aspect of identity that is constituted by the tacit assumptions of society and tradition, or what Crossan calls, world. In other words, the unconscious itself, dreams, and the shadow, can be seen to have a function that is phenomenologically similar to what Crossan describes as the eschatological permanence of God. Careful attention to, and interpretation of, dreams and projections, among other manifestations of the unconscious (i.e., God), can be experienced as God's advent, the subsequent reversal of our idea of our past, thereby leading to the integration of new meaning in our life, often experienced as "new" life. This phenomenological and structural similarity between Jung's idea of individuation and Crossan's view of

Jesus' idea of the kingdom through the parables can be taken in either of two ways. One, as secondary support for Crossan's view of Jesus by locating Jesus in a particular spiritual tradition that teaches this way of personal transformation, or two, as evidence that a contemporary existential view of life is being retrojected back onto Jesus. In this later case, I would see Crossan as more under the influence of Bultmann's existential interpretation of Heidegger than he lets on.

The Image of Jesus in *Raid on the Articulate: Comic Eschatology in Jesus and Borges*

In *Raid* we find an intensification of Jesus as the iconoclast, but now he is an ironic comic. In this book language itself has become everything for Crossan. World and language, play and language, consciousness and language, are identical. "Forms of language and genres of communication are the iron girders of world and their parody is always eschatological in its full implications."[72] Jesus, through satire, irony, hyperbole and comedy, subverts the hardened and absolutized traditions of Jewish law and wisdom. The goal, or ideal, for Jesus, according to Crossan, appears to be a kind of ironic detachment from world. Crossan says, "There is nothing wrong with making a whole of one's existence as long as one does it in conscious knowledge that world is our supreme play and that we encounter the Holy in its eschatology."[73] For Crossan, now that reality equals language, it is paradox that confesses "our awareness that we are making it all up within the supreme game of language. Paradox is language laughing at itself."[74] Does this mean that for Crossan God only manifests in the shattering end of what we have built, and not in the process of building as well?

In *In Parables* Crossan said he was not interested in "the psychological self-consciousness or even theological self-understanding of Jesus," but that he was interested in the parables, the language, of Jesus.[75] Now, in *Raid*, Crossan feels there is little, if any, distinction,

---

[72]Crossan (1976) 55.

[73]Crossan (1976) 73.

[74]Crossan (1976) 93.

[75]Crossan (1973) xiii.

and that he is "inclined to equate consciousness and language."[76] Crossan finds in his reconstructed language of Jesus the essence of the historic Jesus of Nazareth, and through his understanding of language Crossan seems to imply that he makes direct contact with the intent of the original Jesus of Nazareth, and the God of Jesus. Crossan states, "I find it much more plausible that Jesus knew and spoke from out the comic irony which dictates that only *in* language is language conquered, only *by* language is language humbled, and only *from* language is language transcended."[77] Crossan gives great weight to language itself, but I find this presentation of language in relation to Jesus to be too abstract and overbearing. The person of Jesus diminishes behind the "paradox of language."

Crossan also argues for the language of Jesus, that is, his reconstructed parables and sayings of Jesus, being the everlasting essence of Jesus that transcends the local and particular historic Jesus of Nazareth. An important part of this argument is theological. He is arguing against the traditional spatial Christian metaphysics that posits the personality of Jesus continuing on in a literal heaven somewhere. Crossan cannot accept this theological view and so he locates the "persona" (read essence) of Jesus in language.[78] Language is here taking the place of traditional theological and metaphysical constructs. The significance of the historic person of Jesus of Nazareth shrinks in comparison to the value invested in "his" language by Crossan. Of course, this makes the interpretation of Jesus more important that Jesus himself, which is the direction of my own position, and implied by Crossan's 1983 article, "The Hermeneutical Jesus." But Crossan, as noted in Chapter Two, has landed himself in an epistemological contradiction, because he claims that his historical reconstruction of the language of Jesus *is in fact* the original language of Jesus.

I do have some sympathy for Crossan's view of language and the comic, but I cannot follow him all the way in his linguistic ontology, and I do not think it makes any historical sense whatsoever to impute a postmodern ironic sensibility to Jesus. Certainly Jesus used language to convey his own view of life, and even if this included

---

[76]Crossan (1976) 178.
[77]Crossan (1976) 179.
[78]Crossan (1976) 178.

radical challenges to the religious and social conventions of his contemporaries, the idea that Jesus had a meta-self-consciousness about language itself is highly doubtful. This is a modern literary and philosophical consciousness *we* are saddled with. While Jesus the radical comedian, the sardonic and joyful comic and satirist, is a wonderfully prosaic image of the man, Crossan's preoccupation with modern literary and philosophical perspectives on language forces this image of Jesus to slip its historic moorings in first-century Palestine. I find the prosaic possibilities of this image of Jesus eroding under Crossan's tendency to idealize his image of Jesus.

The Image of Jesus in *The Historical Jesus: The Life of a Mediterranean Jewish Peasant*

In this book Crossan presents Jesus as a "peasant Jewish Cynic"[79] who operates as a magician-healer and a social revolutionary (but not a political revolutionary). Crossan portrays Jesus as a man whose "ecstatic vision and social program sought to rebuild a society upward from its grass roots but on principles of religious and economic egalitarianism...."[80] Crossan carefully defines these images of Jesus with his methodological interweaving of sociological, historical and textual vectors. In contrast to his linguistic and literary Jesus in *In Parables* and *Raid*, the Jesus who emerges in *The Historical Jesus* is a sociological Jesus. Overall, it is Crossan's use of sociological categories that defines the social and religious situation in first-century Palestine and Jesus' role in that situation. In general, this situation is defined in terms of a conflict between different social orders of power. The hierarchical and oppressive structures of official social and religious power are seen in conflict with the free and creative individual, and the social movement that derives from this individual, who is in direct contact with the transcendental power of the divine. While the categories have changed in Crossan's work, from literary to sociological, the structural dynamics remain the same—just as paradox and irony subvert the conventional and assumed worlds of meaning in the sayings of Jesus, Jesus as egalitarian magician subverts the entrenched power of the prevailing social institutions of culture and religion.

---

[79]Crossan (1991) 421.
[80]Crossan (1991) xii.

For Crossan, Jesus is a peasant who comes from the lower classes, and is himself one of the "nobodies" in the Mediterranean world, that, we should remember, is Crossan's Mediterranean world that he constructs with sociological models. As a peasant nobody, Jesus knows firsthand the oppression and inferior status that haunts this social class. But we never find Crossan imagining how Jesus himself might have personally suffered this oppression and inferiority. Jesus appears, in Crossan's depiction, to have simply transcended absolutely these conditions, socially and psychologically, because of his own immediate and direct contact with God. In Crossan's eyes, Jesus does not just teach egalitarianism, he simply is able to ignore all social distinctions in practice.[81] Does Crossan mean to imply that Jesus transcends all of the constraints of his particular social location absolutely? I am certain he would never claim this, but this is the impression. For me, while the language of sociology, like the language of history, has a certain realism to it that appeals to my modern consciousness, I find this image of Jesus leaning far more toward the ideal than the prosaic end of the spectrum.

Crossan views the egalitarian and subversive practice of Jesus taking place in terms of very specific behavioral themes. Jesus' behavior as a "magician," his inclusive "open commensality," and his chosen itinerancy, are the basic images for Crossan's definition of Jesus' social presence. I will comment on each in turn.

Crossan chose the word "magician" to characterize Jesus' healing power and activity quite intentionally. For him it is equivalent to other terms such as "thaumaturge, miracle worker, charismatic, holy one"[82] and shaman. The "magician" is the individual who has personal and direct access to "transcendental power" and who can make this power present immediately and directly to others. This individual and autonomous function of the magician stands in strong social contrast to the officially approved and controlled forms of communal symbol and ritual. This is the basis of the distinction Crossan draws between magic and religion. Religion is socially approved and corporate access to divine power. Magic is unsanctioned, individual and direct access to divine power, and as such, is characterized by Crossan as deviant and

---

[81]Crossan (1991) xii.

[82]Crossan (1991) 138.

threatening to the official religious forms. For Crossan, the idea that magic, like myth, is specious and false, is the point of view of official religion—"Our religion is true. You dabble in magic and myth." Crossan makes clear that both magic and religion have quackery and deception as well as authentic depth and meaning. But still, the major contrast between them is one of conflict. For Crossan, "magic is to religion as banditry is to politics," and "magic, simply, is what any socioreligious ascendancy calls its deviant shadow."[83] Crossan also points out that even in antiquity, the word magic was used to discredit unapproved miracle workers who operated outside officially sanctioned practices. Jesus as magician, by which Crossan means miracle worker as healer and exorcist, and not as one having power over nature or the dead, makes present the radical religious egalitarianism central to Crossan's image of Jesus.

The word "egalitarian" functions for Crossan as the central definition of Jesus' understanding of the kingdom. This means that God's presence is unmediated and unbrokered, available equally to anyone, thereby making the official social and religious institutions that mediate access to power and God irrelevant. For Crossan, it is the radical egalitarianism of Jesus' view of the kingdom of God that makes his vision, practice and movement so dangerously subversive to the hierarchical power and privilege of the Mediterranean world.

Part of the function of "Jesus as magician" is also to subvert and challenge contemporary traditional Christian piety. Crossan takes a dig at Christian theologians who make great efforts to describe Jesus as a miracle worker, but not a magician, and then struggle to define any real differences between the two. For Crossan this illustrates another instance where there is an "ideological need to protect religion and its miracles from magic and its effects."[84] Certainly this image of Jesus as magician is critical of the traditional modes of religion in his own historic setting as well as contemporary traditional Christian images of Jesus, but is it prosaic? It is prosaic to the extent that it places Jesus in a real and concrete cross-cultural and trans-historical spiritual tradition that can be described quite well phenomenologically and has many practitioners. But as a sociological type it is by definition ideal, and because of the way he presents this ideal, I find Crossan's treatment of Jesus as magician curiously lacking. He never directs any significant

---

[83]Crossan (1991) 309.

[84]Crossan (1991) 305.

attention to the problem of the real effect of direct contact with transcendent power on the person of Jesus.

In his chapter on Jesus as magician, "Magic and Meal,"[85] there is
no indication that direct contact with transcendental power was at all
problematic for Jesus himself. Because the whole discussion remains
primarily at the level of sociology and social forces, and so maintains a
level of abstraction and thus idealization, the complex, ambiguous and
difficult problems that accompany individual unmediated experience of
the divine are completely overlooked. There is only one quotation Crossan uses in his earlier chapter, "Magician and Prophet,"[86] where he
introduces the holy man type in the context of Judaism, that refers in
general to the personal psychological dangers of being a magician.
Crossan cites Gildas Hamel as saying that the deeds of holy men, their
"prayers and miracles, had the particularity of being 'out of season,' or
at least outside of the prescribed way of relating to God. They even
displayed the hubris towards God (or the Gods) by accepting the
danger to their life, or *sanity*, of an immediate relationship with the
divine powers...."[87] But it is never suggested by Crossan that Jesus
might have had any such problem or struggle with his own sanity.

In the light of the problem of sanity and God contact it is interesting to see how Crossan handles one of the very few instances in the
gospels that opens the door to at least speculate about Jesus' suffering
under some psychological difficulties. It is found at Mark 3:19b-21:

> Then he [Jesus] went home; and the crowd came together again, so
> that they could not even eat. And when his family heard it, they went
> out to seize him, for people were saying, "he is beside himself."

Crossan refers to this passage in passing by simply asserting that it is
an "intercalation" deriving from Mark's "very severe criticism of the
family of Jesus."[88] The literary context of this passage in Mark is
obviously very important, but whether or not this perception of Jesus
was created by the author of Mark is not so easily decided. This image
of Jesus being "beside himself" stands alone without apology or
defense. If it is only an intercalation, or a misperception on the part of

---

[85]Chapter 13, 303-32.

[86]Chapter 8, 137-167.

[87]Crossan (1991) 137-38; italics added.

[88]Crossan (1991) 299.

those near Jesus, then we do not have to deal with it. But whatever its ultimate textual status, it is an image of Jesus that can lead to varied critical prosaic interpretations of the person of Jesus. Was Jesus healing and/or speaking in some kind of trance state, and therefore literally out of his mind? Is Jesus' unbalanced emotional intensity given to fits and outbursts that seem dangerous, or that really are dangerous? Perhaps Jesus is prone to archetypal (I could say psychotic) seizures, of which this is a typical example, and for which the polarized terms sane and insane are too simplistic, yet nevertheless places him in a frightening, to himself and others, borderline condition. Of course none of this is decidable, but it points to what I mean by imaging a prosaic Jesus in contrast to the ideal. Such imagining also makes Jesus and his situation more real by portraying its ambiguity and complexity. Crossan dismisses this text too easily.

The passage that immediately follows in Mark is obviously very important and bears a relationship to the statement that Jesus is beside himself. In verses 3:22-30 we find the Beelzebul controversy in which religious officials from Jerusalem accuse Jesus of being able to cast out demons because he is possessed by the prince of demons, Beelzebul. In Mark the implication is that Jesus casts out demons by the Holy Spirit, and in Matthew Jesus is found stating that it is by the "Spirit of God" (Mt 12:28). My point is that whatever it is called, Spirit of God, Holy Spirit, or Beelzebul, this archetypal divine power dwarfs the ego on a scale not unlike the sun to the earth. What happens to the limited human ego when it comes in direct contact with such an awesome power? Does it experience states of "being beside itself"? Jung helps us understand the psychological danger because of the clinical and phenomenological overlap between inflation and psychosis.

I can imagine Crossan saying that Jesus' degree of sanity or insanity is not the point, and that in itself it is finally undecidable. What seems to be exclusively important to Crossan is Jesus' message and the social implications of God's presence as radical social egalitarianism. It could be claimed that these matters exist with some degree of independence from Jesus' personality and psychology. However, Crossan's own insistence on integrating Jesus' message and Jesus' practice means to me that other aspects of his personality cannot be bracketed, and I would claim that personality and practice are integrally related. If Crossan is to remain consistent methodologically he cannot exclude Jesus' psychology because what he omits explicitly will return implicitly in unrealistic and idealized terms.

This is the reason I claim it is necessary to include Jesus' personality in the creation of the myth of the historical Jesus, and why the prosaic dimension of this creation should not be overwhelmed by the ideal. I agree that Jesus' mental status is completely undecidable, but I believe it is as vital to think about and imagine the psychology of Jesus as it is to do the same for his message and practice, which is equally undecidable. Jesus' psychology, message and practice are not discrete entities. The psychological-archetypal issue, the ontological issue, is that the image of Jesus bears a significant relationship to our self-image, that is, our self-image in relation to the divine and the world. This is because, for those of us in the Christian West today, Jesus has been identified with the divine Christ of Christian tradition for two-thousand years of our being. And our being, as we should understand from Jung and his idea of the collective unconscious, is indefinite in extent in space and time. Jesus Christ has been the archetypal image of life itself for two-thousand years. Human beings are life itself, and the core depth of human being, human identity, that is expressed in the symbol of Jesus Christ, is two-thousand years deep for those of us who inherit this Christian tradition. The image of Jesus Christ is historically implicated in our self-understanding and self-consciousness. The aspects of this image that we do not envision and imagine consciously remain unconsciously entwined in both historical and childhood memories that will continue to influence our contemporary and adult world in inadequate and inappropriate ways. Because a significant aspect of our ontological self-understanding is symbolized by the realism particular to historical and psychological discourse, I suggest that it is only by imagining a fully realistic (prosaic) historical and psychological Jesus that we can serve continuing incarnation. This theme of the unconscious influence of the image of Jesus Christ on our social and individual identities will be examined more closely in chapter six when I explore the value of the differentiation of consciousness for both God and world.

Crossan is convinced that Jesus had a mission, and its literal and symbolic modes involved "open commensality" and wandering from home to home without a fixed home oneself, and without a traveling bag. Open commensality places the shared meal at the heart of the egalitarian kingdom. Those traveling, including Jesus, are "healed healers," and visit individual homes (not towns and cities as such), bringing a "miracle and a Kingdom" and receiving lodging and meal in return. For Crossan, this is "the heart of the original Jesus movement, a shared egalitarianism of spiritual and material resources."[89]

The itinerant nature of the mission is to prevent any locale from becoming famous as a broker mediating the kingdom. And the prohibition against carrying a bag, presumably for food and provision, while wandering, which Crossan believes derives from Jesus himself, is to guard against self-sufficiency, and thereby maintain a mutual openness and dependency that is commensality. For Jesus,

> commensality was...a strategy for building or rebuilding peasant community on radically different principles from those of honor and shame, patronage and clientage. It was based on an egalitarian sharing of spiritual and material power at the most grass-roots level. For that reason, dress and equipment appearance was just as important as house and table response.[90]

Crossan gives only a positive interpretation to Jesus' itinerancy. Other interpretive options are possible. Psychologically, Jesus' wandering could be interpreted as a basic instability, as well as the inability to make long term commitments to people or place. Recall too Jung's comment on the "wandering philosophical tramp" who has little or nothing to teach those of us who must live in a fixed place with job, family, etc. On the other hand, as a modern symbol it could lend religious significance to our increasingly mobile and transient culture. Not only has the United States, since Jung's time, become more and more of a mobile and transient culture, but the growing global economy is increasingly encouraging a kind of world itinerancy. At any rate, itinerancy is an ambiguous theme or symbol, but Crossan, with historic conviction, justifies it with a univocal ideological, sociological and theological meaning that belies its more complex, and finally undecidable significance.

The only other place where we get a hint that Crossan's Jesus is a struggling and limited human being, who may have had to contend with greater than usual emotional intensity, which, according to Jung, is often one of the costs of being close to God, is in Crossan's view of Jesus' relationship to the Jerusalem Temple. Citing Jonathan Smith, Crossan first establishes that "Temple and Magician were one of the

---

[89]Crossan (1991) 341.
[90]Crossan (1991) 344.

characteristic antinomies of Late Antique religious life."[91] In brief, temple-focused religion, with its fixed sacred space and rites, was in decline throughout the ancient world, and the magician, or divine man, was a kind of mobile "entrepreneur" of the sacred. In Jesus' wandering, magical and egalitarian commensality, his going to the people rather than the people going to him, Crossan sees the perfect antithesis to the Temple and its singular control of religious tradition and practice. Crossan states that it does not "matter...what Jesus thought, said, or did about the Temple, he was its functional opponent, alternative, and substitute...."[92]

Nevertheless, Crossan goes on to examine the textual traditions that portray Jesus' sayings and actions against the Temple. He comes to the conclusion that Jesus did indeed make statements and take an action against the Jerusalem Temple during Passover that could have led to his execution. Crossan characterizes Jesus' actual relationship to the physical Temple building this way:

> I think it quite possible that Jesus went to Jerusalem only once and that the spiritual and economic egalitarianism he preached in Galilee exploded in indignation at the Temple as the seat and symbol of all that was nonegalitarian, patronal, and even oppressive on both the religious and the political level. His symbolic destruction simply actualized what he had already said in his teaching, effected in his healings, and realized in his mission of open commensality.[93]

Here Jesus explodes with powerful emotion. We see a Jesus who is youthful, spirited, idealistic and maybe naive. Could this be an image of Jesus breaking down, "losing it" ('beside himself'), under fierce social and emotional pressures? Could this be a hot headed reaction showing a serious lack of judgment? These are prosaic possibilities. But Crossan's symbolic interpretation seems to fully justify Jesus' action, and his depiction does not include any personal complexity or ambiguity in Jesus himself. In fact, the situation is idealized in terms of Jesus the "good guy" and the Temple as the "bad guy."

Throughout *The Historical Jesus* this is one of the recurring limitations of the use of sociological types to describe Jesus and his sit-

---

[91]Crossan (1991) 355.

[92]Crossan (1991) 355.

[93]Crossan (1991) 360.

uation. Good and evil are simplistically polarized by ideal social types. Crossan acknowledges some awareness of this problem indirectly, although he is not talking about the problem of good and evil, when he says "comparative anthropology should never obscure discrete historicity, but neither should particular traditions and situations obscure human constancies and continuities."[94] Ideal types will always obliterate discrete historicity that, in my view, is only realistic when it includes human ambiguity, or, what Bernstein called "side-shadowing." Crossan never addresses the idealizing tendency of typology as a serious problem.

The particular paragraph about Jesus and the Temple is paradigmatic of the problem I have with the whole book, and for me it also illustrates Jung's frustration with the merely historical biographies of Jesus. First Crossan believes he has sufficient historic epistemo-logical warrants to accept the Temple statements and action as historic in some way if not exactly as recorded in the gospels. He then explains the motivation for this central event in the life of Jesus in only psychological and sociological terms. I am not against the use of psycho-logical and sociological realism in trying to understand the historical Jesus, and I must admit that one person's "realism" can be another's poison. But in Crossan's hands, the sociological explanations not only have their inevitable idealizing tendency, but they also reflect a certain reductive and materialistic outlook because social categories remain the final explanatory category. The "God" of Jesus, though supposedly very real, very present and active, remains curiously abstract, and somehow outside of Jesus' personality.

What is profoundly unsatisfying to me in Crossan's image of Jesus is the absence of any personal struggle on Jesus' part with the transcendental power he was in contact with. Without speculation about this dimension of Jesus, it is the suffering and inner struggle of Jesus, so prominent in the Christian depiction of the Christ, that is completely missing from Crossan's Jesus-image.

Perhaps Crossan does not want to speculate about Jesus' personality because he believes there are no epistemological warrants for doing so, while he does believe there is such evidence for deriving the social and historical situation of Jesus. If this is Crossan's position, and I do not think it is far-fetched to assume it could be, it parallels the split he maintains between traditional epistemology and hermeneutics,

---

[94]Crossan (1991) 159.

and between the traditional idea of history as factual and the traditional idea of myth as just made-up story. And, Crossan's self-contradiction in this area is extreme because, as we have seen in *Raid*, he joyfully proclaims that all of reality is made up by us with language. If Crossan was consistent with his own premise that reality is made up by us with language then he would need to acknowledge that historical criticism is just another language game and does not establish "facts" independently of its own assumptions.

My point is that the "epistemological warrants" for historical and psychological interpretation of, and speculation about, Jesus are exactly the same. Just as we can never know the psychology of Jesus and our psychological interpretations will be mythic, so we can never know the original historic Jesus of Nazareth and our historical interpretations will be mythic. I can agree with Crossan that some of the epistemological warrants for interpreting Jesus are created by bringing together history, cross-cultural studies and the texts of the Jesus traditions, but I do not mean it in the same positivist way Crossan seems to. The difference is that the basis of the epistemological warrants for such "knowledge" is not positivistic but hermeneutic. From the philosophical and psychological perspectives elaborated up to this point, what counts for "knowledge" is fundamentally interpretive, no matter how elaborate the methodology used to create it. All our "facts" are mythic constructions, created as they are by plots of meaning. It is "faith" that creates history—faith in a plot of meaning, faith in the historical *sinngebild*, that creates the "facts" of history.[95]

Summary of Crossan's Images of Jesus

Crossan presents two overlapping images of the historical Jesus. The first is the literary Jesus, who, brilliant and witty with language, shocks his hearers into the kingdom with paradox and irony. The second is the sociological Jesus of magic and meal, on a mission of spreading egalitarian, open commensality among the rural poor of

---

[95]Published during the writing of this book, John Miller's (1997) *Jesus at Thirty: A Psychological and Historical Portrait* (Minneapolis: Fortress) is an important contribution to bringing psychological models to the study of the historical Jesus. He does not, however, address the mythic nature of these constructions.

Galilee. In both cases Jesus is seen as challenging and attacking the hierarchical and oppressive powers of the world. The literary Jesus does not give any clues about how one is to live the new way of life he is presenting, while the egalitarian Jesus is much more specific about social practice.

Overall, I find Crossan's Jesus alternating between the prosaic and the ideal. In principle, a socially located Jesus should be quite prosaic. Jesus the "peasant Jewish Cynic" is located quite specifically and prosaically in contrast to traditional Christian images of the Christ, even though each of these three types are ideals inviting the imagination to deepen their specificity. But in Crossan's methodological practice the ideal types of sociological construction tend to predominate. And, I believe, an ideal theological type also unwittingly intrudes. I am intrigued by many aspects of Crossan's Jesus, but find myself finally unsatisfied. However, I believe the method Crossan employs and his image of Jesus holds the potential from which alternate realistic and complex images of Jesus can be created.

The other way in which Crossan's Jesus is more ideal than prosaic is that Crossan never offers any criticism of Jesus' message or mission. I get the impression that the message and mission of Jesus that Crossan believes goes back to the historic Jesus is self-evidently the highest ideal for how to be in the world. In fact, Crossan is brave enough to publish an imagined dialogue between himself and the Jesus of *The Historical Jesus*, in which Jesus criticizes him:

> "I've read your book, Dominic, and it's quite good. So now you're ready to live by my vision and join me in my program?"
>
> "I don't think I have the courage, Jesus, but I did describe it quite well, didn't I, and the method was especially good, wasn't it?"
>
> "Thank you, Dominic, for not falsifying the message to suit your own incapacity. That at least is something."
>
> "Is it enough, Jesus?"
>
> "No, Dominic, it is not."[96]

Apart from the self-serving quality of this little dialogue—in which Crossan is implying, "I did not create a Jesus in my own image because this Jesus makes me uncomfortable and disturbs my own com-

---

[96]Crossan (1994) xiv. The dialogue originally appeared in The Christian Century (1991 December 18-25) 1204.

placency"—there are other problems. The Jesus of this dialogue leaves Crossan with the message that he does not measure up to Jesus' expectation that Crossan join his program—Crossan ends up being inferior to this "Jesus," not an equal. If equality is the message of the radical sociological "Jesus" of *The Historical Jesus*, I can imagine that the ironic "Jesus" of Crossan's *In Parables* and *Raid* might make him truly uncomfortable. That "Jesus" might say something like, "Dominic, your writing and scholarship are good enough. Why don't you get a cup of coffee and relax." Would this be more "egalitarian"?

The other significant problem that haunts Crossan's image of Jesus and that pervades his overall methodology is the subtle onto-logical priority he gives to history over myth. Crossan seems to find in the historical fact something more real and more substantial than what he finds in story, which is made up by us and contaminated with ideology and propaganda. Somehow, for Crossan, the scientific histori-cal fact is untainted by ideology.

I find evidence for this subtle uneven valuation of history over myth in the following. At the end of *The Historical Jesus* in the Epilogue Crossan states that there always have been and always will be multiple Jesuses and multiple Christs, and that they exist together in a dialectic. He argues that "the structure of a Christianity will always be: *this is how we see Jesus-then as Christ-now*," and he states that this dialectic is at the heart of tradition and canon. The sequence of the italicized words is significant—the historical Jesus is first and the theological Christ is second, as if the historical Jesus is the primary phenomena and the theological Christ is secondary and derivative.

In defense of his method Crossan states that his method assumes there will always be multiple Jesuses, in contrast to the nineteenth century's dream of "uncommitted, objective, dispassionate historical study," and that this nineteenth century dream was a "methodological screen to cover various forms of social power and imperialistic con-trol." In other words, Crossan's method is supposedly untainted by ideology. He then says that his own method "presumes that there will always be divergent historical Jesuses, [and] that there will always be divergent Christs *built* upon them."[97] I emphasize the word "built" because its use suggests Crossan's implicit bias for the priority of

---

[97] Crossan (1991) 423; italics added.

history. Does this mean that for Crossan the historical Jesus is primary and the theological Christ is secondary and derivative? Does this derive from Crossan's view that stories are made up while facts are apparently "discovered?"

However, the situation is much more complex and best characterized by the structure of the hermeneutic circle and projection. History and myth are each primary and influence each other. Myth is necessary in order to create the facts and facts are necessary to embody the myth. Every historical Jesus is already informed by the Christ as the archetype of the self, and the story of Jesus gives shape to the self as the image of Christ. I would be much happier with Crossan's dialectic if he would say that divergent Jesuses and divergent Christs build upon, or reinterpret, each other.

I also find this subtle tendency toward the priority of the reality of history in his use of the word "reconstruction." Certainly the word "construction" is a typical metaphor in relation to ideas and theories and models, etc. But Crossan's use of it, in contrast to a word like "reinterpretation," leaves me with the impression he is pounding nails and building something more substantial than a mere reinterpretation. It is interesting to me that we would probably not tend to say that we are "reconstructing" an archetypal image, such as reconstructing the mythical Christ (in spite of the above reference to the "built" Christ). We tend to use the word "reinterpret" in relation to archetypal images and theological ideas. But we do say we are reconstructing, rather than reinterpreting, the historical Jesus. If we talked about the *idea* of the historical Jesus it would be more appropriate to speak of reinterpretation, rather than reconstruction, of an idea. But Crossan never talks about the historical Jesus as an *idea* although this is certainly implicated in his admission of multiple Jesuses. In the word "reconstruction" are the not-so-faint echoes of the imperial tyranny of positivism that has not yet completely faded away from our collective psyche.

In my estimation, one of the great values of Crossan's books and methods is that they demonstrate ways to think critically and closely about the problem of Jesus, and they reveal the kind of work and effort that goes into interpreting Jesus. Crossan shows us how a fertile imagination is indispensable to depicting the possible realities of Jesus' historical situation. And Crossan is an exemplary model of thinking closely and critically about the literary structures and problems of the texts.

Conclusion

Why does the image of the historical Jesus matter and what effect does the image of Jesus have on the psyche? In my view these questions are central and decisive because in Western Christian civilization the image of Jesus is always connected, consciously or unconsciously, and mostly unconsciously, to the archetype of the self through the symbol of the Christ. Jesus and the Christ are an ontological and archetypal unity and, Jesus-Christ as an archetypal image constitutes the psyche of the Christian West. Analytical thinking can separate them for discussion, but in reality they are not separable. Therefore, the image of the historical Jesus we have will have a bearing on our personal relationship to the self, conscious and unconscious. In the image of Jesus we cannot help implicating the image of the ego-self relationship and the history-myth relationship.

The contemporary quests for the historical Jesus that do not address the problem of a fully complex, ambiguous and imperfect, by which I mean realistic, picture of Jesus struggling with himself and a god, leave themselves open to being undermined by unconscious Christ images. Ignoring the fundamental ambiguity of Jesus' personality, activity and his historic situation, leaves uncriticized some still idealized aspects of the Christ to implicitly authorize the image of Jesus presented. The quest for the historical Jesus will always have a christological agenda—either for some christ or against some christ. Denying the christological agenda simply allows it to remain an unconscious ideology.

Another reason the image of Jesus is important is because the image of Jesus always implies a story. The power of story comes from the structure of narrative. And the structure of narrative is itself the image of the archetype of the self. The structure of narrative creates coherence, consistency and completeness with its beginning, middle and end. All the parts of the narrative are related to the whole and all the parts are interrelated to each other through their relationship to the whole. Narrative, in terms of its archetypal structure, is a god-image. For this reason our image of Jesus and its story are basic to our self-understanding and our way of being with each other and in the world.

The image of Jesus as the reflection at the bottom of a deep well is a source of self-understanding when we realize that the process of projection moves in two directions and at multiple levels. There is the projection of our personal subjectivity into the image of Jesus, and then there is the projection of the self from the other side, which is why we work on the image of Jesus in the first place. The image of Jesus can also reveal this deep-subjectivity, which is also the *Zeitgeist* of our own aion, or the god of our own era. Examining the image of Jesus in the light of both historical criticism and a phenomenology of images can make us more aware of the tension between the historical time of Jesus and our own historical time, as narrative images that are both "outside" of us and "inside" of us. As archetypal images they both transcend our consciousness and shape our consciousness; and in turn, our consciousness also shapes these historical images of Jesus. Even as we try to better understand Jesus in relation to his own time and place we are creating this image of him in terms of our own historical self-understanding that remains in large measure opaque to us. When we grasp that our concepts of projection and the hermeneutic circle affirm in a positive way our fundamental unconsciousness of ourself, we must accept the basic tension and ambiguity between our images of the past and our images of the present and realize that together they contribute to a deepening understanding of both self and world.

CHAPTER SIX

THE MYTH OF THE HISTORICAL JESUS

Review of Major Themes

In this chapter I will suggest an integration of historical criticism and analytical psychology that will make sense of the otherwise conventionally contradictory, and therefore meaningless phrase, "the myth of the historical Jesus." However, before moving to the possibility of reframing historical criticism in a new myth of meaning I will summarize the ground covered thus far.

The phrase "the myth of the historical Jesus" is meant to unsettle the traditional and popular associations to the words "myth" and "history." I understand the conventional sense of myth and history as follows. The term "myth" tends mostly to mean false and illusion, or at best it means "just a story." Likewise, "history" connotes objective truth, real facts and empirical data. Hovering about the idea of history is the aura of science and its rational armory used in the war of critical Reason against dogma, superstition, myth and mere subjectivity—a war against relativism. In short, this conventional state of affairs pits "soft story" against "hard facts," and "hard facts" always wins the contest about which is more real, reliable and certain. It is my contention that this bias about reality is a deeply ingrained historic and cultural perspective more or less shared by most of us in Western societies. (Is it this *war* of Reason against the relativism of subjectivity that echoes in Crossan's choice of military terms—"campaign, strategy, tactics"—to characterize his triple triadic epistemological method?)

The thrust of this work has been to revise the positivist Cartesian understanding of myth and history in the light of critical historiography and a phenomenological reading of Jung with illumination from Heidegger, as my response to the methodological crisis in historical Jesus studies. In chapter one I introduced the methodological crisis of historical Jesus studies in terms of what some scholars identify as a "bewildering," "confused," "hopeless" and "embarrassing" prodigal proliferation of images of the historical Jesus. Both historical critical methodology and the scholar's hermeneutic bias are identified as being at the root of the problem.

In identifying the multiple images of Jesus as an "academic embarrassment," and citing methodology and scholarly subjectivity as the twin culprits, the implication is that an academic discipline like historical studies "should" be able to yield better results. As I read this situation, the implied result would be one depiction of Jesus of Nazareth that is historically accurate, objective and agreed upon by enough scholars so as to secure the integrity of the discipline, and the validity, and therefore authority(?), of the Jesus-image. However, framing the problem of multiple Jesus-images in terms of a conflict between historical critical methodology and the scholar's subjectivity also indicates that the problem is being conceived of in traditional epistemological terms that rely on the Cartesian traditions of positivism that overvalue rationality and facts and view subjectivity with suspicion. This epistemological tradition believes that in general, rational, "scientific" methods can overcome and eliminate bias, point of view, prejudice, etc., from the methods and results of research and investigation. It is my contention, regardless of explicit assertions to the contrary by historical Jesus scholars, that the so-called Third Quest for the historical Jesus is bogged down in subtle and unwitting assumptions deriving from the legacy of historical positivism, and the deeper ontological problems of Cartesian metaphysics. The deeper ontological problem is that the problem of knowledge became the central problem for philosophy because of an implicit and absolute split between subject and object (person and world).

Reality was divided into two incommensurate substances, mind and matter, and the conundrum of how mind could know matter or how matter could influence mind was conceived. Because of this gulf, epistemology was preoccupied with establishing rational foundations that could secure final and certain knowledge of the world and of human beings that would transcend the relativism of historical and cultural particularism. In my view it is the ghost of positivism, still lingering around the concept of "history" and its methods and viewing subjectivity in general as "mere subjectivity,"—as "*only* one's own reflection at the bottom of a deep well"—that is at the heart of the methodological crisis of historical criticism.

My proposed solution to the methodological crisis in historical Jesus studies is to suggest a conceptual alternative to our conventional notions of history and subjectivity in the light of contemporary historiographical, hermeneutical and depth-psychological theories of the ontological nature of the historical and the self, and finally to view history as myth. And within the perspective of the *myth* of the historical Jesus I propose that, among other things, one possibility for the tool of historical criticism in conjunction with a phenomenological analytical psychology is to participate in the differentiation and evolution of consciousness understood as a mode of incarnation.

In chapter two I undertake a close examination of Crossan's overall method specifically in relation to the quest for the historical Jesus. First I review the historical context of the quest in which Crossan participates as a part of the so-called Third Quest. While many Third Quest scholars are critical of nineteenth-century historical positivism and its assumptions about history, I believe Cartesian assumptions about reality still subtly and unconsciously influence their idea of history. The Third Quest uses new methods and tools but is still influenced by some positivist views. From my perspective, the real source of the methodological crisis in historical Jesus studies is that new buildings are being constructed while the three-hundred-year-old-only-partially-inspected foundations continue to crumble.

I began my close reading of Crossan's method with his work *The Historical Jesus*. The method he explicitly mounts in this work is largely in response to the "academic embarrassment" at the multiplicity of Jesus images in biblical scholarship. I maintain that the very way in which he introduces and then structures the epistemological criteria for determining the voice and actions of Jesus implies a reliance on a positivist understanding of historical reality. I also claim that the very word "reconstruction" in large measure hangs on positivist assumptions about the past.

Crossan's hierarchy of chronological stratigraphy and attestation for the sources, texts and complexes of the Jesus tradition attempt to establish, if not definitively at least suggestively, the "hard facts" about the historic Jesus. A close reading of this method not only reveals its unwarranted assumptions, but also the pervasive and decisive presence of Crossan's own scholarly judgment (read, subjectivity) at every point. I raise the question as to whether or not Crossan's own hermeneutical bias is either deliberately hidden, or merely unwittingly obscured, by the impressive and persuasive rhetoric of his method.

My reading of Crossan's method in *In Parables* and *Raid* leads me to believe Crossan is not trying to deceive the reader with any rhetorical or epistemological sleight of hand, but that he really believes in the traditional epistemological validity of historical critical methods with regard to recapturing the past and the original Jesus. In both *In Parables* and *Raid* I find a methodology deeply split between traditional historical critical "positivism," used with confidence to determine the voice and intent of the original Jesus of Nazareth, and postmodern literary, hermeneutic and linguistic perspectives to interpret this determination of "hard facts."

Crossan is by no means a naive positivist, and he is one of the more creative and innovative interpreters of the Jesus tradition. He claims to know that history is reconstruction and interpretation rather than objective certainty, and asserts that faith can only be based on interpretation and not facts. But he continues to oppose faith and fact, theology and history, autobiography and methodology, as if these can be neatly and discretely separated. In spite of himself, his brilliant literary analyses and interpretations, his hermeneutic sophistication and his genuine desire for an open and honest dialectic between history and faith, Crossan, in my view, in the final analysis, gives the ontological nod to history over myth, to fact over interpretation, and preserves the ontological problematic of these traditional Enlightenment polarities.

Crossan devoted all of his methodological attention in *The Historical Jesus* to the problematics of the Jesus traditions. Of notable interest was that he treated history in general as if it were completely unproblematic. Because of both this omission as well as the positivist assumptions guiding his method in general I next explored in chapter three the contributions from critical historiographers.

The discussion among critical historiographers reveals that the struggle between positivism and hermeneutic perspectives has received explicit attention for several decades in the general field of historical studies. Also of note is that while the hermeneutic and subjective dimensions of historiography have been noticed and acknowledged by many historians, this awareness has had a varied impact on the practice and writing of history. Some historians still write calmly and securely about the past as if they were reporting actual events.

Philosophers of history looking at the process of historiography note that unwarranted presuppositions of objective certainty and the stability of facts still influence history writing in large measure. But what is in fact revealed by critical historiography is that narrative, plot and *Sinngebild* (or, what I call myth and deep-subjectivity) are the thought structures that form the discourse called history. It is these thought structures that give rise to and shape the "facts." Historical "facts" are in fact constituted by a faith in an *a priori* narrative that gives the facts their shape and meaning—in this sense positivism itself is a kind of "narrative."

There is a significant and unclosable gap between the tremendous complexity and density of real life and the written record called history. History as discourse and memory is never what actually happened—it is a written account of how something was remembered, and therefore includes a significant dimension of subjectivity. The confusion about the reality status of history as discourse, the confusion about the nature of the relationship between written history and what actually happened, is due in part to the realism we associate with the narrative structure of historical discourse. In my view, the confusion about the realism of written history is also due in large part to the deeply ingrained assumptions deriving from Cartesian epistemology and metaphysics. In the context of Enlightenment metaphysics the clear and distinct idea that derives from rational thought and measurable quantities (traditional empiricism) is equated with objective historical facts. And the subject-object split assumes that a subject can observe an object without bias and without influencing it.

The critical review of historiography leads to seeing its fundamental hermeneutic and narrative foundation. The past is not an object we can observe. It is an idea we have in the present about the past, and while our idea of the past is in significant measure a product of the influences of history, it is also an idea that is largely determined by the needs and perspectives of the present. History is constantly being rewritten from within history. There is no perspective available outside of history that could provide a final truth of history. History is a river of being and meaning that will never catch up with itself. History is not a static ground of definitive objects. All so-called facts are the creations of the meaningful narratives they serve.

These realizations lead to my contention that Jesus of Nazareth, as a real person who once lived but now no longer exists, is unapproachable by historical critical methods. Obviously it is possible to continue to reinterpret the documents that reveal his one-time presence in history. But this is a reinterpretation of meaning in the present and not a reconstruction of the past. The perspective of the myth of the historical Jesus opens new possibilities for approaching the image of the historical Jesus as *historical image*.

The understanding that historical thinking is only one particular "shape" we can give to time leads me to conceive of history in terms of myth. In this sense "myth" is conceived of as both the structure of narrative and the structure of meaning. The structure of narrative and the structure of meaning link-up with deep-subjectivity that, in the light of Jung, we can also understand as archetypal-subjectivity. These overlapping ideas lead me to Jung's thought and the cross fertilization that occurs by reading Jung and Heidegger together as hermeneutic phenomenologists.

The insights of critical historiography anticipate my reading of Jung as more of a psychological hermeneutic phenomenologist than a "scientific" psychologist. This reading seeks to both rescue Jung from being interpreted in the context of traditional Cartesian metaphysics, and to show how he was involved in overcoming the subject-object split of Cartesian epistemology.

My comparison of Jung and Heidegger suggests that the primordial basis of mind is not rationality but fantasy, image and interpretation, through which we are immersed in a world of significance before any rational thought emerges. The mind, or subject, is first constituted by a world, and is at first identical with its world of practices and beliefs, before it is able to observe the world critically as other. Another way of saying this is that we are constituted by already existing narratives that determine our ways of knowing.

The Cartesian ontological split between subject and object, between person and world, that also leads to the ontological split between fact and meaning, and the unwarranted presupposition of the neutral observer, is overcome in Jung's view of *psyche* and Heidegger's view of *Dasein*. As being-in-the-world *Dasein* is primordially constituted by mythic structures that appear as images that are modes of being human. These mythic structures, the archetypes for Jung and existential structures like *understanding* and *meaning* for Heidegger, are not eternal or absolute truths. They are purely formal possibilities that receive specific and changing meaning content throughout history and in different societies. The world of meaning that constitutes psyche is mythic. I draw the conclusion that our *a priori* myths determine our "facts"—that is, in general, our view of reality shapes our knowledge. Rational evaluations are a secondary procedure and cannot determine absolute and transcendent knowledge or truth. In fact, much of knowledge, can be viewed as an ontic, or empirical, manifestation of far larger ontological and archetypal worldviews or *Zeitgeisten*. Both knowledge and worldviews are subject to the transitory transformations of time and place.

I suggest that Jung's archetypal understanding of projection is a structural analogue to Heidegger's ontological view of the hermeneutic circle as the basic existential constitution of *Dasein*. This means that we are not isolated subjects who impose interpretations on a mute world, but that we and the world are an ontological unity, and that the world first imposes itself on us. We grow to self-consciousness gradually through images and interpretations. And just as we are constituted by an unconscious world or myth, the process of becoming conscious is that of a world or myth, becoming conscious.

Jung interprets the Christ story in terms of the process of individuation with the premise that self-realization *is* incarnation. Jung views ego and self as a complex ontological or archetypal unity, and not as two different and separate substances or entities. Jung interprets the idea of "God" in terms of the archetype of the self which is the unconscious, larger and encompassing identity of the person. It is because God and self are overlapping concepts that point to the same fundamentally unknowable being of human being that Jung can say self-realization *is* incarnation.

Heidegger realizes the fundamental unity of being and human being in the structure of *Dasein* as the there-of-being. Borrowing the structure of *Dasein* but not imputing any theology to Heidegger, we might say that the human individual is the there-of-God. I would also suggest that the relationship between history and myth is similarly structured in that history is the there-of-myth. It would be possible then to say that Jesus Christ, in the light of Jung's interpretation, is a projection of this universal structure of human being—Jesus Christ as a symbol of the historical individual as God's "there."

In my view, Jung and Heidegger each present a view of life and human being as fully involved in "given" ontologically hermeneutic worlds. This basic transformation of our self-understanding alters our understanding of the historical object and subject. The subject and object of history is nothing more than human being itself. This perspective supports the view that the quest for the historic Jesus and its historical critical methods can not retrieve the original Jesus of Nazareth. But the process of historical criticism can contribute to the differentiation of consciousness, the continuing withdrawal of the projection of the self from Jesus, for the self-realization of "God" in the individual.

My investigation of the multiple images of Jesus in the work of Jung and Crossan began with the realization that images of Jesus cannot be evaluated for accurate historic correspondence with the actual Jesus. Therefore, different criteria are needed and I suggested a phenomenological approach to the Jesus-image as *image* based on the working criterion of a prosaic-ideal continuum. With this schema the image is evaluated in terms of its impact on the psyche, and whether the image will aid or hinder self-realization. (Another possible direction for this work would be to correlate images of the historical Jesus with psycho-spiritual stages of development.)

Images of Jesus are fundamentally interpretations and projections, and as such are revealing of the personal and collective psyche. While aspects of one's own personal psychology will infuse the image of Jesus, I believe that characteristics of the aion or the *Zeitgeist*, what I consider to be aspects of deep-subjectivity, will also reveal themselves. Since the collective unconscious, or soul, projects itself into what is unknown to us, Jesus is a perfect object for projection. How we see Jesus can reflect characteristics of our own relatedness to ourself, world and God. The discourse of historical and psychological *realism*, in contrast to any attempts at historic accuracy, are necessary components of this imaginal work if the image of Jesus is going to have any relevance for people today.

The specific content of the images of Jesus put forward by Jung and Crossan show an attempt to deepen the psychological and historical realism with which Jesus is imagined. The content of their images is not important in terms of any objective truth about Jesus, but they are helpful to the extent that they foster critical and imaginative reflection about Jesus by others, in the service of self-understanding and world-understanding.

The myth of the historical Jesus opens the possibility of an alternative purpose of historical critical method in relation to the image of Jesus. I will explore this possibility in terms of the integration of projections and the differentiation of consciousness. To this discussion I now turn in the next section.

Projection and Hermeneutic Method

First I will describe the process of the withdrawal of projections in general as outlined by Jung and von Franz. Then I will discuss a possible role for historical critical method in this process.

The idea of "withdrawing projections" is itself problematic because it conjures up the image of taking back inside something we have put outside. This derives from the Cartesian and Freudian perspective that conceives of projection in terms of the subject and object separation. Within a Jungian understanding of projection as an unconscious identity it is more accurate to think in terms of the differentiation of consciousness and the possibility of integrating the unconscious qualities. The spatial metaphor of drawing-in a projection works when we realize that from the perspective of the existential "space," or purview, of consciousness, the unconscious quality is "outside" of its horizon. Therefore, I will speak of integrating or drawing-in those aspects of being that manifest to us as images we call projections. The differentiation of consciousness does not mean only the differentiation (separation) of one's own personal consciousness (ego) from out of the unconscious identity, although this is part of the process, and as we will see, an early stage. The differentiation of consciousness aims to bring the unconscious value and meaning of the projection into one's own personality as conscious self-realization.

The concept of projection as a psychological phenomenon is important because it immediately tells us that there is a personal and moral responsibility in relation to an experience that subjectively feels as if it has nothing to do with me—it is experienced *as if* it is utterly other and objective. The projection of the shadow is a case in point. The enemy is evil and their destruction is fully justified. The projection of the self as profoundly religious images is experienced as even more absolutely objective because it is so completely outside the sphere of personal consciousness. But the idea of projection is a hermeneutic insight that attaches a sense of *mineness* to such experiences.

In general we should distinguish between levels or qualities of projection in terms of the personal and the collective unconscious. Personal projections would in principle be easier to integrate than collective ones. The shadow is more of a personal level projection, although not limited to the personal, and the self is definitely collective, and therefore "farther" from the personal. However, in reality, the psyche is not so neatly delineated. The personal unconscious and the collective unconscious are always intertwined and projections always contain elements of each realm of experience.

A projection is constituted by an unconscious identity that is its ontological ground. Because of Jung's view of the purposeful and compensatory nature of the unconscious in relation to the ego, we also assume that a personal projection has a purpose, guided by the self, in showing up to a particular person at a particular time in their life. Of course, the meaning of the projection is not given in advance. Determining the meaning and purpose is the work of interpretation. Within Jung's understanding of the psyche projections are not arbitrary or accidental. They show up when they do for a reason that is personal and significant. If we are going to accept projection as a hermeneutic tool, we must find the personal component in the projection experience. The hermeneutic turn enabling us to do this can also be described as the psychological shift from "blind literalism to metaphor."[1] Projection as a hermeneutic perspective enables us to make the shift from literal perception to symbolic perception, and experience a conscious emotional connection to the otherness of the world.

Let me repeat that a projection only becomes a projection as such after some disturbance sets in which blocks or challenges the original unconscious, literal perception. Another example will help here. The now-popular notion of the "mid-life crisis" is such a *breakdown* of an unconscious identification with life values and purposes that have contained us and given us innate meaning up to that point. We simply lived the values we developed and accumulated unreflectively during the first part of our life. From our psychological perspective we can refer to this situation as a projection, but for the

---

[1]Brooke (1991) 57.

person living these values they are not a projection until the *breakdown* occurs. The *breakdown* signals the need for a fundamental change in our psychic situation that requires ego reflection, reevaluation and reinterpretation of the very premises of our lives—it pushes us to create a new myth of meaning for ourselves. The term *breakdown* in this context signals an impulse from the self ("God") demanding further and deeper transformation and self-realization through the breaking open of an unconscious projection.

Jung informally identifies five levels in the withdrawal of projections that he associated with cultural and historical development.[2] Marie-Louise von Franz, drawing on Jung, somewhat formalizes Jung's discussion into five stages in the withdrawal of projections.[3] In the following I draw on both Jung and von Franz. Jung refers to an example from Nigeria of a native soldier who heard the voice of an *oji* tree calling to him. He "tried desperately to break out of the barracks and hasten to the tree." The soldier, in attempting to do just this, was caught and questioned. He explained that everyone who carried the name of the tree heard its voice from time to time. At this point Jung describes five levels of the progressive differentiation of consciousness using this example.

The first level is the original, unconscious identity prior to any consciousness, doubt or criticism. In the first stage the soldier, tree and voice are united as an unconscious identity, and the *experience* is literally true as reported.

The second level is the first sense of a separateness, or differentiation, between a subject and an object. At this level the voice and the tree are seen as distinct, and the voice is attributed to a spirit or tree demon. Although this is not yet a modern interpretation, it is a step in the process of differentiation. Jung refers to it as a "higher" level of culture and consciousness in contrast with the primal identity.

The third level is the "moral evaluation" of the specific content of the projection, in this case, the voice. Is it good or evil, and what is my relationship to it? Should I follow it or not? Rather than remaining identified with the voice, now a conscious, moral stance in relation to the voice can be taken. This is a clearer distinction, or differentiation, between subject and object. In this case, the "object" is the experience

---

[2]Jung (1967a) 247–49.
[3]von Franz (1980) 9–11.

of an independent "otherness" that makes an emotional claim on the soldier. Being able to take a critical stance toward the phenomenon and ask questions about its value, differentiates the ego from the unconscious identity. The phenomenon, however, has not yet been turned into a psychic reality with a personal relation to the subject in terms of a psychological metaphor or image. The voice is still a literal "outer" voice, but obedience to it is now a matter of choice rather than compulsion. Another example is that certain ethical standards of Christianity enable people to take a moral stance toward what we might call a projection—"to love an enemy" or "not to commit adultery"—but this situation does not yet enable a psychological, metaphorical interpretation of the content. Individuation as differentiation cannot occur if a tradition remains the unconscious (outer and literal) carrier of moral value and ethical behavior. If a tradition remains the unconscious provider of morality, the individual never has to grow through the struggle and conflict of finding their own moral stance. Another example of the nascent beginnings of this level of differentiation is when the small child starts saying "No" to her or his parents.

The fourth level corresponds to our modern Enlightenment and Freudian consciousness, which denies demons and spirits outright and calls the whole thing an illusion or hallucination, and reduces it psychologically to an unconscious personal motivation. The voice might be interpreted as the desire of the soldier to escape military service. In this case the ontological value of the voice is reduced to insignificance and ignored. This level destroys the original intimate connection between person and world. It is here that the *ontological* split between subject and object occurs, while the process of differentiation in general does not necessitate an ontological separation. The subjective experience of being personally and intimately at one with the world is cut off. We become an isolated subject with inner psychological dynamics and the world becomes a dead and utterly other mechanism without any inherent meaning. In another context, Jung comments on this state of affairs as the "despiritualization of nature."[4] However, it is also true that at this level the ego achieves an independent ontological status all its own that is crucial in the evolution of consciousness. At first the freedom is heady, but later the isolation is devastating. Jung believes that it is only by way of the experience of the death of the original meaningfulness of the world and the radical autonomy and

---

[4]Jung (1968) 54.

isolation of the ego in its identification with rationality that leads to the new interpretation of *psyche* as an objective phenomenon in its own right. This development leads to level five.

At the fifth level, whether or not the reality of spirits is accepted, the phenomenon as such is taken seriously as a psychic reality. While the language used to describe such an experience as "talking trees" is very different if we are speaking literally or psychologically, phenomenologically any distinction on the ontological level is false. If we are going to take the objective reality of the psyche seriously, then trees do talk, but we are going to interpret it and understand it very differently than the Nigerian soldier. Trees do not actually talk, but one's *experience* of the voice is as real as one's experience of the actual tree (perhaps even more "real" than the literal tree because of the emotional and numinous component of the voice). At this level, psychologically and metaphorically the "talking tree" becomes a real conflict of conscience. The moral struggle is intensely personal, and the problem of good and evil may not be clear at all. This is the level of the individual's lone moral choice based on personal moral authority. But it is not the alienated individual of level four. It is one who knows the support of life and the wealth of being. At the fifth level, the unconscious is known to be a real objective actuality, and therefore what is called "spirit" also has to be taken as real. This reality is the reality of our experience, and we must wrestle with it hermeneutically, and find its personal meaning in relation to our world, and not simply obey it or dismiss it.

I will summarize, below, the five levels in the integration of projections provisionally in terms of how I view the ego-other relationship. The "other" stands for the unconscious, or self, and its powerful emotional dynamics. It also stands for the world or object that is experienced as numinous and fascinating. The object in the above example is the *oji* tree, but it can be anything that fascinates us or grips us. In our cultural context the "other" could be an object such as the Bible or an automobile, an idea such as "history," or an image such as Christ or Jesus.

Summary of the Five Levels of Projection

1. Ego–other identity: literal perception and compulsive obedience; emotional claim on ego is complete.

2. Ego in partial outer separation from the other: no moral conflict; uncritical obedience to emotional claim by the other.

3. Ego more separate and struggles with moral evaluation of the emotional claim of the other as outer reality: non-psychological and non-symbolic level.

4. Ego is completely separate from the other and the other is an "it"; ego is identified with rationality and rules supreme; emotional claim of the other is destroyed.

5. Ego and other are differentiated and relativized in relation to each other as well as archetypally (i.e., ontologically) united. The emotional claim of the "other" is taken seriously as a personal responsibility for self-realization. The ego combines symbolic and rational perception into a new complex dialectic. At this level the aspect of *world* illuminated as projection can be integrated into consciousness through the hermeneutic medium of projection as psychological metaphor.

With the fifth level it is possible to *integrate* the projection into one's own personality, thereby transforming its "functioning and effects" and oneself. Von Franz reminds us that the process of integration is a "remarkable and complicated" feature of modern psychology, and far too easy to take for granted. It is hard work requiring a great deal of time. The unconscious content must be "brought repeatedly into the view of the conscious ego and recognized as belonging to its own personality."[5] The process entails considerable emotional and moral effort and patience, because the boundaries and structures of one's own personality are at stake.

It is also important to remember that the withdrawal of all projections is not a goal. In fact, such a goal is impossible, just as it is

---

[5]von Franz (1980) 11.

impossible to get out of the hermeneutic circle. And just as impossible is the withdrawal of all the unconsciousness out of any but the most superficial projections. Something of the unconscious will always adhere to our projections, and our consciousness will always be partial. Interpretation is never ending. This is another way of saying that hermeneutic-psychological perception recognizes the inexhaustible wealth of associations attaching to life experience. Such is the richness of symbolic perception. We need to recognize the hermeneutic fact that all our perception and knowledge always rests on fundamentally unknowable projections. If we accept this condition as our own, then the fundamental attitude of ego-consciousness is altered, and we will be more modest and open toward our feelings, ideas and interpretations.[6] This position means we know there is always more to discover, and that understanding is never final.

Projection enables the self as World, in all its multiple and partial aspects, to light up intimately as a reflection of our own face. Not simply our ego-face, that literal reflection in the literal mirror, but the reflection of our unknown face, the world's circulating desire to enter becoming as our involvement with an ever expanding world of joy, suffering and enchantment.

Imagination is at the heart of projection, and is an important function of archetypal-subjectivity, if it is not the main function of the collective unconscious. As such, it is this deep sense of imagination that plays a central role in creating images of Jesus. Analytical psychology can provide both the appreciation of the ontological value of the unconscious function of imagination and the psychologically critical perspective that can ground imagination existentially and ethically. The idea that all knowledge is dependent on myth and interpretation does not dissolve all interpretations or values into a sea of relativism or nihilism. This is the natural anxiety of a postfoundational world. In my view, postfoundationalism should be a new awareness that while there are no absolute and ultimate foundations, there are still foundations we all rely on—they are just unconscious and temporary, that is, subject to change and transformation. And by "temporary" I do not mean simply local fads and fashions, nor only the shifts from generation to generation. We need to think in terms of scales of being and borrow the larger sense of scale found in modern

---

[6]von Franz (1980) 199.

geology and astronomy. The tectonic plates we build our homes on are temporary, and the starry constellations we navigate by are temporary, but from our personal ontic perspective these "temporary" realities are "permanent." For example, I "know" the earth is both moving through space and rotating on its axis at great speeds, but one would be hard pressed to convince me of this experientially. That is, I "see" the evidence of the earth's movement, but I do not "feel" this movement personally. In the same way I know that the ontological assumptions I rely on are historical and temporary, but as far as I am concerned they are absolutely real, and I base my life on them. Even so such awareness makes possible a critical perspective on any view of reality, and this is crucial for ethical considerations within hermeneutics. Such perspectives of scale help us from being glib when we say, "everything is interpretation." To think that the fundamentally hermeneutic foundation of being leads to complete relativism and nihilism is a form of solipsism and fails to appreciate how the scale of the archetypal unconscious depths dwarfs the ego. The archetypal foundations of being constitute the most unconscious projections, and therefore they are the most difficult to become conscious of if at all. There is an intimation of this level of being in Heidegger's statement "in the circle is hidden a positive possibility of the most primordial kind of knowing."[7] The differentiation of consciousness is a process that leads in this direction, and the historical critical method has a hand in this process. Both historical criticism and analytical psychology can work together to identify the varied narrative and archetypal themes that influence our understanding of history. Hayden White's work in identifying the literary themes of tragedy, comedy, romanticism, etc. in historical writing is the result of applying historical criticism to nineteenth-century historiography.[8] White refers to this process of inquiry as "metahistory," a kind of philosophical historical criticism. In this instance historical criticism differentiates these heretofore unrecognized and unconscious narrative themes and makes them conscious. Such narrative themes are also archetypal themes that condition historical self-understanding.

Our ability to identify archetypal themes in historical writing increases our consciousness about the underlying influences that inform our historical stories that are at first unconscious. One possible example in historical Jesus studies is that archetypal themes associated

---

[7]Heidegger (1962) 195.
[8]White (1978) 41–62.

with Hermes/Mercury can be seen in two contemporary scholar's approaches to Jesus. Both John Meier and Robert Funk, each in a different way, finds in the historical Jesus (which each acknowledges is a construction) a mercurial iconoclast. Funk believes this image describes the actual historic Jesus, and Meier characterizes the "quest for the historical Jesus" itself with this image. Meier admits the real Jesus is fundamentally unattainable, but states that the primary characteristic of the constructed "historical Jesus" is its radical historicality and "refusal to be held fast by any given school of thought."[9] Funk calls the real Jesus a "vagabond king," and states, "The real Jesus escapes now and again from the scriptural and creedal prisons in which we entomb him."[10]

The word "king" as it is used by Funk is not meant in a literal political sense, but rather in a metaphoric or mythological sense, that is, as a term of value, which we would not assert about just any historical person. But the historic fact is that Jesus the person is not an infinitely variable and changeable entity. The historic person of Jesus is limited, particular and incomplete. Informing these contemporary pictures of Jesus is an image that correlates with Hermes. The Hermes of Greek mythology and the Mercury of Roman and alchemical mythology are equivalent. Hermes/Mercury is a boundary crosser, a thief, a paradox, always in motion, a "vagabond king," breaking free of any attempt to encase him in ideology, i.e., mercurial.

Bernie Neville, writing in the *Journal of Analytical Psychology*, suggests that our current postmodern culture is the "manifestation of a specific archetypal image, familiar to us in the myth of Hermes."[11] The postmodern ethos of deconstruction, relativity of values, polytheism and endless change is characteristic of the mythology of Hermes. While the lack of boundaries can lead to great anxiety and nihilism, it also makes room for play, imagination and transformation. Neville suggests our culture is in the "grip of a Hermes inflation," perhaps in counter reaction to our long worshipping of Apollo as a god of light, reason and fact.

Another way in which historical criticism differentiates understanding is in the recognition that "Christos" had many different

---

[9]Meier (1990) 24.
[10]Funk (1993) 5, 9.
[11]Neville (1992) 353.

meanings in the first-century writings we have about Jesus. The term "christ" in Matthew, Mark, Luke, John and elsewhere means something different in each of its contexts. The historic term "christ" in the first-century does not mean the same thing that "Christ" came to mean in the later, unified Christian tradition. Jung's global interpretation of the Christian tradition is flawed because the varied meanings of "christ" in the first-century are not the same as the "Christ" of nineteenth-century Switzerland. Jung's attempt to find meaningful continuity between the beginnings of Christianity and the present has limitations in relation to a more nuanced historical understanding of Christian origins, even though Jung made a real attempt to understand the psyche of other historical epochs.

The idea of "history" is itself an archetypal theme in contrast to metaphysical and religious worldviews. The historical development of non-religious and naturalistic approaches to our understanding of our place in the world, the scientific explanation of the nature of reality and of ourselves in contrast to religious and theological explanations, is part of the emergence of the idea of history as a prominent "shape of time" determining self-understanding. The basic attitude that historical criticism embodies is also what enables us to recognize *history* as *myth*, as only one of the "shapes of time." Historical criticism has both negative and positive value. On the one hand it has the force to destroy unconscious identifications with received meanings through its differentiation of historical particularity, and on the other, it has the power to both reveal the meanings of ancient narratives, as well as the power to create new meaningful narratives today. I will now explore this double nature of historical criticism in relation to the historical image of Jesus.

The Value of Historical Criticism

Over twenty years ago Walter Wink, a New Testament scholar including himself among other voices in the biblical field, declared "Historical biblical criticism is bankrupt."[12] Also over twenty years ago, both Hayden White and Peter Munz referred to the sad and deteriorating state of contemporary historical studies in general. White stated that historiography's need to appear objective and scientific has

---

[12]Wink (1973) 1.

led to the lose of its origins in the literary imagination, its source of strength and renewal.[13] Munz lamented historiography's rejection of the speculative philosophy of history as part of its rightful practice. He believed that its continued rejection would lead to the death of the discipline of history under a growing and meaningless pile of dry and dusty facts.[14] All three, among others,[15] declared in their own ways that academic historical understanding and practice had cut itself off from the profound vital and imaginal depths of myth, by which I also mean deep-subjectivity. This *breakdown* and disturbance in the meaningfulness of historical practice signals the projection of unconscious assumptions that I have discussed throughout this book. The positivist assumptions that have guided, and continue to guide, historiography are suffering a serious disturbance and require a new myth of meaning within which to continue practicing. The old myth that historical criticism was a valued part of—the emancipation of reason from the tyranny of dogma and tradition, the freedom of the individual to think independently and critically, and the establishment of democratic governments, not to mention the achievements of science among other positive developments—is no longer adequate by itself to our cultural and historical situation. We can say seriously that historical criticism is suffering a mid-life crisis. Therefore, historical critical practice requires a new narrative of purpose that will reestablish a meaningful relationship with psyche. In what follows I suggest one possible role for historical criticism in relation to the Jesus traditions.

If the meaning of the Christian texts, and therefore the Christian myth, is moribund in major part because of the rise of historical consciousness and the effects of the historical critical method itself, the solution to this death of meaning, for some, is not to abandon the historical critical approach to the figure of Jesus, but to create alternative myths within which it can operate.

Critical historiographers have in effect turned the historical critical method toward historiography itself and have revealed the hermeneutic foundation under its positivist assumptions. This per-

---

[13]White (1978) 62.

[14]Munz (1977) 246–251.

[15]In 1975 (again, over twenty years ago) the American Academy of Religion published the papers of its Myth Seminar under the title, "Myth and the Crisis of Historical Consciousness." At least three of those brief papers brought Jung, or a Jungian perspective, into the discussion to a limited degree.

spective reveals the fallacy of the goal to achieve accurate historic knowledge of the original Jesus of Nazareth, and affirms the constructive and narrative nature of history in general. This view undermines the unwarranted confidence placed in, and the ontological security sought in, the "hard facts" of history—the myth of history is revealed, that is, the narrative of history is realized.

The value of historical criticism is both negative and positive, and I mean this in terms of the function of historical criticism to both take apart and put together the narratives of history. The function of "criticism" in this context—the word "critical" means "to judge"—is to make judgments about the meaning of historical documents and narratives, and this involves questioning their received meaning. Within the perspective of our understanding of projection, the "received meaning" of a text or narrative (the gospels for example) is usually an unconscious identification with that meaning. To question the received meaning is to disturb the unconscious projection, and this has a negative, or destructive, effect on the person. Historical criticism has disturbed and destroyed the faith of many in the gospels as accurate reports of Jesus' sayings and actions. In part, seeing the narrative structure of history through the judgments of historical criticism is a kind of taking apart, a dismembering and deconstructing of our original assumptions about history in general, or a particular historical narrative. This negative value of historical criticism also has a positive side. At the same time, historical criticism shows us the creative power of narrative, and helps us to realize that each historical epoch has its own type of narrative with terms and meanings particular to it. And it helps us to recognize the wholeness of narrative, that it is a particular whole, that is at the same time, related to narratives that came before it and that will come after it. Historical criticism also differentiates between the narratives of different historical periods, and helps us to realize that each needs to be understood both on its own terms as well as in the light of our contemporary self-understanding. This differentiation attempts to preserve the tension between the distinctiveness of the past as well as its continuity with the present.

In relation to the Jesus texts themselves, my own view at this point is to suggest a phenomenological perspective on the use of historical criticism, in contrast to its function in the context of traditional epistemology. A phenomenological perspective continues the tradition of scientific observation but no longer under the illusion of the neutral, uninvolved observer. In this case, a critical historical criticism, is undertaken by a self-aware observer who knows he or she is an involved and interpreting investigator. The self-aware observer is also aware that they are not alone in creating new meaning. The objective otherness and autonomy of the collective unconscious is a respected partner in the work. Those invisible structures of the psyche, the archetypes, will project themselves spontaneously and continuously throughout the process, and this is the work of imagination.

Crossan provides an example of the careful and painstaking historical critical and literary analysis of the Jesus-texts. His work of transmissional analysis for example, undertaken explicitly in four books, *In Parables, In Fragments, Four Other Gospels,* and *The Cross That Spoke*, does not have to be a true or correct reconstruction of the original historic textual situation nor of Jesus' language in order to have value. However, within the phenomenological context the goal is not to uncover or discover the original voice and actions of Jesus. One of the things the critical procedure does is to deconstruct and dismember the original unity of the received meaning of the Christian narrative. This negative impact of the historical method prepares the way for other narratives to be created in relation to the original Christian narratives. Thus historical criticism helps us see that there never was just one Christian narrative in the first century, but many.

To carry the operation of historical critical dismemberment forward is to disturb the received meaning of the texts, and at first, leaves the texts atomized and stripped of their meaningful context in any narrative. What is left? Naked textual fragments, sayings, parables, etc.—we might call them the dry bones of the image of Jesus. Within a phenomenological context, this analysis makes no assertion or assumption that these remains, or textual bones, derive from the actual historic Jesus. We only know that they derive from textual images and the narrative myths of Jesus. Having destroyed the received narrative meaning, these naked textual bones are at first meaningless in themselves. Stripped of all context they stare back at us blank and mute. They have become abstractions, mere markings on a page. However, this is not only an operation performed on an external text. It is also a critical and destructive operation on the psyche of the critic. While a text is relatively easy to cut up, all that is required is a pair of scissors, the archetypal nature of the narrative structure, the myth, that constitutes the psyche of the critic (that is, anyone) is another matter all together. This is why this process takes years, and why we need to know we are not only working on texts, but deeply on ourselves. The real challenge at this point is to not rush to new meaning, nor to regress to received meaning. To be able to leave these bones lying in the desert of meaninglessness is to tolerate and suffer a kind of atheism toward them and within oneself. This is a state of depression, grief, anger, despair and death. This negative state comes before the fragmented bones can be embodied again in a new myth of meaning, a new narrative. The next step is to recreate new meaning and narrative for these fragments. There are many ways to approach this. I will suggest one.

This procedure for creating a new myth for the bones of Jesus is to allow the psyche's imaginative capacity to project unbidden fantasies and images into the bones. It is to intentionally encourage fantasy without restriction. This is not a function of intellect or conscious thought, but of what Jung called "active imagination." This is a contemplative and meditative process that one tries not to control consciously. One reflectively allows the spontaneous arousal of image and fantasy in relation to the now fragmented and dead texts.

There is a historic precedent for this operation of the imagination in relation to an object—Renaissance alchemy, a field Jung studied in depth. Jung's understanding of the alchemists he studied was that for them matter and its chemical transformations were both an unknown quantity and quality from the perspective of our knowledge of matter today. Into the dark unknown of matter the alchemists projected the natural states, qualities and transformations of the psyche. As Jung states,

> The real nature of matter was unknown to the alchemist: he knew it only in hints. In seeking to explore it he projected the unconscious into the darkness of matter in order to illuminate it. In order to explain the mystery of matter he projected yet another mystery—his own unknown psychic background—into what was to be explained. This procedure was not, of course, intentional; it was an involuntary occurrence.[16]

Many alchemists knew they were not just doing chemical experiments, but also saw that they were involved in a mystic and obscure process of self-transformation. The literal view saw the alchemists attempting the impossible operation of turning lead into gold. Others knew that this gold or philosopher's stone was a spiritual goal and that the real transformation occurred in the alchemist. The

---

[16]Jung (1968a) 345.

operation of the imagination in this case was not simply the alchemist's personal fantasy. Imagination had more to do with the soul and God than with the individual. In the following citations Jung highlights this feature of alchemy.

> The concept of imaginatio is perhaps the most important key to the understanding of the opus. The author of the treatise "De sulphure" speaks of the "imaginative faculty" of the soul.... The soul functions in the body, but has the greater part of its function outside the body (or, we might add by way of explanation, in projection). This peculiarity is divine, since divine wisdom is only partly enclosed in the body of the world: the greater part of it is outside, and it imagines far higher things than the body of the world can conceive. And these things are outside nature: God's own secrets. The soul is an example of this: it too imagines many things of the utmost profundity outside the body, just as God does.

> The soul, says our author, is only partly confined to the body, just as God is only partly enclosed in the body of the world. If we strip this statement of its metaphysics it asserts the psyche is only partly identical with our empirical conscious being; for the rest it is projected and in this state it imagines or realizes those greater things which the body cannot grasp, i.e. cannot bring into reality.

> The imaginatio, as the alchemists understand it, is in truth a key that opens the door to the opus. We now know that [the alchemical work] was a question of representing and realizing those "greater" things which the soul, on God's behalf, imagines creatively and extra naturam—or, to put it in modern language, a question of actualizing those contents of the unconscious which are outside nature, i.e., not a datum of our empirical world, and therefore an a priori of archetypal character.[17]

Bringing the operation of *imaginatio* to the image of the historical Jesus affirms that the historic Jesus is almost as much of an unknown to us as matter was to the alchemists. Because as an historic person he remains fundamentally unknown to us, he can function as a *symbol* or *image* of the ontological unity of human and divine. However, as a broken and fragmented image stripped of its traditional content and meaning, it is a *dark image*, an *obscure symbol,* and as such it is an apt one for projections. What the alchemists did unintentionally, it is possible to do today intentionally with the broken image of the historical Jesus.

---

[17]Jung (1968a) 396, 399, 400.

The alchemists also amplified their work with mythological imagery as part of the operation of *imaginatio*. The process I am proposing also has obvious mythological parallels. The myth of Osiris and Isis was at times used to amplify the alchemist's experience, as was the myth of Christ. The critical analysis of the Jesus-texts, a kind of cutting them up, corresponds to the dismemberment of Osiris by Set (Typhon), as well as the crucifixion of Christ. Isis, who gathers up the scattered pieces for Osiris' regeneration, and Christ's corresponding resurrection, are metaphors for the spontaneous operation of the imagination, the work of self-realization, and the awakening of one's deeper self, through the creation of new Jesus-narratives.[18]

The destruction of the meaning of the texts by criticism may allow heretofore rejected and repressed aspects of psyche, both personal and collective, to attach themselves to the now broken bones, if we, in silent contemplation, allow them to appear spontaneously. Some of these images may be unsavory and shadowy. On principle, no image should be excluded. Whatever imagery appears, an ego is required to interpret and shape it into a new myth of meaning.

At a deeper level, and over time, such work with Jesus may help to integrate the self. Just as the "resurrection" of Osiris is the achievement of "immortal" life, and not the return to mortal existence—he becomes the Lord of the Underworld—the revivification of the bones of Jesus is not the recovery of the historic Jesus, but the discovery of one's own myth, one's own self, one's own "eternal" and "immortal" identity. To this extent does the face reflected at the bottom of the well become the face of the self, one's own self, that is, that which one is meant to be. And the multiple images of Jesus are the positive manifestation of the multiple historical possibilities of the self. There does not need to be any quest for the one true image unless one desires one's own "true" image, but even this image, if it is true to its hermeneutic foundation, will change over time.

The only reason this destructive, creative and imaginative operation with the image of Jesus could have any value at all is because the image of Jesus is inescapably bound up with the archetype of the self in our Western culture. In itself, the historic Jesus can only be a hypothetical thought or image of the actual Jesus as he might have been before any early forms of Christianity. But, it is in practice impossible to have any thought at all about Jesus without the influence of the

---

[18]Jung refers to the Osiris myth many times throughout the Collected Works. For his interpretation of it under the theme of rebirth see (1967) 349–61.

mythic or theological Christ (the archetype of the self) being involved. It is only because of the Christ that we would even think about Jesus at all, and therefore, any thinking about the historic Jesus always has a theological or christological agenda, either explicit or implicit. There are two basic hermeneutic positions—For or Against[19] with a variety of alternatives in between. No matter whether one takes an affirming view of Jesus or a devaluing view of Jesus, it is always going to be in order to support a particular view of life, a theology or philosophy. By and large I would say the arguments, historical, theological, or psychological, are at bottom finally christological. That is, they are attempts to change one image of Jesus, probably the one we grew up with, by proposing or opposing an alternative image of Jesus. The only reason to do this is because of the implicit authority and power the Christ myth gives to any image of Jesus.

The Differentiation of Consciousness

At this point I will explore what the differentiation of consciousness looks like, in part, from a historical perspective. The historical view, as does the view of the five levels in the integration of projections, suggests that the differentiation of consciousness is also a development or evolution of consciousness. I offer the following as a speculative interpretation of the historical shift in our experience of the Bible from a mythological perception to a historical perception, from purely religious and theological understanding to more "naturalistic" perspectives such as the historical. Conventionally, this change is often referred to as a shift from "pre-critical" to "critical," but this fails to do justice to the fact that each era has its own unique critical perspective. Martin, for example, suggests substituting "Symbolic" and "Analytic" for "pre-critical" and "critical," and I will borrow his terms.[20] I will also view this shift in terms of the historical change from Catholicism to Protestantism. To speak of Catholicism and Protestantism in this way I will borrow Jung's informal phenomenological view of Catholicism and Protestantism.

---

[19]Nietzsche (1967) 267.
[20]Martin (1987) 381.

The Symbolic reading of the Bible has been described as the immediate and direct experience of the presence of God. Hans Frei described the Symbolic reading of the Bible as "strongly realistic." The text was read as "...at once literal and historical, and not only doctrinal or edifying. The words and sentences meant what they said, and because they did so they accurately described real events and real truths and were rightly put only in those terms and no others."[21] Harrisville and Sundberg note "the Bible was immediate to the reader, not a distant document. Its influence was intensely felt. At a given moment, any passage or combination of passages, even from widely divergent sources within the scriptures, could disclose God's will." "This sense of the Bible's uncanny presence as literally containing 'heaven on earth' was augmented by premodern notions of the nature of reality."[22]

Within the Symbolic experience, the Bible and revelation share identical ontological status, the word of God and God are one and the same. This is a direct and immediate unconscious identity with a world of myth. In Jung's language, the Bible, as the immediate experience of the reality and presence of God, embodies the self. Within Jung's perspective we would say the Bible is a symbol of the self, or a projection of the self. But for the one who experiences the biblical reality *as* God this is no projection, it is simply *the case*—the Bible is not symbolic, it *is the word of God.* In terms of the levels in the process of withdrawing projections this represents the first level of unconscious subject-object identity. And the text as word of God is to be obeyed as literally and uncritically as the voice of the *oji* tree by the Nigerian soldier. At this point I will not try to trace levels two and three in relation to the Bible, but I imagine they could be traced. With the advent of historical critical consciousness we jump to level four.

Under the influence of historical criticism and the force of the sciences in general, the sacred power of the Bible gradually diminishes and the power of critical rationality increases. As the divine voice grew softer the human voice grew louder, resulting in an inflation of the human with reason. Jung has this to say about such a process:

> the increase in self-knowledge resulting from the withdrawal of impersonal projections—in other words, the integration of the contents of the collective unconscious—exerts a specific influence on the ego-personality. To the extent that the integrated contents are

---

[21]Harrisville (1995) 1.
[22]Harrisville (1995) 14.

parts of the self, we can expect this influence to be considerable. Their assimilation augments not only the area of the field of consciousness but also the importance of the ego, especially when, as usually happens, the ego lacks any critical approach to the unconscious. In that case it is easily overpowered and becomes identical with the contents that have been assimilated.[23]

Although Jung is talking about the individual person here, I am interpreting this as occurring on a cultural and historical level as well. I believe this is what has happened with the rise of historical critical consciousness in relation to the biblical texts and the numinosum of mythic and divine reality (their ultimate ontological value) the texts carried. Historical critical consciousness withdrew the impersonal projection of the sacred power (the self) that the texts embodied. At the level of the withdrawal of these projections as a general cultural development, the whole process is basically unconscious because it is a collective phenomenon. Therefore, there was no individual ego to stand back and take a critical awareness of the reality and nature of the unconscious into account. This allowed another projection to occur.

The sacred power and value (its status as ultimate reality) of the Bible was withdrawn from the texts, and was then projected into history and historical critical consciousness. The heavens and the spirit as the former ultimate reality were replaced by the earth and matter becoming ultimate reality. The human person, as the sole agent of history, became inflated, that is, unconsciously identified, with the power of rationality. History, in opposition to myth and theological dogma, became the location of the ultimate ontological value, the location of what was really real. Interestingly enough, a close look at historiography reveals the phenomenological structures and the ontological values of the Self: unity, coherence, the center, a grand plan, continuity, plot (mythos), and unquestioned, unproblematic, natural, given realism. With the Enlightenment, the ontological pendulum has swung from myth to history, unconsciously, uncritically. We could say that the Enlightenment enjoyed its own "Symbolic" reading of history as the unambiguous presence of the real. Jung describes this state of affairs:

...the more numerous and the more significant the unconscious contents which are assimilated to the ego, the closer the approx-

---

[23] Jung (1951) 43.

imation of the ego to the self, even though this approximation must be a never ending process. This inevitably produces an inflation of the ego, unless a critical line of demarcation is drawn between it and the unconscious figures. But this act of discrimination yields practical results only if it succeeds in fixing reasonable boundaries to the ego and in granting the figures of the unconscious—the self, anima, animus, and shadow—relative autonomy and reality (of a psychic nature) [that is, of an ontological nature].[24]

Jung's last sentence states again what he described as the fifth level in the withdrawal of projections. Perhaps this state represents a more conscious relationship to myth. In other words, the relations between the ego and the unconscious need to achieve a differentiated and critical dialogue in which each side is granted equivalent ontological value in relation to each other. Naturally in practice this is never an ideal process, but often unbalanced, messy and confused. But the aim is to achieve a mutually critical and constructive dialogue. In brief, we see an unquestioned Symbolic experience of myth become an unquestioned Symbolic experience of history, that perhaps now can become an inclusive Symbolic-Analytic experience of myth and history, or what I playfully sometimes think of as "mythistory." A similar shift can be seen in the transition from Catholicism to Protestantism that roughly corresponds to the historical differentiation of consciousness. I will now apply this perspective to an interpretation of Crossan's image of Jesus.

Crossan's Phenomenological Shift to Protestantism

I offer what follows in the spirit of a speculative interpretation that is meant to be suggestive. In *Parables* and *Raid* I detect a movement within Crossan himself toward a modern form of Protestantism. I will discuss this in the light of Jung's view of the modern Protestant's religious dilemma. What do I mean by Crossan's "Protestant" tendencies? I suggest that Crossan's image of Jesus reveals a shift within him, archetypally, from a "Catholic" worldview to a modern "Protestant" worldview. Catholic and Protestant are in quotes because I do not mean any of their specific historical and social manifestations because there are many forms of Catholicism and Protestantism. Borrowing from Jung, I am using the terms phenome-

---

[24]Jung (1951) 44.

nologically to describe in general different ways of being related to the collective unconscious.

Jung defines modern Protestantism in terms of what it has lost in relation to traditional Christianity, i.e., Catholicism: "the mass, confession, the greater part of the liturgy, and the vicarious function of priesthood."[25] Because the dogma and rites, that traditionally provide mediation of and protection from the powerful effects of the collective unconscious, have lost their authority and efficacy, Jung sees that "the Protestant is left to God alone." For Jung the Protestant is "defenseless against God" and has the "unique spiritual opportunity for immediate religious experience."[26]

In this light, I suggest that Crossan's Jesus is the "first Protestant." Crossan says, "Comic eschatology sends us out repeatedly into that chaos where alone we can encounter a God who is not just our own projected vanity."[27] And again Crossan states that Jesus admonishes us "to act wisely, prudently, decisively," but never tells us "what such action means or entails." "Jesus does not specify because such application is our personal fate and our own individual destiny. It will always depend on what treasure it has been given us to find."[28] These citations suggest that Jesus' view of the kingdom, in Crossan's interpretation, points to the same kind of individual, unmediated and unprotected encounter with the unpredictable and uncontrollable reality of God, that Jung sees as the fate and opportunity of the modern Protestant. Crossan's Jesus, the radical and seemingly anarchic iconoclast, shares characteristics with some early radical Protestant groups and their rejection of images. Is Jesus' action against the Temple prophetically "Protestant"?

From Jung's autobiography it is obvious that when he talks about the contemporary Protestant experience of God he knows he is talking about himself. But Crossan in his own eyes is definitely not talking about himself—he is talking about the historical Jesus, and he also believes to some degree, the historic Jesus. Crossan tells us in the Epilogue of *Who Killed Jesus?* that, after he completed high school in Ireland, he spent nearly twenty years in a medieval religious order, the

---

[25]Jung (1940) 33.
[26]Jung (1940) 86.
[27]Crossan (1976) 174.
[28]Crossan (1976) 162.

Servites. Ordained a priest in 1957 he spent his entire priestly career as an academic in the United States.[29] Certainly the theology and religiosity of traditional Catholicism had a profound impact on Crossan, and that he was likewise drawn to it. It would follow that the metaphysical Christ of Catholicism is the psycho-spiritual context within which Crossan began his journey with the image of Jesus.

My own theory about Crossan in this regard is that the meta-physical Christ of Catholicism lost its numinosity under the critical glare of Crossan the intellectual. In Jung's terms we would understand this as the dissolution of the projection of the self. But this process remained unconscious, and the self did not become integrated into Crossan. But it did shift its location to the historic Jesus, the material, earthly Jesus of historical fact (in contrast to the spiritual, heavenly Christ of dogma). Historically, Protestantism itself shifts the authority of the self from its location in the church and dogma of Catholicism, and its singular interpretation of the Christ, to the Bible and the resulting plural interpretations of the texts. For Crossan, as we have seen, language is numinous, and in the combination of the *historic lan-guage* of Jesus, I surmise, Crossan projects and makes contact with, not Jesus, but the self. However, for him this is not a symbolic process involving the self, but Jesus of Nazareth.

Crossan's fascination with digging back through the texts, back through time, to the original words of Jesus, is like a passionate quest for a fragment of the true cross, a material relic. In this we can see that the projection of the Christ has shifted for Crossan from out there in the Catholic metaphysical heavens to down here, on earth, but back there in time, into the actual, real, concrete words of Jesus. As we have noted, the words of Jesus have no special value unless they are imbued with the self, or the Christ. So it is my hypothesis that Crossan's tre-mendous efforts at digging and sorting through the words attributed to Jesus in order to isolate the true words of Jesus is the longing to get close to the concrete incarnation of the self. However, this is still in a state of projection, albeit a Protestant one rather than Catholic.

The whole process of using the historical critical method and literary analysis under the mantle of Cartesian epistemology in order to isolate the original "words" (i.e., voice) of Jesus is to me not unlike someone who is determined to isolate a fragment of the true and pure wheat before it became distorted with the water, egg, yeast and salt in

---

[29]Crossan (1995) 214. For more biographical detail see Forum 1 (1985) 59–61.

the final loaf of bread. So they probe all the way down to a molecule or atom of wheat and feel they now *have* a piece of the *original, pure, undistorted* wheat. However, an atom of wheat, or even a molecule of wheat, is not wheat in any sense at the practical human scale. An atom of wheat is an abstraction, an *idea* (ideal) of pure and undistorted wheat. The only reason to argue otherwise, keeping the analogy with the voice of Jesus, would be because the realty and numinosity of the self is at stake. So it is for the words of Jesus. The true and undistorted words of Jesus can never be isolated or recovered, but because the idea of contact with the pure and undistorted original historic Jesus is so gripping arguments are mounted, and will continue to be mounted, in order to convince ourselves that epistemologically and ontologically, we have *touched* the original Jesus. Is it a bit ironic that for Crossan it seems the brokerless kingdom is being brokered by the historic Jesus?

Directions for Future Research

Are there specific genres appropriate for telling the story of the myth of the historical Jesus that do justice to our contemporary self-understanding? Certainly, contemporary self-understanding is not univocal, and no one genre would be appropriate as multiplicity is the nature of our situation. However, the attempt to combine contemporary "scientific" self-understanding and literary imagination was modeled by Freud himself. James Hillman has noted that Freud's official psychoanalytic writing is actually a hybrid of interpretive literature and medical-scientific discourse. And Freud presented his texts as science, not literature. Freud struggled with the two traditions of the sciences and the humanities when he was writing his case *histories*. His literary style and conventions were more akin to fiction, but he also employed the analytic distance and language of the medical scientist. Freud was inventing a genre that had no precedent. Hillman, who describes this literary invention more fully in his article "The Fiction of Case History: A Round," makes this comment, "[Freud's] psychoanalysis could make no further headway in the world at which he aimed it, medicine, unless it could find a suitable form of "telling" that gave the conviction, if not the substance, of medical empiricism."[30] Hillman

---

[30]Hillman (1975) 126.

notes that when Freud writes a case history he tells us he is describing the "intimate structure of a neurotic disorder."[31] Such medical-scientific language objectifies the most personal emotions and sufferings of a human being, and gives us the illusion we are reading science, when we are really reading Freud's fiction.

Could this be what is happening with Crossan's "fiction"? Is the combination of his elaborate methodology and his own literary style a new genre of "fiction"? What would happen to our general impression of Crossan's methodology in *The Historical Jesus* if the entire work was reframed within a larger work that was a novel? What would happen if he said outright at the beginning of the book, without changing anything else, that this whole work is a "fiction" or a *myth*? Of course, we do not realistically expect Crossan to say any such thing about his research and book, but in another place Crossan does speak of "fictional realism" when he compares parable and gospel. First he states that Jesus' parables are fully realistic about everyday life, but that this "core of realism cannot turn parable into history." He then states,

> The narrative gospel focuses on words and deeds, on teachings and healings, on passion and resurrection. It deals with a person's totality and it does so in a format that looks like biography and history but is actually parable and fiction. Of course it is based on historical facts, both possibilities and actualities, but so also are the parables.

His term "fictional realism" occurs in the following rhetorical question: "Is the basic continuity between historical Jesus and ecclesiastical Christ established not so much in discussions about orthodox and heterodox contents as in the fictional realism with which Jesus spoke in parables and with which they spoke about him as parable itself?"[32] The distinction Crossan draws here between parable and history is, in the light of history as myth, a surface one. Crossan's own historical work on Jesus is also a "fictional realism," his own form of "gospel."

Robert Funk, the founder of the Jesus Seminar and a colleague with whom Crossan has worked closely, states explicitly that all our narratives of self-understanding are fictions and refers directly to telling the story of the historical Jesus. Funk stated, during his opening remarks at the Seminar's first meeting in 1985, that we now recognize

---

[31]Hillman (1975) 128.
[32]Crossan (1985) 186–87.

that all narrative accounts of ourselves, as a nation, as the Western tradition, the history of the world, the Bible, are fictions. He says that while our stories are made out of material that is real enough to us, they are still narrative, and therefore fictional, constructions. Funk is actually using the word "fiction" in a way similar to my use of "myth." We abandon fictions in any field, including the sciences, when "they fail to account for enough of what we take to be real in the everyday course of events." Our fictions are changed "when they no longer match our living experience of things." The present determines the criteria for the *real* because obviously we create our stories about ourselves in the present, and we use contemporary terminology to describe reality.

Funk continues to say that our traditional grand narratives have collapsed, that they are no longer adequate to our modern world view, and speaking to his biblical colleagues, he admits that we are hard pressed to create a new coherent narrative for Jesus of Nazareth. The fiction that has contained Jesus has broken apart. And echoing a now-decades-old theme, he states, "Our stories are eroding, under the acids of historical criticism." His answer to this crisis is to "retell our stories." He proposes the following:

> What we need is a new fiction that takes as its starting point the central event [Jesus] in the Judeo-Christian drama and reconciles that middle with a new story that reaches beyond old beginnings and endings. In sum, we need a new narrative of Jesus, a new gospel, if you will, that places Jesus differently in the grand scheme, the epic story.

> We require a new, liberating fiction, one that squares with the best knowledge we can now accumulate and one that transcends self-serving ideologies. And we need a fiction [about Jesus] that we recognize to be fictive.

In large measure, this perspective agrees with my own, up to this point. But in the next sentence he surprises me with the following, "Satisfactions will come hard. Anti-historicist criticism, now rampant among us, will impugn every *fact* we seek to establish. Every positive attribution will be challenged again and again."[33] He has talked at length about fictions that we know to be fictive, and now suddenly talks about "facts." He does not say "every *fictional* fact we seek to

---

[33]Funk (1985) 11–12; italics added.

create." Because this talk is so brief and obviously a sketch, it is not at all clear how Funk proposes to reconcile his "fictions" with his "historical facts." That the facts about the original Jesus are indeed his aim is made clear in his opening paragraph: "We [the Jesus Seminar] are going to inquire simply, rigorously after the *voice* of Jesus, after what he really said." It is also not at first clear whether the "anti-historicist criticism" is coming from conservative and fundamentalist Christians or radical postmoderns, or both. However, if the "facts" are our modern fiction about the real then why not say so explicitly? It sounds like Funk is himself engaged in an Enlightenment battle against the "anti-historicist" readers of the Bible. In fact, Funk states that part of the program of the Jesus Seminar is to publicly oppose the fundamentalist literal interpretation of the Bible. It seems he himself is engaging a positivist interest in Jesus. Or, when he says "what Jesus *really* said" does he mean that the *real* for *us* is the *fiction of the historically real*? It is not clear whether Funk is an unwitting historical positivist, not narrowly but in intent, or whether he is self-consciously creating a "real" historical fiction. With regard to Funk I will have to leave his ambiguity ambiguous. But I will now return to Crossan.

Regarding my question of the genre appropriate to the task of creating the new fiction/myth of Jesus, has Crossan created such a new fiction in his accumulated work that is both historical critical and fully creative? In a way he has, but rather than call it a fiction at the beginning, he calls it a "reconstruction" at the end. It would seem that Crossan, like Funk, also inhabits a borderline area where it is difficult to determine what he is really doing. But, for myself, the evidence I have seen clearly points to his being a "closet positivist."

With regard to future exploration of new genres appropriate to the problem of the image of Jesus for our time, I would suggest that some experiment with a self-conscious return to a "gospel" form.[34] By this I mean a narrative that is both fully subjectivized and undertaken

---

[34]Three such works I am aware of have been attempted recently. Theissen's (1987) *The Shadow of the Galilean* alternates a narrative style for telling the story of Jesus with scholarly commentary and debate about the "historical facts." Two current works, published recently, reveal the difference between the work of an author who is not informed by historical criticism and one who is. The novelist Norman Mailer's (1997) *The Gospel According to the Son* (NY: Random House), adopts the form of an autobiography by Jesus, and is not informed by historical criticism. James Carse's (1997) *The Gospel of the Beloved Disciple* (HarperSanFrancisco) is based on some current historical critical perspectives and intentionally employs imagination in re-telling the story of Jesus in a self-consciously gospel form.

within our modern discourses of historical and psychological realism but with a different attitude toward the apparatus of "method." The person undertaking such a subjectivized narrative should be aware of the historical critical analysis of the received gospel texts and will choose the aspects of the traditions they will work with. A "gospel" form implies a large role for the imagination, and the author needs to be open to their own deep-subjectivity and its inexhaustible flow of images. This genre requires a balance of human and archetypal dimensions without idealization. One purpose of such a genre is to serve an alchemical-like work, a conscious working with projections from the unconscious for the purpose of the differentiation of consciousness and self-realization as incarnation.

The question of training and disciplining subjectivity is an important area needing investigation. In academic writing the convention has been to make the subject disappear, and to raise the question of subjectivity borders on questioning the integrity of academic colleagues. On the one hand, simply raising the issue of subjectivity makes it more visible and has a disciplining effect on it. On the other hand, as Tony Kelly suggests, we might look to the training of psychotherapists and artists where it is common for the apprentice to "undergo hours and even years of criticism of their subjectivity: they are scrutinised by the panel, continuously challenged by the instructor or the master in the field," until it is hoped they have sufficient self-knowledge so that they will not misuse, nor abuse, their power, skill or gifts.[35] The task is to develop self-knowledge that goes deeper than our conscious autobiography and our social location, which although are now more and more recognized as important elements in hermeneutics, are not all there is to subjectivity. And there will always be that which remains unconscious and can only be perceived by others—this dimension must be acknowledged and allowed for as well.

Jung's own writing style, especially in *Answer to Job*, deserves examination in terms of genre and writing about Jesus. Although he is not writing about the historical Jesus as such, he self-consciously combines his own emotion with historical knowledge, religious imagery, reflection and judgment—he is both critical and imaginative. The traditional distinctions between history, theology and psychology

---

[35]Kelly (1991) 208.

tend to dissolve in Jung's writing and this style and direction could use more investigation.

In general, I would suggest that the modernist ontological distinction between history and theology may be a non-issue, just as the ontological distinction between fact and interpretation is a non-issue. This point of view with regard to history and theology requires more research in relation to the deep-subjectivity in which both are rooted. If history is seen to be fundamentally mythic, and its "facts" are as dependent on a faith in a narrative as are theology's assertions dependent on faith in a particular narrative, then perhaps the nature of the relationship between history, theology and psyche needs rethinking. It would seem that Jung's thought contains the possibility for an integration of historical and theological ways of thinking that remain a problem in thinking about the historical Jesus.

Conclusion

I suggest that a new paradigm for the quest for the historical Jesus that combines a phenomenological and hermeneutic analytical psychology with a historical criticism that is aware of history as myth is truer to the actual epistemological situation of both history and psyche. That is, that both history and memory are creative constructions having a great deal to do with the value-creating and significance-creating power of emotion, and that both are structured by the archetype of narrative that we understand as overlapping with the archetype of the self. This paradigm participates in the contemporary transition toward a postfoundational world and suggests that the traditional aim to which the historical critical method has been put by the quest for the historical Jesus, that of recovering the one true Jesus, is not warranted in the light of the understanding that history is myth, i.e., narrative. This understanding releases the historical critical method from attempting to pin-down the Jesus of the past as some kind of discrete and external object unrelated to the present and the needs and desires of the historian. Historical criticism can still inform an interest in Jesus of Nazareth, but its heightened awareness of history as mythic should eliminate its scientific positivist aspirations, while deepening and sharpening its awareness of the subjective nature of historical understanding and historical particularity. Hopefully, the historical critical awareness of the mythic nature of history will help the historian accept the role of archetypal-subjectivity, that is, imagination and projection, in the narrative creation of history. This means that the so-called methodological problem of multiple images of the historical Jesus is not something to be overcome or fixed—from the point of view of the mythic view of history, nothing is broken. Rather, multiple historical-Jesus-images are an unavoidable necessity in the light of the narrative and mythic essence of history—as such, it is not to be struggled against but embraced. Our view of archetypal-subjectivity and projection reveal these multiple "reflections in the bottom of a deep well" as revelations of the meaning of being, world and particular historical epochs, as well as aspects of the self and God.

Historical criticism, in conjunction with analytical psychology, can work toward uncovering primordial but unrecognized understandings of being and the world that constitute particular historical epochs. However, the deepened psychological awareness of archetypal-subjectivity, projection and the hermeneutic circle should also make the historian aware of the unavoidable role of the unconscious in general in historical research and free the historian from viewing subjectivity and projection as only obstacles.[36] In fact, this perspective shifts the perception of projection as an obstacle to the experience of projection as a gift from the unconscious (i.e., God). It is only through historical awareness, that is, the historical awareness of time, that the unconscious can reveal itself and become conscious—this function of historical time is just as true for culture as for the individual. As the present becomes the past and we gain the distance of time, a quality of reflection and judgment on experience and memory is possible that is not possible when we are simply living the present. The unconscious projections of a former age become conscious to us, and our own unconscious projections will become conscious to later ages.

A psychologically aware historical criticism should allow itself an appropriate degree of unconsciousness to the extent that the hermeneutic circle we are always in is always larger than our individual consciousness. Our own necessarily limited horizon of conscious understanding is expanded and deepened when we approach the narrative self-understanding of former ages on their own terms. In this way, by

---

[36]Loughlin (1984), in a reference to the large element of projection in all accounts of Jesus, states "There is really no getting round this problem; it is an obstacle for us all."(325)

differentiating and deepening our consciousness of the past, historical criticism enables a participation in what Jung calls individuation, or the evolution of consciousness, both for the individual and for culture.

One approach I propose in relation to the historical Jesus is to approach the Jesus-texts with the combined awareness of historical criticism and archetypal-subjectivity, that holds in tension an awareness of the past and an awareness of the present, and to realize the figure of Jesus as a projective field for *imaginatio* as an archetypal activity of God for the continuing creation of contemporary gospels. In this way the image of Jesus acts as a mirror, facilitating the incarnation of the self, not in Jesus, but in the individual. Any contemporary myth of the historical Jesus also needs to fully engage the terms of our modern world, and this includes historical, psychological and scientific consciousness as modern myths. We require a capacity to understand the mythic dimension of our modern discourses. As Jung admits,

> Psychology, as one of the many expressions of psychic life, operates with ideas which in their turn are derived from archetypal structures and thus generate a somewhat more abstract kind of myth. Psychology therefore translates the archaic speech of myth into a modern mythologem—not yet, of course, recognized as such— which constitutes one element of the myth "science."[37]

This suggests a paradox. From a historical perspective, Jung's own myth of individuation suggests a level five awareness in the withdrawal of projections in relation to former myths and worldviews. But as a historical perspective on past myths this view depends in part on achieving a distance in time from the worldview that is now seen as symbolic and/or no longer adequate for contemporary understanding. The same is true in personal psychology. A projection is really only recognized after the passage of time. If our present time and worldview is also a myth in its own right, but "not yet recognized as such," then we also have to admit we are simultaneously in some way at level one and completely unconsciously identified with our new myth. This would in fact be the understanding that best accords with the fact of the unconscious being *unconscious*. Levels one through five in the differentiation of consciousness are not a progressive linear development that leaves the previous levels behind with any finality. They describe a circular process with the levels overlapping one another and shifting back and forth as well. This reflects the phenomenology of the

---

[37]Jung (1968) 302.

hermeneutic circle as our ontological "ground," and suggests the mo-desty needed by consciousness in the face of the vast unconscious. So also is our consciousness of history severely limited by the reality of the vast and complex density of actual lived historic reality—our his-torical stories about the past, so necessary for our being, are always finite and partial, and so always changing, expanding and deepening. The *myth of the historical Jesus* also suggests that we will, and can only, have *many* stories about the historical Jesus, many different kinds of *gospels*. To continue to strive for the "one true gospel," or the "one true historical Jesus," actually cuts us off from the reflections at the bottom of the deep well that are not obstacle, but gift, and potential revelations of self, world and God.

BIBLIOGRAPHY

American Psychiatric Association. (1994). *Diagnostic and statistical manual of mental disorders (4th ed.). Washington, DC: Author.*

Andreski, Stanislav. (1972). *Social Sciences as Sorcery.* New York: St. Martin's.

Atwood, George E. & Tomkins, Silvan S. (1976). On The Subjectivity of Personality Theory. *Journal of the History of the Behavioral Sciences.* 12 (1976), 166-177.

Aziz, Robert. (1990). *C. G. Jung's Psychology of Religion and Synchronicity.* Albany: State University of New York.

Batdorf, Irvin W. (1984). Interpreting Jesus since Bultmann: Selected Paradigms and Their Hermeneutic Matrix. *Society of Biblical Literature Seminar Papers 1984.* 187-215.

Bailey, Lee Worth. (1986). Skull's Lantern: Psychological Projection and the Magic Lantern. *Spring 1986.* 72-87.

Bedford, Gary S. (1981). Notes on Mythological Psychology: Reimagining the Historical Psyche. *The Journal of the American Academy of Religion.* XLIX, 2, 231-247.

Berguer, G. (1923). *Some aspects of the life of Jesus from the Psychological and Psycho-analytic Point of View.* (E. S. Brooks and V. W. Brooks, Trans.) New York: Harcourt, Brace.

Bernard, Henry Norris. (1888). *The Mental Characteristic of the Lord Jesus Christ.* New York: Thomas Whittaker.

Bernstein, Michael Andre. (1994). *Foregone Conclusions: Against Apocalyptic History.* Berkeley: University of California.

Borg, Marcus J. (1984). *Conflict, Holiness & Politics in the Teachings of Jesus.* Lewiston, NY: Edwin Mellen.

263

————. (1987). *Jesus: A New Vision.* San Francisco: Harper & Row.

————. (1994). *Jesus in Contemporary Scholarship.* Valley Forge, PA: Trinity Press International.

Boring, M. Eugene. (1985). Criteria of Authenticity: The Lucan Beatitudes as a Test Case. *Forum.* 1, 4, Dec., 3-38.

Braaten, Carl E. & Harrisville, Roy A. (Eds.). (1964). *The Historical Jesus and the Kerygmatic Christ: Essays on the New Quest of the Historical Jesus.* New York: Abingdon.

Breech, James. (1983). *The Silence of Jesus: The Authentic Voice of the Historical Man.* Philadelphia: Fortress.

————. (1989). *Jesus and Postmodernism.* Minneapolis: Fortress.

Breisach, Ernst. (1994). *Historiography: Ancient, Medieval, and Modern.* (2nd ed.) Chicago: University of Chicago.

Brooke, Roger. (1991). *Jung and Phenomenology.* London: Routledge.

————. (1991a). Psychic Complexity and Human Existence: A Phenomenological Approach. *Journal of Analytical Psychology.* 36:505-518.

————. (1991b). Phenomenological Analytical Psychology: a clinical study. *Harvest.* 37, 88-100.

Brown, James A. C. (1961). *Freud and the post-Freudians.* Baltimore: Penguin.

Brown, Clifford A. (1981). *Jung's Hermeneutic of Doctrine.* Chico, CA: Scholar's Press.

Browning, Don S. (1987). *Religious Thought and the Modern Psychologies: A Critical Conversation in the Theology of Culture.* Philadelphia: Fortress.

Buss, Allan R. (1975). The Emerging Field of the Sociology of Psychological Knowledge. *American Psychologist.* 30, 10, October 1975, 988-1002.

Calvert, D. G. A. (1971/72). An Examination of the Criteria for Distinguishing the Authentic Words of Jesus. *New Testament Studies.* 18, 209-218.

Carlson, Jeffrey & Ludwig, Robert A. (Eds.). (1994). *Jesus and Faith: A Conversation on the Work of John Dominic Crossan.* Maryknoll, NY: Orbis.

Certeau, Michel de. (1988). *The Writing of History.* New York: Columbia University.

Charlesworth, James H. (1988). *Jesus Within Judaism.* New York: Doubleday.

Charlesworth, James H. (1994). Jesus Research Expands with Chaotic Creativity. In J. H. Charlesworth & W. P. Weaver (Eds.), *Images of Jesus Today* (pp. 1-41). Valley Forge: Trinity.

Chilton, Bruce & Evans, Craig A. (Eds.). (1994). *Studying The Historical Jesus: Evaluations of the State of Current Research.* Leiden: E. J. Brill.

Clarke, J. J. (1992). *In Search of Jung: Historical and Philosophical enquiries.* London: Routledge.

Collingwood, R. G. (1946). *The Idea of History.* London: Oxford University.

Connolly, John M. & Keutner, Thomas. (Eds.). (1988). *Hermeneutics Versus Science: Three German Views, Wolfgang Stegmuller, Hans-Georg Gadamer, Ernst Konrad Specht.* Notre Dame: University of Notre Dame.

Cook, Albert. (1988). *History/Writing: The Theory and Practice of History in Antiquity and in Modern Times.* Cambridge: Cambridge University.

Covington, Coline. (1995). No Story, No Analysis?: The role of narrative in interpretation. *Journal of Analytical Psychology.* 40, 405-417.

Cramer, Raymond. (1959). *The Psychology of Jesus and Mental Health.* Los Angeles: Cowman.

Crossan, John Dominic. (1973). *In Parables: The challenge of the historical Jesus.* New York: Harper & Row.

―――. (1975). *The Dark Interval: Towards a theology of story.* Niles, IL: Argus Communications.

―――. (1976). *Raid on the Articulate: Comic Eschatology in Jesus and Borges.* New York: Harper & Row.

―――. (1979). *Finding is the First Act: Trove Folktales and Jesus' Treasure Parable.* Philadelphia: Fortress.

―――. (1980). *Cliffs of fall: Paradox and polyvalence in the parables of Jesus.* New York: Seabury.

―――. (1983). *In Fragments: The Aphorisms of Jesus.* San Francisco: Harper & Row.

―――. (1983a) The Hermeneutical Jesus. *Michigan Quarterly Review.* Summer. 237-249.

————. (1985). *Four Other Gospels: Shadows on the contours of canon.* Minneapolis: Winston.

————. (1988). *The Cross That Spoke: The origins of the Passion narrative.* San Francisco: Harper & Row.

————. (1988a). Materials and Methods in Historical Jesus Research. *Forum.* 4, 4, 3-24.

————. (1988b). Divine Immediacy and Human Immediacy: Towards a new first principle in historical Jesus research. *Semia 44.* 121-140.

————. (1991). *The Historical Jesus: The life of a Mediterranean Jewish peasant.* New York: HarperSanFrancisco.

————. (1991a). The Historical Jesus: An Interview with John Dominic Crossan. *The Christian Century.* December 18-25, 1991, 1200-1204.

————. (1994). *Jesus: A revolutionary biography.* San Francisco: HarperSanFrancisco.

————. (1994a). *The Essential Jesus: Original sayings and earliest images.* San Francisco: HarperSanFrancisco

————. (1995). *Who Killed Jesus?: Exposing the roots of anti-semitism in the gospel story of the death of Jesus.* San Francisco: HarperSan-Francisco.

Cummins, R. (1983). *The Nature of Psychological Explanation.* Cambridge: MIT.

Davies, Philip R. (1995). Method and Madness: Some Remarks on Doing History with the Bible. *Journal of Biblical Literature.* 114, 4, (Winter), 699-705.

Dilthey, Wilhelm. (1988). The hermeneutics of the human sciences. (Selections from vol. 7 of his collected works.) In Kurt Mueller-Vollmer (Ed.), *The Hermeneutics Reader: Texts of the German tradition from the Enlightenment to the present* (pp. 148-164). New York: Continuum.

Dolto, F. & Severin, G. (1979). *The Jesus of Psychoanalysis: A Freudian Interpretation of the Gospel.* (Helen R. Lane, Trans.) Garden City: Doubleday.

Doniger, Simon (Ed.). (1962). *The Nature of Man in Theological and Psychological Perspective.* New York: Harper & Brothers.

Dourley, John P. (1981). The Search for the Nonhistorical Jesus. In *The Psyche as Sacrament: A comparative study of C. G. Jung and Paul Tillich* (pp. 61-78). Toronto: Inner City.

Downing, F. G. (1987). *Jesus and the Threat of Freedom.* London: SCM.

Dreyfus, Hubert. (1991). *Being-In-the-World: A commentary on Heidegger's Being and Time, division I.* Cambridge: MIT.

Drury, John. (1977). Bible Today: Answer to Jung. *The Modern Churchman.* 20, 3, 62-70.

Edinger, Edward. (1973). *Ego and Archetype: Individuation and the Religious Function of the Psyche.* Baltimore: Penguin.

———. (1987). *The Christian Archetype: A Jungian Commentary on the Life of Christ.* Toronto: Inner City.

———. (1984). *The Creation of Consciousness.* Toronto: Inner City.

Ellenberger, Henri F. (1970). *The Discovery of the Unconscious.* New York: Basic.

Fiorenza, Elisabeth Schussler. (1983). *In Memory of Her: A Feminist Reconstruction of Christian Origins.* New York: Crossroad. (pp. 72-159)

Fowl, Stephen. (1989). Reconstructing and Deconstructing the Quest of the Historical Jesus. *Scottish Journal of Theology.* 42, 319-333.

Freud, Sigmund. (1927). *The Future of an Illusion.* New York: Vantage.

Frey-Rohn, Liliane. (1974). *From Freud to Jung: A Comparative Study of the Psychology of the Unconscious.* New York: G. P. Putnam's Sons.

Funk, Robert W. (1985). The issue of Jesus. *Foundations & Facets Forum* 1, 1, March, 7-12.

———. (1993). The Gospel of Jesus and the Jesus of the Gospels. *The Fourth R* 6,6:3-10.

Funk, Robert W., Hoover, R. W. and The Jesus Seminar. (1993). *The Five Gospels: The Search for the Authentic Words of Jesus.* New York: Macmillan.

Gadamer, Hans-Georg. (1977). *Philosophical Hermeneutics.* (David E. Linge, Trans. and ed.). Berkeley: University of California.

———. (1986). *Truth and Method.* New York: Crossroad.

Gager, J. G. (1974). The Gospels and Jesus: Some Doubts about Method. *Journal of Religion* 54, 244-272.

Garvie, Alfred E. (1907). *Studies in the inner Life of Jesus.* New York: George H. Doran.

Gelven, Michael. (1989). *A Commentary on Heidegger's Being and Time* (Rev. ed.). DeKalb, IL: Northern Illinois University.

Georgi, Dieter. (1992). The Interest in Life of Jesus Theology as a Paradigm for the Social History of Biblical Criticism. *Harvard Theological Review.* 85:1, 51-83.

Gibbs, Lee W. & Stevenson, W. Taylor (Eds.). (1975). *Myth and the Crisis of Historical Consciousness.* Missoula: Scholars Press.

Giegerich, Wolfgang. (1980). Der Sprung nach dem Wurf: Uber das Einholen der Projektion und der Ursprung der Psychologie. *Gorgo* 1, 49-71.

Goss, James. (1981). Eschatology, Autonomy, and Individuation: The Evocative Power of the Kingdom. *Journal of the American Academy of Religion.* 49, 363-381 S.

Gossman, Lionel. (1978). History and Literature: Reproduction or Signification. In R. H. Canary & H. Kozicki (Eds.), *The Writing of History: Literary Form and Historical Understanding* (pp. 3-39). Madison: University of Wisconsin.

Guignon, Charles B. (1983). *Heidegger and the Problem of Knowledge.* Indianapolis: Hackett.

Hall, Granville Stanley. (1917). *Jesus, The Christ, In The Light of Psychology.* Garden City, NY: Doubleday, Page.

Harrington, Daniel J. (1987a). The Jewishness of Jesus: Facing Some Problems. *Catholic Biblical Quarterly.* 49, 1, 1-13.

————. (1987b). The Jewishness of Jesus. *Bible Review.* 3.1, Spring, 33-41.

Harrisville, Roy A. & Sundberg, Walter. (1995). *The Bible in Modern Culture: Theology and Historical-Critical Method From Spinoza to Käsemann.* Grand Rapids, MI: William B. Eerdmans.

Harvey, A. E. (1982). *Jesus and the Constraints of History.* Philadelphia: Westminster.

Heidegger, Martin. (1962). *Being and Time.* (John Macquarrie and Edward Robinson, Trans.) New York: Harper & Row.

————. (1969). *Discourse On Thinking.* New York: Harper & Row.

————. (1971). *On The Way To Language.* (Peter D. Hertz, Trans.) San Francis-co: Harper & Row.

————. (1975). *Poetry, Language, Thought.* New York: Harper & Row.

————. (1977). *Basic Writings.* (David Farrell Krell, Ed.) San Francisco: Harper & Row.

Heisig, James W. (1979). *Imago Dei: A Study of C. G. Jung's Psychology of Religion.* Cranbury, NJ: Associated University.

Hewison, D. S. (1995). Case History, Case Story: An Enquiry Into the Hermeneutics of C.G. Jung. *Journal of Analytical Psychology.* 40, 383-404.

Hiley, David R., Bohman, James F., Shusterman, Richard (Eds.). (1991). *The Interpretive Turn: Philosophy, Science, Culture.* Ithaca: Cornell University.

Hillman, James. (1972). *Emotion: A comprehensive phenomenology of theories and their meanings for therapy.* Evanston, IL: Northwestern University.

————. (1975). The Fiction of Case History: A Round. In James B. Wiggins (Ed.), *Religion As Story* (pp. 123-173). New York: Harper & Row.

Hitchcock, Albert W. (1907). *The Psychology of Jesus: a study of the development of His self-consciousness.* Boston: Pilgrim.

Hobbs, Edward C. (1962). Self-Understanding vs. Self-Consciousness. [Paper]. Berkeley: Pacific Coast Theological Group.

Hoeller, Keith (Ed.). (1988). *Heidegger and Psychology.* A Special Issue from the *Review of Existential Psychology & Psychiatry.*

Holt, David. (1975). Projection, Presence, Profession. *Spring 1975.* 130-144.

Homans, Peter (Ed.). (1968). *The Dialogue Between Theology and Psychology.* Chicago: University of Chicago.

————. (1969). Psychology and Hermeneutics: Jung's Contribution. *Zygon: Journal of Religion and Science.* 4, 4, 333-355.

————. (1970). *Theology After Freud: an interpretive inquiry.* Indianapolis: Bobbs-Merrill.

————. (1975). Psychology and Hermeneutics: An Exploration of Basic Issues and Resources. *Journal of Religion.* 55, 327-47.

————. (1979). *Jung in Context: Modernity and the Making of a Psychology.* Chicago: University of Chicago.

————. (1982). A Personal Struggle with Religion: Significant Fact in the Lives and Work of the First Psychologist. *Journal of Religion.* 62, 128-144.

Horsley, Richard. (1987). *Jesus and the Spiral of Violence.* San Francisco: Harper & Row.

————. (1994). Innovation in Search of Reorientation: New Testament Studies Rediscovering Its Subject Matter. *Journal of the American Academy of Religion.* Winter, LXII, 4, 1127-1166.

Howard, Roy J. (1982). *Three Faces of Hermeneutics: An Introduction to Current Theories of Understanding.* Berkeley: University of California.

Howes, Elizabeth B. (1984). *Jesus' Answer to God.* San Francisco: The Guild for Psychological Studies Publishing House.

Hoy, David Couzens. (1978). *The Critical Circle: Literature, History, and Philosophical Hermeneutics.* Berkeley: University of California Press.

Hurt, Kathy Fuson. (1982). The Quest of the Psychological Jesus (Jungian reading of Mark). *The Unitarian Universalist Christian.* 37, 1-2, 21-31. Spr-Sum.

Jarrett, James L. (1981). Schopenhauer and Jung. *Spring 1981.* 193-204.

————. (1990). Jung and Nietzsche. *Harvest: Journal for Jungian Studies.* 36, 130-148.

————. (1992). Jung and Hermeneutics. *Harvest: Journal for Jungian Studies.* 38, 66-83.

Johnson, Cedric B. (1983). *The Psychology of Biblical Interpretation.* Grand Rapids: Zondervan.

Johnson, Luke Timothy. (1996). *The Real Jesus: The misguided quest for the historical Jesus and the truth of the traditional gospels.* San Francisco: HarperSanFrancisco.

Jung, C. G. (1953-1979). *The Collected Works of C. G. Jung.* [CW] (20 vols.). (H. Read, M. Fordham, & G. Adler, Eds.; R.F.C. Hull, Trans.). Princeton: Princeton.

————. (1916). The Transcendent Function. CW 8 (pp. 67-91). (2nd ed.).

————. (1931). Archaic Man. CW 10 (pp. 50-73). (2nd ed.).

————. (1935). The Tavistock Lectures. CW 18 (pp. 5-184).

———. (1940). Psychology and Religion. CW 11 (pp. 3-105). (2nd ed.).

———. (1946). The Bologna Enigma. *Spring 1979.* 189-200.

———. (1948). A Psychological Approach to the Dogma of the Trinity. CW 11 (pp. 107-200).

———. (1951). *Aion: Researches Into the Phenomenology of the Self.* CW 9ii.

———. (1952). Answer to Job. CW 11 (pp. 355-470).

———. (1954). Transformation Symbolism in the Mass. CW 11 (pp. 201-296).

———. (1957). The Undiscoverd Self. CW 10 (pp.245-305).

———. (1961). *Memories, Dreams, Reflections.* (Aniela Jaffé, Recorder and ed.; Richard and Clara Winston, Trans.) New York: Vintage.

———. (1966). *Two Essays On Analytical Psychology.* CW 7. (2nd ed.).

———. (1967). *Symbols of Transformation.* CW 5. (2nd ed.).

———. (1967a). *Alchemical Studies.* CW 13.

———. (1968). *The Archetypes and the Collective Unconscious.* CW 9i. (2nd ed.).

———. (1968a). *Psychology and Alchemy.* CW 12. (2nd ed.).

———. (1970). *Mysterium Coniunctionis.* CW 14. (2nd ed.).

———. (1971). *Psychological Types.* CW 6.

———. (1973). *C.G. Jung Letters.* Vol. 1: 1906-1950. (Gerhard Adler, Ed.). Princeton: Princeton.

———. (1975). *C.G. Jung Letters.* Vol. 2: 1951-1961.

———. (1977). *C. G. Jung Speaking: Interviews and Encounters.* (William McGuire & R.F.C. Hull, Eds.). Princeton: Princeton.

———. (1983). *The Zofingia Lectures.* (Jan Van Heurck, Trans.). London: Routledge & Kegan Paul.

———. (1984). *Dream Analysis: Notes of the seminar given in 1928-1930.* (William McGuire, Ed.). Princeton: Princeton.

———. (1988a). *Nietzsche's Zarathustra: Notes of the seminar given in 1934-1939.* (James L. Jarrett, Ed.). Volume One (pp. 1-764). Princeton: Princeton.

————. (1988b). Volume Two (pp. 765-1578).

Käsemann, Ernst. (1964). The Problem of the Historical Jesus. In *Essays On New Testament Themes* (pp.15-47). London: SCM.

Kelly, Sean M. (1993). *Individuation and the Absolute: Hegel, Jung and the Path Toward Wholeness.* Mahwah, NJ: Paulist.

Kelly, Tony. (1991). The Historical Jesus and Human Subjectivity: A Response to John Meier. *Pacifica.* 4, 202-228.

Koch, Sigmund. (1985). The Nature and Limits of Psychological Knowledge. In S. Koch & D. E. Leary (Eds.), *A Century of Psychology as Science.* New York: McGraw-Hill.

Koester, Helmut. (1994). The Historical Jesus and the Historical Situation of the Quest: An Epilogue. In Bruce Chilton & Craig Evans (Eds.), *Studying the Historical Jesus: Evaluations of the State of Current Research* (pp. 535-545). Leiden: E. J. Brill.

Krentz, Edgar. (1975). *The Historical-Critical Method.* Philadelphia: Fortress.

Krieger, Murray (Ed.). (1993). *The Aims of Representation: Subject/Text/History.* New York: Columbia.

Kunkel, Fritz. (1952). *Creation Continues: A Psychological Interpretation of the First Gospel.* New York: Charles Scribner's Sons.

Leavy, Stanley. (1988). *In the Image of God: A psychoanalyst's view.* New Haven: Yale.

Leslie, Robert C. (1965). *Jesus and Logotherapy: The Ministry of Jesus as Interpreted through the Psychotherapy of Viktor Frankl.* Nashville: Abingdon.

Lindauer, M. S. (1974). *The Psychological Study of Literature: Limitations, Possibilities and Accomplishments.* Chicago: Nelson-Hall.

Loughlin, Gerard. (1984). On Telling the Story of Jesus. *Theology 87*, September, 323-329.

Mack, Burton. (1988). *A Myth of Innocence: Mark and Christian Origins.* Philadelphia: Fortress.

Martin, Brice. (1990). Reflections on historical criticism and self-understanding. In David Hawkin (Ed.), *Self-definition and self-discovery in early Christianity.* Lewiston, NY: Edwin Mellen.

Martin, James P. (1987). Toward A Post-Critical Paradigm. *New Testament Studies*, 33, 370-385.

Martin, Luther H. & Goss, James (Eds.). (1985). *Essays On Jung and the Study of Religion.* Lanham, MD: University Press of America.

McConnell, Frank (Ed.). (1986). *The Bible and the Narrative Tradition.* New York: Oxford.

McGann, Diarmuid. (1985). *The Journeying Self: The Gospel of Mark through a Jungian Perspective.* New York: Paulist.

Meier, Carl Alfred. (1977). *Jung's Analytical Psychology and Religion.* Carbondale: Southern Illinois University.

Meier, John P. (1990). The Historical Jesus: Rethinking Some Concepts. *Theological Studies.* 51, 1, 3-24.

———. (1991). *A Marginal Jew: Rethinking the Historical Jesus.* Vol. 1. New York: Doubleday.

———. (1991a). Reflections on Jesus-of-History Research Today. In James H. Charlesworth (Ed.), *Jesus' Jewishness.* New York: Crossroad.

Meyer, Ben F. (1979). *The Aims of Jesus.* London: SCM Press.

Miller, David (1981). *Christs: Meditations on Archetypal Images in Christian Theology.* New York: Seabury.

———. (1987). "Attack Upon Christendom!" The Anti-Christianism of Depth Psychology. In Murray Stein & Robert Moore (Eds.), *Jung's Challenge to Contemporary Religion.* Wilmette, IL: Chiron.

Mogenson, Greg. (1989). *God Is a Trauma.* Dallas: Spring Publications.

Mueller-Vollmer, Kurt (Ed.). (1988). *The Hermeneutics Reader.* New York: Continu-um.

Munz, Peter. (1977). *The Shapes of Time: A New Look at the Philosophy of History.* Middletown, CT: Wesleyan.

Nagy, Marilyn. (1991). *Philosophical Issues in the Psychology of C. G. Jung.* Albany: State University of New York.

Nations, Archie. (1983). Historical Criticism and the Current Methodological Crisis. *Scottish Journal of Theology*, 36, 59-72.

Neill, Stephen & Wright, N. T. (1988). *The Interpretation of the New Testament 1961-1986* (pp. 360-449). New York: Oxford.

Neville, Bernie. (1992). The Charm of Hermes: Hillman, Lyotard, and the Post-modern Condition. *Journal of Analytical Psychology.* 37, 337-353.

Nietzsche, Friedrich. (1967). *The Will To Power.* (Walter Kaufmann & R. J. Hollingdale, Trans.). London: Weidenfeld and Nicolson.

Novick, Peter. (1988). *That Noble Dream: The "Objectivity Question" and the American Historical Profession.* Ideas in Context. Cambridge: Cambridge University.

Oakman, Douglas E. (1986). The Nature and Difficulties of the Study of the Historical Jesus. In *Jesus and the Economic Questions of His Day* (pp. 221-252). Lewiston: Edwin Mellen.

Oates, W. E. (1950). The Diagnostic Use of the Bible: What a Man Sees in the Bible Is a Projection of His Inner Self. *Pastoral Psychology.* 1, 43-46.

Ott, Heinrich. (1964). The Historical Jesus and the Ontology of History. In C. E. Braaten & R. A. Harrisville (Eds.), *The Historical Jesus and the Kerygmatic Christ: Essays on the New Quest of the Historical Jesus* (pp. 142-171). New York: Abingdon.

Packer, Martin J. & Addison, Richard B. (Eds.). (1989). Entering The Circle: Hermeneutic Investigation in Psychology. Albany: State University of New York.

Palmer, Richard E. (1969). *Hermeneutics: Interpretation Theory in Schleiermacher, Dilthey, Heidegger, and Gadamer.* Evanston: Northwestern.

Papadopoulos, Renos (Ed.). (1993). *Carl Gustav Jung: Critical Assessments.* Four Volumes. London: Routledge.

Perrin, Norman & Duling, Dennis C. (1982). *The New Testament: An Introduction.* (2nd ed.). New York: Harcourt Brace Jovanovich.

Polkow, Dennis. (1987). Method and Criteria for Historical Jesus Research. *Society of Biblical Literature 1987 Seminar Papers.* 336-356.

Provan, Ian W. (1995). Ideologies, Literary and Critical: Reflections on Recent Writing on the History of Israel. *Journal of Biblical Literature.* 114, 4, (Winter), 585-606.

Rabinow, Paul. (1977). *Reflections on Fieldwork in Morocco.* Berkeley: University of California.

Rabinow, Paul & Sullivan, William M. (Eds.). (1987). *Interpretive Social Science: A Second Look.* Berkeley: University of California.

Richardson, William J. (1988). The place of the unconscious in Heidegger. *Heidegger & Psychology* (pp. 176-198). (Keith Hoeller, Ed.). A Special Issue from the *Review of Existential Psychology & Psychiatry.*

Riches, John. (1982). *Jesus and the Transformation of Judaism.* New York: Seabury.

Ricoeur, Paul. (1970). *Freud and Philosophy: An Essay on Interpretation.* New Haven: Yale.

———. (1980). *Essays On Biblical Interpretation.* (Lewis S. Mudge, Ed.) Philadelphia: Fortress.

———. (1987). *Hermeneutics and the Human Sciences.* (John B. Thompson, Ed. & Trans.). Cambridge: Cambridge.

Rieff, Philip. (1966). *The Triumph of the Therapeutic: Uses Faith After Freud.* New York: Harper & Row.

Rizzuto, Ana-Maria. (1979). *The Birth of the Living God: A Psychoanalytic Study.* Chicago: The University of Chicago.

Robinson, James M. (1979). *A New Quest of the Historical Jesus.* Missoula, MT: Scholars Press. (Reprint of the 1959 ed.)

Robinson, James M. & Cobb, John B. (Eds.). (1964). *The New Hermeneutic.* New York: Harper & Row.

Rollins, Wayne G. (1983). *Jung and the Bible.* Atlanta: John Knox.

Sanders, E. P. (1985). *Jesus and Judaism.* Philadelphia: Fortress.

Sanford, John A. (1970). *The Kingdom Within: A study of the inner meaning of Jesus' sayings.* New York: J. B. Lippincott.

Sanford, John A. (Ed.). (1984). *Fritz Kunkel: Selected Writings.* Ramsey, NJ: Paulist.

Schacter, Daniel (Ed.). (1995). *Memory Distortion: How minds, brains, and societies reconstruct the past.* Cambridge: Harvard.

———. (1996). *Searching for Memory: The brain, the mind, and the past.* NY: BasicBooks.

Schleiermacher, Friedrich D. E. (1988). Foundations: General theory and art of interpretation. (Selections from *Hermeneutics and Criticism* and his published manuscripts.) In Kurt Mueller-Vollmer (Ed.), *The Hermeneutics Reader: Texts of the German tradition from the Enlightenment to the present* (pp. 72-97). New York: Continuum.

Schwartz-Salant, Nathan. (1982). *Narcissism and Character Transformation.* Toronto: Inner City.

Schweitzer, Albert. (1906/1968). *The Quest of the Historical Jesus: A critical study of its progress from Reimarus to Wrede.* (Introduced by J. M. Robinson). New York: Macmillan.

————. (1948). *The Psychiatric Study of Jesus.* (Charles R. Joy, Trans.). Boston: Beacon.

Scott, Bernard Brandon. (1981). *Jesus, Symbol-Maker for the Kingdom.* Philadelphia: Fortress.

Shanks, Hershel (Ed.). (1994). *The Search for Jesus: Modern scholarship looks at the gospels.* Washington: Biblical Archaeology Society.

Shapiro, Gary & Sica, Alan (Eds.). (1984). *Hermeneutics: Questions and Prospects.* Amherst: The University of Massachusetts.

Slusser, Gerald H. (1986). *From Jung to Jesus: Myth and consciousness in the New Testament.* Atlanta: John Knox.

Spence, Donald P. (1982). *Narrative Truth and Historical Truth: Meaning and interpretation in psychoanalysis.* New York: W. W. Norton.

Spurling, Laurence (Ed.). (1989). *Sigmund Freud: Critical Assessments.* Four Volumes. London: Routledge.

Steele, Robert S. (1982). *Freud and Jung: Conflicts of interpretation.* London: Routledge.

Stein, Murray. (1985). *Jung's Treatment of Christianity: The Psychotherapy of a Religious Tradition.* Wilmette, IL: Chiron.

————. (1987). Jung's Green Christ: A Healing Symbol for Christianity. In Murray Stein & Robert L. Moore (Eds.), *Jung's Challenge to Contemporary Religion* (pp. 1-13). Wilmette, IL: Chiron.

Stevenson, W. Taylor. (1969). *History As Myth: The Import for Contemporary Theology.* New York: Seabury.

Stock, Brian. (1990). *Listening for the Text: On the Uses of the Past.* Baltimore: Johns Hopkins University.

Strenger, Carlo. (1991). *Between Hermeneutics and Science: An Essay on the Epistemology of Psychoanalysis.* Madison, CT: International Universities.

Telford, William R. (1994). Major Trends and Interpretive Issues in the Study of Jesus. In Bruce Chilton & Craig A. Evans (Eds.), *Studying the Historical Jesus: Evaluations of the State of Current Research* (pp. 33-74). Leiden: E. J. Brill.

Theissen, Gerd. (1987). *The Shadow of the Galilean: The Quest of the Historical Jesus in Narrative Form.* Philadelphia: Fortress.

Thiselton, Anthony C. (1984). *The Two Horizons: New Testament Hermeneutics and Philosophical Description.* Grand Rapids: Wm. B. Eerdmanns.

Thompson, Thomas L. (1995). A Neo-Albrightean School in History and Biblical Scholarship? *Journal of Biblical Literature.* 114, 4, (Winter), 683-698.

Tillich, Paul. (1959). *Theology of Culture.* (Robert C. Kimball, Ed.). London: Oxford.

Tyrrell, George. (1909). *Christianity at the Cross-Roads.* London: Longmans, Green.

Ulanov, Ann Belford & Barry. (1975). Jesus as figure and person, symbol and sacrament. In *Religion and the Unconscious* (pp. 97-117). Philadelphia: Westminster.

van Beek, Franz Jozef. (1994). The quest of the historical Jesus. In Jeffrey Carlson & Robert A. Ludwig (Eds.), *Jesus and Faith: A conversation on the work of John Dominic Crossan* (pp. 83-99). Maryknoll, NY: Orbis.

Vermes, Geza. (1973). *Jesus the Jew: A Historian's Reading of the Gospels.* Philadelphia: Fortress.

———. (1993). *The Religion of Jesus the Jew.* Minneapolis: Fortress.

Veyne, Paul. (1984). *Writing History: Essay on Epistemology.* Middletown CT: Wesleyan.

von Franz, Marie-Louise. (1975). *C. G. Jung: His Myth In Our Time.* New York: G. P. Putnam's Sons.

———. (1980). *Projection and Re-Collection In Jungian Psychology: Reflections of the Soul.* La Salle, IL: Open Court.

White, Hayden. (1973). *Metahistory*. Baltimore: Johns Hopkins.

————. (1978). The Historical Text as Literary Artifact. In R. H. Canary & H. Kozicki (Eds.), *The Writing of History: Literary Form and Historical Understanding* (pp. 41-62). Madison: University of Wisconsin.

————. (1987). *The Content of the Form: Narrative Discourse and Historical Representation*. Baltimore: Johns Hopkins.

Wink, Walter. (1973). *The Bible in Human Transformation: Toward a new paradigm for biblical study*. Philadelphia: Fortress.

————. (1978). On Wrestling with God: Using Psychological Insights in Bible Study. *Religion in Life*. 47, 136-147.

————. (1980). *Transforming Bible Study: A Leader's Guide*. Nashville: Abingdon.

Witherington, Ben III. (1994). *Jesus the Sage: The Pilgrimage of Wisdom*. Minneapolis: Fortress.

————. (1995). *The Jesus Quest: The Third Search for the Jew of Nazareth*. Downers Grove, IL: InterVarsity.

Wolff, Hanna. (1987). *Jesus the Therapist*. Oak Park, IL: Meyer-Stone.

Wright, N. T. (1992). *Christian Origins and the Question of God*. Vol. 1, *The New Testament and the People of God*. Minneapolis: Fortress.

————. (1993). Taking the Text with Her Pleasure: A Post-post-modernist Response to J. Dominic Crossan's *The Historical Jesus: The Life of a Mediterranean Jewish Peasant*. *Theology*, 96, Jl-Ag. 303-310.

Wuellner, W. H. & Leslie, R. G. (1984). *The Surprising Gospel*. Nashville: Abingdon.

Wulff, David M. (1991). *Psychology of Religion: Classic and Contemporary Views*. New York: John Wiley & Sons.